# *The* GIRL *from* COPENHAGEN

*A memoir*

*by*

GLENN PETERSON

Library of Congress Control Number:     2018914268

ISBN:   Softcover        978-1-9845-7018-5
        Hardcover        978-1-9845-7019-2
        EBook            978-1-9845-7017-8

Print information available on the last page

Rev. date: 12/04/2018

To order additional copies of this book, contact:
Xlibris
1-888-795-4274
www.Xlibris.com
Orders@Xlibris.com

IN MEMORY

OF

INGE E. PETERSON

1923-2018

# SYNOPSIS: THE GIRL FROM COPENHAGEN

*The Girl From Copenhagen* is a memoir. It includes a photo section that follows my mother's life from childhood into old age. Born in Denmark in 1923 on the island of Falster ("Amid thunder and lightening," as she was fond of saying), Inge Buus had an idyllic life growing up with her brother and sister on their father's farm. All three siblings learned to ride a horse by the age of eight or nine. Inge, however, was anything but a farm girl. She never mastered the art of milking a cow. She refused to drink milk. During the fall slaughtering time, she would stay in her room and close the door so she would not hear the squealing of the fattened pigs. She avoided gathering eggs because the hens would peck her fingers. After graduating at the top of her high-school class, she moved to Copenhagen to study nursing. Unfortunately, her nursing career was cut short when her ankles began swelling up on her long shifts, rendering her as infirm as some of her patients. She subsequently found employment as a bookkeeper at Burmeister and Wain, the largest shipbuilder in Denmark.

Inge and her family witnessed the German invasion of Denmark on April 9, 1940. At first, the occupation did not seem all that bad. The Danish economy, in a recession at the time, prospered with the German wartime demand for produce and machinery. But then the Nazis began to tighten the screws, revealing their true intentions as they attempted to round up and deport Denmark's Jewish population to concentration camps. This was the last straw for the Danish people, who considered their Jewish neighbors as Danes first and Jews second, and succeeded in smuggling most of Denmark's 8,000 Jews to neutral Sweden on a flotilla of small fishing boats. After this blatant act of defiance, Hitler ordered a crackdown on his Danish "protectorate." On her way to work, Inge would pass by German tanks stationed in Copenhagen's town square. Helmeted German soldiers armed with machine guns demanded to see her *Ausweis.* There were almost daily bombings in the heart of the city, some conducted by the Danish Resistance, others conducted by the Germans in retaliation. Inge had mixed feelings about working in the shipyard, which was producing engines for German U-boats, making the yard a target for Allied bombers as well as the Danish Resistance. But the pay was much higher than she would be able to obtain elsewhere, so she chose to stick it out.

The Danes celebrated when the five years of Nazi occupation came to an end. At a dance in Copenhagen, Inge met a dashing young GI, Sergeant Bob Peterson. After a whirlwind courtship, Inge decided to marry her GI. In 1946, leaving behind a loving family and friends, she packed up her belongings in a large wicker basket and sailed to the United States. Bob was employed by Gibbs & Cox, a shipbuilding company in New York City. In the late 1940s and early 1950s he worked on the design of the S.S. United States. Living in an apartment in Jersey City until 1954, Inge and her resourceful mate would drive every Friday night to an undeveloped plot of land in rural New Jersey and work through the weekend. Lacking running water and electricity, they built their dream house with their own hands.

In 1965, with the house completed to Bob's satisfaction, he grew restless and set his sights on greener pastures. Over the next twenty-five years there would be a total of seven more moves, some dictated by the necessities of employment opportunities, others simply places where Bob had aspired from his youth to settle down in. ("A house is just a place to hang your hat," Bob once said.) Inge never uttered a word of complaint during all of these moves. No doubt, like her husband, she had the spirit of wanderlust in her blood—after all, she had gone off to America with a man she had known for no more than a week. During these many moves, Inge made a total of twenty-five trips back to her native Denmark. The love of her life collapsed and died shortly after moving into their new home in Pennsylvania.

"We're staying here," Bob promised a few days before his sudden death. "No more moves."

Living with her son, Glenn, Inge would make two more trips to Denmark after Bob's death. She would outlive almost all of her contemporaries, dying of dementia at the age of ninety-four.

# PREFACE

By her ninety-fourth year my mother's memory problems were becoming more and more evident. She would misplace her watch, her ring, her glasses. She could not tell me what day of the week it was, or even the year. But she always knew the date and year of her birth. She could not remember what she had eaten for supper the day before. Although she like to snack on grapes, she was often unable to remember what they were called. But when looking through one of her photo albums, she could still recall the names of her childhood friends back in her native Denmark. One day she surprised me by rattling off the telephone number at Klostergaarden, her father's farm—a number she had not used since the farm was sold in 1942.

# THE FARMER'S DAUGHTER

Inge Elizabeth Buus was born on July 29, 1923 in the small town of Stubberup, located near Nykøbing on the island of Falster. She was delivered by a midwife in the home of her mother's parents—"amid thunder and lightening," as she was fond of saying. Her father, Lars Buus, came from a long line of farmers. His father, Peter Buus, owned a farm in western Jutland called Risgaard. One of Lars' uncles, Jens Buus, wrote the first textbook in Danish covering all aspects of farming and animal husbandry. In 1920 Lars married Ella Johanne Pedersen. They had three children, Knud, Inge, and Anna Lise, who grew up on their father's farm, Klostergaarden—so named because of its resemblance to a medieval cloister, with four main buildings enclosing an open courtyard. It was a good-sized farm with perhaps fifteen to twenty permanent workers, more during the sowing and harvesting seasons. There were cooks and servants. Pictures of Lars Buus taken at the time show him wearing a suit and tie, looking more like a country squire than your typical farmer.

For young children growing up on a farm there was no lack of things to see and do. One day Inge and her siblings might gather by the pen of a prized sow and watch it give birth to a litter of squealing piglets. (Which would have to be removed for the night lest the sow roll over in her sleep and accidentally crush her offspring.) The next day the children might witness a newborn foal taking its first hesitant steps. They would gather by the cow stalls and watch the men milk the cows. Now and then they would try their hand at a butter churn—a tiring job even for a grownup once the butter began to thicken. Harvest time was always an exciting event for the children, with extra hands arriving to pick the maturing cabbage and lettuce, and to dig up the sugar beets, turnips, and potatoes. The wheat harvest was no longer labor-intensive as it had been at Risgaard, when the the sheaves of wheat had to be cut, bundled, and stacked by hand. Here at Klostergaarden the work that had formerly employed dozens of men was accomplished by only two men in a mere fraction of the time: one man operated the huge combine harvester that cut, threshed, and separated the grain from the chaff; the other man steered a tractor with an attached wagon that stored the processed wheat to be later bundled into sacks. The harvest had to be done promptly lest the fat seed heads became moldy, and this was a chancy proposition at best, as the combine, traveling from farm to farm, had to be reserved weeks in advance of the actual harvest. The arrival of the combine was a stirring sight. It looked and sounded with its engine roaring like some monster advancing slowly and menacingly as it consumed the rows of wheat. "*Lukke* øjnene! (Close your eyes!)," Lars would say by way of teasing his children when the long-awaited combine made its appearance. As on all of these harvests, the hope was that the weather would be dry. Rain could be a curse as well as a blessing, making all the difference between a good crop and a failed crop. Whatever the outcome of the harvest, there was always next year to prepare for. A farmer's day is never done. Pulling on stout boots, the children would accompany their father as he surveyed the muddy spring fields, impatient for the ground to dry out so the next crop of wheat could go in.

From an early age the three siblings were expected to perform a daily quota of chores. At the ages of four and five, Inge and Anna Lise would help their mother hang up their wash on the clothesline behind the farmhouse. All three siblings would tend the chickens, scattering feed on the bare ground of the chicken coup. Every morning they would gather the eggs, placing them carefully in a straw-lined basket. Inge, however, did not possess the knack of gently prodding the reluctant, angrily clucking hen to reveal her little clutch of eggs. The disturbed bird would peck forcefully and repeatedly at the back of her hand, inducing Inge to withdraw. Excused from the responsibility of gathering eggs, Inge fared better in the garden, where there were peas, string beans, strawberries, raspberries, gooseberries, and plums to be picked in their respective seasons. Anyone who has traipsed through soggy fields on a farm will know that it is impossible to keep the mud and the occasional cowpat from soiling one's footgear. It fell to older brother, Knud, to scrape and brush clean the three siblings' dirty boots and shoes at the end of the day.

But aside from their daily chores, the children had plenty of time left for play. They had any number of cute puppies to spoil. They had a cat, which was technically a working animal, kept for its prowess at killing mice, and it often distressed the children when tabby toyed with its intended victim, repeatedly swatting it and then letting it run off, only to corner it again before delivering the final *coup de grâce*. There was a tame dove that would come to the children when they called out to it, "doo-di, doo-di," and take kernels of corn from their outstretched hands—even from Inge's hand, her run-on with the hens notwithstanding. Klostergaarden provided a great venue for a game of *skjul* (hide-and-seek). There was a wooded area near the farmhouse where one could conceal oneself behind a tree or a bush. Or one could lay prostrate in the wheat field and be completely invisible from the outside. There were barns, sheds, and other outbuildings—so many hiding places, in fact, that the game of hide-and-seek usually ended with the two searchers giving up and going inside, leaving it up to the target to figure out that he or she had long since been abandoned.

Despite her reluctance to stand up to the hens (nor did she care much for the task of plucking the feathers off a slaughtered bird, preferring to shell peas as an alternative), Inge was actually something of a daredevil, leading her brother and sister in the game of *Rolf og hands kæmper* (Rolf and his warriors, which sounds a bit edgier than its American counterpart, follow-the-leader.) They would jump, one after the other, over a raspberry bush in the garden, then proceed to the side of the road and spring over a water-filled ditch. The sport of climbing up onto a haystack and sliding down the steep slope, however, was quickly curtailed, as Lars feared that the children might contaminate the cows' fodder with their muddy boots. Looking for a more difficult challenge, Inge scrambled up onto a fence and tottered with arms outstretched along the top rail, daring her siblings to follow suit. They were hard-put to keep up with her. Unfortunately, the next time Inge attempted the act, she lost her balance and fell headlong onto the rail. No bones were broken, but the force of the impact loosened her front teeth. She vowed to take fewer risks in the future. But this was a vow made to be broken.

The bicycles the children learned to ride were full-sized, adult versions. In those days there were no pint-sized bikes, no training wheels. You simply hopped onto the bike, pushed off, and peddled as hard as you could. Shortly after Inge had mastered her bicycle, she was riding along the road in front of Klostergaarden. Suddenly, a fat goose appeared from nowhere and waddled out into her path. Inge jammed on the brakes, but was unable to stop in time. She ran over the unfortunate goose, breaking its neck. Feathers went flying everywhere. Crying as she ran into the house and expecting to be punished for killing the goose, Inge explained to her mother what had happened. But her mother told her not to be upset, and dried Inge's tears with her apron. The goose was cooked and served for dinner that very evening. Inge wasn't able to eat a single mouthful of it. She was similarly squeamish when the fattened pigs were slaughtered in the fall, staying in her room with the door closed so she would not have to hear the animals' piteous squealing. Nor would she partake of any of the choice cuts of pork served on that first dinner after the slaughter. Only after the passage of a day or two did she finally consent to put a sausage and a slice of bacon on her plate.

The farmer's daughter was anything but a farm girl. From an early age, she refused to drink milk, preferring soda or tea. She picked at her eggs, mashing them up with her fork and spreading them about on her plate to make it appear as if she had eaten more than she really had. Little was known at the time about the physical effects of a diet deficient in vitamin D. Had they known these facts, Inge's parents would no doubt have insisted that she drink her milk and eat her eggs. As a result of a lack of vitamin D, Inge developed rickets, which would lead to some troublesome health issues later on in her life.

Though Inge would come to enjoy riding a horse (bareback, no saddle—which required a considerable amount of horsemanship), she never learned to milk a cow; she was never able to get the flow of milk started after any number of tugs on the cow's teats. Chiding her older sister for her clumsy efforts and reminding her of her failure with the hens, Anna Lise would push Inge away from the cow and take over. In no time she would have the pail half full. Nothing to it.

There was one activity, however, at which Inge always bested her sister. Whenever a marzipan bar or other confection came their way, Anna Lise would eat hers immediately, right down to the last bite. Inge, to her sister's consternation, would consume only a little bit of her candy, saving most of it for later, often stretching it out for a day or two. *"Jeg kunne altid hold hus med det,"* Inge would say years later when recalling the friendly rivalry. (Roughly: "I could always make it last.")

Inge may not have been cut out for life on a farm, but she picked up many useful household skills from her mother. In addition to cooking and baking, she became proficient in knitting, crocheting, and sewing. She learned to knit socks and sweaters, and would eventually use a paper pattern to make her own coats and dresses. A treasured item Inge brought with her when she came to America was a pillow that her mother had made from scraps of old clothing that had been worn by the three children. More than half a century later Inge would be able to point to each triangular patch on the pillow and recall, "The gray patch was from Knud's scarf. The red patch was from Anna Lise's sweater. This green patch was from one of my sweaters." The pillow, as colorful to this day as it was when Ella Buus knitted it, was stuffed with the down from several geese. (Including, perhaps, the one that Inge had run over.) Nothing goes to waste on a farm. Recycling is nothing new.

There were hints of the coming storm from Denmark's belligerent neighbor to the south. Mother recalled hearing one or two of Hitler's longwinded speeches on the radio in which he taunted the American president: "Roosevelt, Roosevelt, *wo bist Sie,* Roosevelt?" But for the most part, the 1930s marked a halcyon period. Photos in one of my mother's albums document regular visits to Risgaard, the farm in Jutland where Lars Buus had been born. Lars' mother, Severine, continued to live there after her husband's death until the late 1930s. The farm, with its thatched straw roofs, was constructed back in the 1700s. Typical of Danish farms, the farmhouse, barns, and stables were laid out in a square, leaving a cobblestone courtyard in the center. This arrangement provided protection, especially in the winter, from the prevailing north wind.

The three siblings had an idyllic childhood. By the age of eight or nine they would all learn to ride a horse. On hot summer days they would often go by horseback to nearby Guldborg Sound to cool off. They made longer trips by horse and buggy to the east coast of Falster, where they enjoyed the fine, white-sand beaches at Tromnæs or Marielyst—the latter, a mile or so to the south. After their swim, they would have a picnic under the shade of a stand of beech trees, while the horse that had brought them would be treated to a feedbag.

Mother once told me of an incident that happened when the whole family was on an outing at the beach. I don't recall where it took place, but the year 1930 sticks out in my mind. Everyone on that summer day was enjoying the cooling breeze blowing ashore from across the water. Suddenly there was a loud splash. Someone had fallen off the end of the pier. Lars Buus reacted instantly, running down to the end of the pier and jumping into the water. He didn't know who he was rescuing until he pulled the struggling victim out of the water. It was Anna Lise.

In the 1930s, a trip from Nykøbing Falster to Jutland took about half a day. (There were no bridges at the time connecting the islands.) To visit their grandmother Severine Buus at Risgaard the siblings would have to coordinate their journey by ferry (nearly an hour's voyage between Lolland and Langeland) and then by train. But the long trip was well worth the effort. Farmor (literally, father's mother) would prepare glasses of lemonade for the thirsty travelers, then she would entertain them on the veranda with stories of days gone by. Her sons, Lars, Niels, and Alfred, had been taught by a succession of private tutors from Copenhagen, which perhaps accounted for the fact that none of the brothers spoke with even a trace of the distinctive—and sometimes difficult to understand—Jutland accent. I don't know for certain if Severine's daughters, Stinne and Margrethe, received a similar education, but I suspect that they did, for neither of them, when I heard them speak in later years, was burdened with the Jutland dialect. From 1891 to 1892 Severine's husband, Peter, served in Copenhagen as a member of the First Company Life Guards, a cavalry regiment under the command of King Christian the Eighth. Peter also did duty as a Royal Guard at Amalienborg Palace, which was a distinct honor. A photo in Mother's album shows Peter wearing a large bearskin hat and holding a rifle with an attached bayonet. Not many soldiers were admitted to the Royal Guards. In addition to having an exemplary service record, you had to be at least six feet tall. So Peter Buus must have been a towering figure among his fellow soldiers, when the average height of a man in the 1890s was perhaps five feet, six inches. Lars Buus would follow in his father's footsteps, serving in a cavalry regiment in 1916. A photo, made into a postcard as was frequently done at the time, shows him mounted on a horse, his saber glistening at his side. Though both Peter and Lars looked as if they would have made formidable soldiers, neither of them was destined to fight in a battle. If they had, the chances are that I would not have been here to write about their lives.

The farmhouse at Risgaard, with its thatched straw roof and cobblestone courtyard, was like a museum. Inge, Knud, and Anna Lise were fascinated when their grandmother gave them a tour of the interior: a potbellied stove; a shiny copper samovar; a grandfather's clock standing as tall as a man; fading family photographs that preserved, however tenuously, a bygone age. Drawing back a window curtain as if to reveal a sacred relic, Farmor would point to one of the few glass panes that remained of the farmhouse's original window panes, which, over the course of 200 years under the constant pull of gravity, was now visibly thicker at the bottom than at the top. Each of these visits to Risgaard was like stepping back into an earlier century. It is no wonder that photographs from the thirties show Severine surrounded by an adoring flock from among her many grandchildren.

Klostergaarden, by contrast, with its combination of red-tile and concrete-board roofs, was a modern farm for its time. (Milking machines, however, still lay many years off in the future.) Unlike Risgaard with its straw roofs and white-washed, half-timbered walls, Klostergaarden was constructed of red brick. There were no drafty windows, no outhouses, no need for a chamber pot to be kept under your bed at night. Klostergaarden had electricity, central heating, hot-and-cold running water, a telephone, and indoor toilets. The three siblings wanted for nothing. They each had their own room. A photo in my mother's album shows Lars Buus perched confidently on the veranda of the farmhouse with his dog, Rolf, sitting beside him, the very picture of a country gentleman.

When Inge, who was left-handed, went off to school, Her teachers made her hold her pencil or pen in her right hand—which was the standard practice in those days. Writing with your left hand, the logic went, would cause the still-wet ink on the line you were working on to smudge. Moreover, it looked awkward to be pushing the pen along rather that dragging it neatly across the page. Inge bore these corrections with her customary good nature, never complaining, never tempted to switch hands when her teacher's back was turned. Even outside school, when she could have reverted to her left hand, she chose not to, realizing that if she failed to practice using her right hand she would only delay her ability to write properly and thus fail to please her teachers. Mother was no rebel, even in the privacy of her own home. Come to think of it, if I had been left-handed and some teacher had told me to switch over to writing with my right hand, I would have not been so amenable as my mother was. There would have been a confrontation, a showdown. Unlike my mother, I never liked being told what to do. But Mother's easy-going nature served her well. She quickly learned to produce a fluid script with her right hand, becoming ambidextrous as a result. Which would prove not to be a bad outcome after all. (Mother would continue to write with her right hand as an adult, switching to her left hand only temporarily after falling on the boardwalk at Belmar, New Jersey and badly spraining a finger in her right hand.)

Inge was an excellent student; she was always first or second in her class, vying for top honors with a shy, bespectacled boy who sat in the front row so he could better see the blackboard. Inge's straight red hair, cut in a distinctive pageboy style during her grade-school years, made her even more of a standout. For this reason, there was no hiding from the teacher's gaze among her predominantly blond classmates. When no hands were raised in response to a question, the teacher would invariably call on Inge, which kept her on her toes and motivated her to be fully prepared with the day's lessons.

In her early teens Inge abandoned her pageboy cut, letting her hair grow longer and having it curled as she transitioned to the more popular style of the day à la Vivian Leigh. But her red hair would continue to make her stand out in a crowd.

In high school, Inge excelled in Danish composition, English, German, math, history, and biology. She saved a composition book from her senior year in 1943 in which she describes a trip she made to Copenhagen with her best friend Bodil. The account bears glowing notations in the margins from her teacher: "Good. Brilliant. Outstanding." There were few corrections: an omitted comma, a minor spelling mistake. Inge was a well-rounded student. The consistency of effort that she displayed academically extended to athletics. She played on the school tennis team. Being able to swing the racket equally well with either hand gave her an edge over her teammates. Inge was popular with both her classmates and her teachers. She was a favorite with her biology teacher, hr. Larsen, who was apparently something of a character, often pontificating on matters beyond the domain of mere biology. Politics, philosophy—he had opinions on everything, but was always careful to couch his comments concerning Denmark's German "guests" in suitably cryptic terms. Years later, Inge was fond of quoting a bit of practical advice that her teacher had imparted to the class: "Never eat until you are filled up. Leave the table when you still feel like you could eat another *frikadeller*." (A meatball made of pork and veal). Good advice.

# OCCUPIED DENMARK

Inge was seventeen when Germany invaded Denmark. Officially, the assault began early on the morning of April 9, 1940, when a massive and carefully coordinated armada of aircraft parachuted troops all around Denmark to seize key airports, railway stations, and communications. Ships disembarked soldiers simultaneously in every major port. But actually, German soldiers had already set foot on Danish soil the day before. Lars and Ella Buus were heading home on their bikes an hour or so after sunset. Ella happened to glance back over her shoulder and saw a long line of bicycle lights coming up behind them. "We'd better hurry," she said, "before all those people catch up to us." They did not learn until the morning of April 9 that the hundreds of bicyclists they had seen the previous night were advance units of the *Wehrmacht,* fanning out over the island of Falster to secure radio stations and police barracks that would have sounded an early warning of the invading army. By noon the following day, radio broadcasts, now firmly under German control, presented the occupation as a *fait accompli.* German planes dropped leaflets all over Denmark proclaiming the benign intentions of the invaders. Denmark was being occupied, they claimed, to prevent an impending British and French invasion. (Really?) In fact, there was a tiny grain of truth to Hitler's justification. In 1807 the Danish island of Helgoland had been occupied by the English, who then handed it over to Prussia in 1890 in exchange for some territorial concessions in Africa. Were the British up to their old tricks again? The German pre-emptive occupation of Denmark had a measure of logic to it. German announcers on the radio, speaking fluent Danish, declared that there was no cause for alarm. The real enemy was England. Germany's only desire was to protect Denmark from British imperialism. Ignoring previous Prussian incursions into Jutland and the annexation of Schleswig-Holstein in 1864, the Nazi propagandists emphasized that Denmark and Germany were both Aryan nations, with shared values. The two countries could live in peace and harmony as brothers. In the pre-dawn hours of April 9 there was some initial scattered resistance. In the south of Jutland, thirteen Danish soldiers were killed when they fired upon a column of advancing German troops. A single aircraft managed to take off from Værlose Airport, on the outskirts of Copenhagen, and was promptly shot down. In the center of Copenhagen, Danish Royal Guards at Amalienborg Palace exchanged gunfire with German soldiers as they marched into the square. At 6 A.M., Realizing the hopelessness of the Danish position, King Christian X gave the order to cease fire, and agreed to Hitler's terms of surrender. The fighting had lasted a scant two hours. A standing joke at the time was that if Denmark, with a mere 14,000 men under arms, was ever invaded, whoever was in charge of the government would simply pick up the phone and declare, "We surrender."

Unlike other countries that Germany occupied, Denmark was given special treatment—at least initially. The Danish government was permitted to remain in place. There were to be free elections. The king could continue to reside in Amalienborg Palace, and would be allowed complete freedom of movement. The Danish armed forces were not disbanded. The Danish police still walked their beats, albeit now in coordination with German soldiers, who had a somewhat different concept of maintaining order. And what was more, Danish Jews would not be required to wear the Star of David on their sleeves, as was mandatory in other countries the Germans had overrun. All things considered, the occupation did not seem all that bad.

The Danish government was roundly condemned by the Allies for its failure to mount any significant opposition to the German invasion. Norway, by contrast, invaded on the very same day, had put up in coordination with British forces a fierce resistance, resulting in some 5,000 German casualties. But in all fairness, the two situations were not strictly comparable. Norway, with its rugged terrain and steep mountains, was much more easily defended than Denmark, whose highest peak rises a mere 500 feet above sea level. German tanks could simply drive around a sabotaged road over the level fields. Not so in Norway, where a compromised road along one of the fjords could take days to clear, only to be closed again by another rockfall. Nevertheless, Denmark's accommodation to the German occupation was seen by many as an act of collaboration. It's agricultural products, formerly shipped mostly to Britain, were now exported exclusively to Germany. Danish shipyards were forced to build and repair ships to support the German war effort. Trucks and armaments were made to specifications dictated by the *Wehrmacht*. The Danish economy, in a deep recession at the time of the invasion, quickly began to revive. Companies were rehiring laid-off workers. People had money in their pockets again. No one was going hungry. A majority of Danes were content to hold their noses and put up with the German invaders.

During the first two years of the occupation, King Christian would ride his horse from Amalienborg Palace through the streets of Copenhagen, unaccompanied by not a single guard. It was a small, but for Adolf Hitler, a stinging act of defiance. Hitler could not travel anywhere in Germany without a heavily armed escort. To see pictures of the Danish king riding alone on his horse rankled Hitler to no end. German soldiers dutifully saluted Christian X, but he ignored them and continued on his regal way. How could the king ride through the streets of Copenhagen without an armed escort? The king's protectors, it was reported, were ordinary Danish citizens, who, seeing their beloved king passing by on his daily ride, would protect him from harm. Christian X further rankled Hitler by responding to an effusive greeting on the occasion of his seventy-second birthday with a terse, "Best thanks. Christian X."

Many years later, I asked my mother if she ever saw the king riding his horse through the streets of Copenhagen. She had walked every day past Amalienborg Palace on her way to the shipyard in 1944. But she never saw the king. In October 1942, Christian X was seriously injured on a fall from his horse, and was brought to his summer palace, Sorgenfri (Sorrow Free), to recuperate. Hitler, seething in fury at the sympathy shown to the Danish king, had him placed under house arrest.

During the beginning of the occupation, the Danish people experienced surprisingly little change in their daily lives. For the most part, the German soldiers who now patrolled the streets of the major cities were courteous and well-disciplined; they were glad to be stationed in Denmark, as opposed to having to endure fighting on the front or being posted on guard duty to other countries that Germany had invaded, where the troops had to deal with fierce resistance fighters. Being in Denmark was almost like being on a holiday. German soldiers, like other tourists, visited Kronborg Castle, Fredericksburg Castle, the Round Tower, and Copenhagen's Aquarium; they waited in line to view the changing of the Royal Guard at Amalienborg Palace; they strolled through Tivoli Gardens and attended performances in its celebrated concert hall. Yes, Germans and Danes could get along.

In movie theaters, mandatory Nazi propaganda newsreels now preceded the main feature, touting the unbroken string of German successes in the war: German troops marching resolutely along snow-covered roads; jut-jawed German soldiers tramping fearlessly to the front; a seemingly endless stream of panzer tanks rolling past the cameras; reports of steady advances in Russia and North Africa; excerpts from Hitler's rambling speeches. These features were often met with gales of laughter from the audience, who knew better from listening to forbidden BBC broadcasts that the Germans were not the supermen that they claimed to be. American films were still permitted to be shown in the theaters, at least for the first year or so of the occupation. *Gone With the Wind* was a big hit. Mickey Rooney, starring in the long-running *Andy Hardy* series was a particular favorite of Lars Buus, who chuckled at the antics of the energetic but naive youth whose exploits somehow always seemed to work out in the end. In a characteristic display of Nazi pettiness, however, it would not be long before even the most innocent American and British films were banned. Movie-goers would henceforth have to be content with a steady influx of mediocre German films. (*Deutschland, Deutschland* überalles.)

In 1942 the Danish economy continued to boom. Farmers were planting their crops on ever-expanded acreage to feed the hungry German army. They might not have liked the people they were dealing with, but what was the alternative? Prices were good. The Germans were willing to pay far more than the British ever did. Prospering along with his fellow farmers, Lars Buus sold Klostergaarden and bought a much larger farm, called Ourepgaard, which he had had his eyes on since 1918, but had not been able to afford even the down payment. The sprawling farmhouse could easily have been mistaken for a country manor house. Four stories high, it had servants' quarters in the attic. There was a good-sized pond that supported a family of swans. Extensive stands of trees protected the fields from the relentless north wind. And to keep tabs on his far-flung acreage, Lars made daily rounds on horseback.

Unfortunately, these good times were not destined to last. After two years, the German occupation would take an ugly turn. Ever since the occupation began, Denmark had been placed under a nightly blackout. But looking out from an apartment window in Copenhagen across the Øresund, one could see the lights From Malmö in neutral Sweden blazing brightly. By 1942 air-raid alerts were a common occurrence. Every night powerful searchlights would sweep the skies as Allied aircraft passed over Denmark on their way to and from bombing missions in Germany, and bursts of antiaircraft fire could be heard in all major cities. People quickly got used to these alerts and went on with their lives.

For the most part during this period of calm before the storm, Inge and her family lived much as they had before the invasion. They experienced no shortages of food, typical of other nations Germany had conquered. They continued to take summer vacations. Norway, France, and other occupied countries, however, were now off-limits; it was illegal to travel to "neutral" Sweden, which venturesome young men were beginning to visit with the intention of joining the Danish Brigade, an underground organization devoted to training volunteers who would eventually return to Denmark and fight the Nazi occupiers. The Danish island of Bornholm provided a worthy alternative for Danes seeking a change of scenery. Lying less than twenty-five miles off the southern coast of Sweden, its inhabitants spoke Danish with a Swedish accent. Bornholm was sparsely inhabited. A six-to-seven-hour ferry ride from Copenhagen concluded with a stunning view of the sheer rocky cliffs at the western end of the island. To the south were long, sandy beaches. Inge, Knud, and Anna Lise brought their dog, Knøs along with them on their visit in 1942. There were numerous hiking trails through the wooded countryside, every turn providing a breathtaking, bucolic vista. On horseback, one could explore the 18-mile-long island from one end to the other in the course of a few days. Orienteering, which originated in Sweden, was a popular sport at the time. It consisted of finding one's way through the countryside guided only by a map and a compass. The siblings' wanderings took them through quaint villages consisting of clusters of half-timbered houses with red-tile roofs. At the end of a day's excursion they might stop in a small fishing port for a hearty dinner of smoked herring. While Bornholm could boast of a number of unique, thick-walled round churches dating back to the twelfth century (the thick granite walls intended as a defense against marauding pirates), there was not a single castle to be seen on the island. But so what? You could visit any number of castles, cathedrals, and concert halls back on the mainland of Denmark. What more could you ask for?

But excursions to scenic Bornholm were to cease soon after Knud's and Anna Lise's final visit to the island in the spring of 1943. (Inge, who did not go along with her siblings, would soon be on her way to Copenhagen to begin a new phase in her life.) For several months there had been sightings of some strange aircraft crashing into the Baltic Sea off the northern coast of Germany. No one knew what they were. On August 22, one of these aircraft happened to crash-land on an isolated field in Bornholm. It turned out to be an early prototype of the V-I rocket. A couple of quick-thinking policemen managed to take photographs of the missile before German soldiers arrived at the scene; the police sent these photos and other intelligence to London. The cat was out of the bag. Based on the information they had received, the British were able to determine that the missiles had been launched from Peenemünde, a secret installation on the coast of Germany. Royal Air Force bombers subsequently destroyed most of the site, as well as radar facilities and banks of cameras on the island of Bornholm that had been monitoring the V I rocket flights. The production of Hitler's secret weapon was thus delayed for many months. It was not until after the Normandy invasion on June 6, 1944 that Germany was able to begin launching its now-perfected guided missiles on London. Bornholm, previously regarded as a backwater, scarcely worth a second thought, was placed in lockdown after August 1943. SS troops were sent to the island to keep watch over the inhabitants. In retaliation for having spilled the beans on his secret missile program, Hitler ordered the arrest and deportation of over a thousand Bornholmers to German prison camps. Unfortunately for Hitler, It was too little, too late, and his crackdown on his Danish "protectorate" would soon backfire on him.

The Germans were increasingly revealing their true stripes. The velvet gloves were off. At Ourepgaard, seeing how Lars Buus had prospered under the occupation, German soldiers were beginning to demand choice cuts of pork and beef. No, there would not even be a token payment. Lars responded to these requests with a forced smile. It would not do to challenge these soldiers. They were snooping about the farm to see what else they could steal (fresh eggs, potatoes, chickens); they were questioning Lars' Polish workers, who had come to Denmark as refugees fleeing the Nazi juggernaut. (Banislav was a name that Inge often mentioned in later years.) They were hoping to uncover the smallest infraction that they might use to their advantage. And what could Lars do but comply with the demands of these German thieves? What repercussions might result if a single German soldier fell ill from a tainted slice of meat that had come from Ourepgaard? Lars was responsible, not only for the safety of his family, but also for the lives of his workers. The smallest act of defiance, even an inadvertent mistake could be catastrophic. The possibility of German reprisals was not to be taken lightly.

As her high-school years were coming to a close, Inge had an important decision to make. She had a good foundation and aptitude in the biological sciences. Should she follow in the footsteps of her aunt Stinne and a couple of older cousins and become a nurse? Or should she strike off in some other direction?

During a spring weekend in 1943, Inge and her best friend, Bodil, took a train to Copenhagen so Inge could check out the nursing school that she was considering applying to and scout out suitable lodgings. Inge was immediately captivated by the hustle and bustle of the big city. Her first glimpse of the sprawling, modern hospital filled her with anticipation. She questioned one of the young nurses coming down the steps of the building. How did she like working there? What were her duties? How many patients did she look after? The nurse answered that the long hours were demanding, but the work was fulfilling. Inge was encouraged by what she heard. And so on that very day, her path was set. There would be no vacillating, no turning back. Inge had her heart set on becoming a nurse.

After graduating from Rødkilde High School in June 1943, Inge began her internship in Amtssyggehuset (County Hospital) in Copenhagen. Despite the long, often hectic hours a student nurse was expected to put in, Inge enjoyed her work. As worn-out as she might be by the end of her shift, she never spared herself in tending her patients. Many years later, she told me about a dying boy she had cared for in his final days. Perhaps eight or nine years old, he was suffering from blood poisoning. He had picked up on the street a packet containing some mysterious powder; it turned out to be highly poisonous phosphorus. The inquisitive boy discovered that the substance glowed in the dark. Unfortunately, he began keeping the packet in his pants pocket so he could show it to his schoolmates. The corrosive powder soon leached through the material of his pants and ate its way into his skin; it then entered his bloodstream, quickly sickening him. His parents rushed him to Amtssyggehuset, but it was already too late. Wracked with pain as the poison coursed through his system, the boy cried out piteously. Inge, supported by other nurses, tended the dying boy day and night, mopping the sweat from his feverish brow and dripping water onto his parched lips. Toward the end, he was unable to swallow. It took the boy two or three days to die. His parents thanked Inge and the other nurses for taking such good care of their son.

Inge would have made a great nurse. Unfortunately, being on her feet all day long was physically exhausting. Her tired legs would give out during the course of her rounds. It was very likely a complication from the rickets she had contracted as a young child. During her eight-hour shifts her ankles would become swollen and painful, forcing her to take every opportunity she had to sit down and put her feet up. She was becoming as infirm as some of her patients. Though Inge had her heart set on a nursing career, she realized that this would be a physical impossibility. A desk job was now her only option. It was the biggest disappointment in her life.

Inge's first glimpse of a German officer wearing a silver skull-and-crossbones on his peaked cap made her uncomfortable. What kind of twisted mind could conceive of such an evil symbol? But Inge quickly became accustomed to the sight. It was just a hat, a symbol of authority intended to put civilians in their place. Surely, the man wearing it was not a monster. And the helmeted German soldiers that Inge passed on the street were for the most part friendly. They were just ordinary men who were required to wear this imposing uniform. Under their uniforms, Inge reasoned, they were no different from anyone else. As tensions between the Danes and the occupiers continued to escalate, German soldiers manning machine-gun posts became a common sight in central Copenhagen. Inge got used to them, too. After all, they were not threatening her but people who were foolhardy enough to oppose the occupation—saboteurs. There was no cause for alarm. Inge liked living in Copenhagen, so a return to Falster was not in the cards. But what was she to do now that her nursing career was out of the question? With her excellent math skills, she considered a position as an accountant at several small firms. Then, setting her sights higher early in 1944, she applied for a position at Burmeister and Wain, the largest shipyard in Denmark. She was promptly hired, and at a good salary. Inge's parents had serious reservations about her new employer. Burmeister and Wain, forced to make and refit ships for the German navy, was a prime military target for the Allies. The Royal Air Force had bombed the shipyard in January 1943. The attack had left the facilities of Burmeister and Wain relatively unscathed, but had resulted in many civilian casualties when bombs missed their intended target and destroyed a sugar refinery and most of a housing tract in Christianshavn. In December of the same year Danish Resistance forces succeeded in blowing up the facility for the production of engines for German U-boats that the RAF had earlier missed, with no loss of civilian life. Clouds of smoke from the sabotaged shipyard drifted over Copenhagen for two days.

Inge countered her parents' concerns with the argument that the RAF was unlikely to attempt another bombing raid on the shipyard. Burmeister and Wain was spread out over a nearly four-mile-long island in Copenhagen Harbor. Its facilities shared the island with two churches, a home for the feebleminded, a seaman's hostel, a tailor's shop that catered to sailors, a merchant bank, a school for merchant seamen, a sea rescue station, a public bathhouse, a playground, and other civilian establishments. The RAF had no stomach for a repeat of its year-ago slaughter of the innocents at the sugar factory and housing tract, preferring to leave future attacks up to the Danish Resistance, which had the ability to target specific installations and minimize civilian casualties. In any case, the resistance fighters would concentrate their sabotage efforts, if any, on strictly military targets, not on the office building in which Inge was now working. The salary was much higher than what she might have earned in a less strategic business. The Germans needed ships and U-boats and were willing to pay whatever it cost to keep their navy up to scratch..

The Burmeister and Wain company ferry left from a dock on the Langelenie promenade, not far from the statue of the Little Mermaid. Inge enjoyed the daily ten-minute crossing across Copenhagen Harbor to her workplace—a refreshing brace of salty sea air. The German soldier aboard the little ferry would ask to see not only your company pass but also the German-issues *Ausweiss,* a pale-green card bearing your photograph, your place of residence, and your religion. The card was first issued in the summer of 1943, ostensibly to protect law-abiding citizens from the actions of terrorist groups. Although few realized it at the time, the identity card was actually a precursor to Hitler's attempted roundup of Denmark's Jews later that year. While Danish Jews, unlike those in other occupied countries, were never forced to wear the Star of David, the *Ausweiss* card served a similar purpose. My mother expressed her regret to me in later years that she had not saved her German-issued *Ausweiss.* She had not preserved any of the leaflets that German planes had dropped all over Denmark on the morning of April 9, 1940; nor had she kept a single issue of the anti-German underground newspapers. At the time she had just wanted to put all such reminders of the occupation behind her. She took no pictures during her years on Copenhagen. If the German soldiers had caught you on the street with a camera, you would have been immediately arrested on suspicion of being a member of the underground. So any photos documenting the Nazi occupation had to be clandestinely taken, and at great risk.

My mother would often describe to me how at the end of September 1943, the word spread like wildfire through the Danish population that the Nazis were planning to round up all of Denmark's Jews on the night of October 1 and deport them to Theresienstadt, a concentration camp in Czechoslovakia. Danish Jews had enjoyed full and equal rights of citizenship for some three hundred years and were universally regarded as Danes first and Jews second. Being Jewish mattered not a jot to anyone—except to the Nazi invaders. The idea that this one segment of the population should be singled out for extermination was totally incomprehensible. Denmark was united as never before before by this latest Nazi outrage. Many Danes offered to hide their Jewish friends and neighbors, most of whom lived in and around Copenhagen. Jews were hidden in the attics of private homes, in unoccupied summerhouses, in churches, in hospitals, in the forests that surrounded Copenhagen.

Lars Buus was in no position to safely hide anyone on his large farm. German soldiers, continued to come to the farm once a week to extract their tribute. Early in October with the roundup of the Jews underway, several extra German soldiers turned up at Ourepgaard, accompanied by a glowering Danish Nazi—a type that was even more despised than the Germans. They were clearly looking for more than produce, searching lofts and barns, a henhouse, a root cellar. They went so far as to stick pitchforks into a suspicious haystack. They interrogated the farmhands. (*Ausweiss, bitte.*") No Jews here.

Mother told me how one day, a car filled with German soldiers drove off from the farm with their cut of fresh meat and produce. They began singing loudly, *"Wir fahren nach England* (We're driving to England)." One of Morfar's farmhands stared disdainfully at the departing Germans. *"Det bliver som lig,"* he said. ("It'll be as corpses.")

Hitler's roundup of the Danish Jews turned out to be an almost total failure. About 95 percent of Denmark's 8,000 Jews were safely smuggled out of the country, most of them ferried by small fishing boats across the Øresund to Sweden under the very noses of the German patrols. Infuriated by the defiance of his orders for a "final solution," Hitler placed further restrictions on Denmark, which were promptly countered by stepped-up acts of resistance. The attempted roundup of the Jews was the final straw, and only served to turn more Danes against their German "protectors." Any pretense that Danes and Germans could live together in harmony had long gone by the wayside.

Defiance of the German occupation had already ramped up early in September 1943 when the entire Danish government resigned in protest of increasingly burdensome restrictions and regulations. On September 8 the Danish navy scuttled its fleet, ensuring that their vessels would never be used by the Germans. Things were fast coming to a head. The Germans began a roundup of the Danish police force. The police either went into hiding or were deported to German concentration camps, their duties taken over by Hippos, a much-despised evolution of the Danish-German auxiliary police force. More German troops were to be seen on the streets of Copenhagen, and these were not the friendly *Whermacht* soldiers from the early days of the occupation, but battle-hardened SS soldiers. They were under strict new orders: they were to step up the hunt for members of the Danish Underground—no holds barred. The killing of a single German soldier would be followed the next day by the shooting of five Danish citizens, chosen at random to serve as an example. Their bullet-ridden bodies were left where they lay on the street until their grieving relatives mustered up the courage to recover them. My mother never told me if she had personally witnessed any of these "examples," but it would have been on the mind of any Dane walking the streets of Copenhagen. Were the SS soldiers up ahead, armed as they were with submachine guns, preparing for an act of retaliation? It would not do the cross over to the other side of the street. That would only serve to attract attention. Better to continue on innocently and produce your *Ausweiss* card if you were stopped.

Convinced that the German soldier on the Burmeister and Wain ferry would be able to prevent any acts of sabotage at the shipyard, Inge continued in her position. Even when the courteous *Whermacht* soldier who had previously checked her out, often waving her on after the briefest of inspections, was replaced by was replaced by a gruff SS soldier, who insisted on pawing methodically through her handbag in a vain search for suspected bomb materials, Inge saw no cause for alarm. She had nothing to hide. She was an essential worker, albeit for the enemy.

By 1943 Copenhagen was beginning to look more and more like a war zone, with bombed-out buildings and rubble in the streets. A restaurant frequented by German soldiers was firebombed. For their part, Germans set off bombs in popular venues, hoping to provoke Danish Resistance fighters into a rash act of retaliation that would allow the Germans to round them up.

German tanks rolled through Raadhuspladsen in a naked show of force on August 28, 1943. After the Danish navy scuttled its fleet, the Germans declared martial law. A curfew was imposed between the hours of 9 P.M. and 5 A.M. Private cars were banned. Doctors had to visit their patients by bike or go on foot. Gatherings of more than five people were forbidden under penalty of arrest. German soldiers were no longer smiling when they demanded to see your *Ausweiss*. They rarely said, *"Danke."*

One morning Inge was on her way to the shipyard. She had just crossed the courtyard at Amalienborg Palace, which was now guarded by helmeted German soldiers, an ominous substitute for the Danish Royal Guards in their quaint bearskin hats. Making her way toward the waterfront, she was startled when an intense-looking young man (no doubt a student, for they were at the forefront of this clandestine anti-German activity), thrust a leaflet into her hands. A brief glance told her that it was one of those mimeographed underground newspapers that had proliferated after the first two years of the occupation. The fresh ink gave off a distinctive, pungent smell. For a moment Inge's curiosity got the better of her. Her fingers touched the clasp of her handbag. Bad idea. Inge imagined the SS guard on the little Burmeister and Wain ferry opening her handbag and discovering the anti-Nazi diatribe. At the very least she would have been subjected to an intense round of questioning, probably at Gestapo headquarters. "Where did you get this? Who gave it to you? Are you a member of the underground?" Inge discretely crumpled up the pamphlet as she walked on and deposited it in a convenient trash receptacle. After this incident she was careful to avoid any student types who happened to suddenly veer into her path. But now as she underwent the increased scrutiny of the SS guard on the ferry, she was beginning to have second thoughts about her place of employment. Perhaps her parents' fears were not unfounded. Perhaps the high pay offered at Burmeister and Wain was not worth the extra risk.

Another day on her way home from the shipyard, Inge was startled by a figure hurtling from a tall building and smashing on the sidewalk right in front of her. Inge never forgot the sound of the woman's body impacting on the pavement, the sound of her last breath escaping from her mouth, the pool of blood forming under her smashed skull. Did she jump from the window? Was she pushed? Was she a member of the resistance? Inge did not hang around long enough to find out. In German-occupied Denmark, it was not wise to ask any questions. Better to move on. Let someone else deal with the dead woman.

Events were progressing rapidly. Every Danish act of resistance was followed by immediate and brutal German retaliation. In Jutland, resistance groups were blowing up trains, severely impacting German efforts to supply armaments via the Danish railway system to their troops in Norway. The Germans began tying Danish hostages to the front of locomotives, but the resistance adapted by detonating their explosives after the first couple of cars had passed. Hitler fumed at such distractions from his main war effort, which were draining scarce reserves from the front. Never at a loss for dreaming up increasingly chilling demonstrations of their ruthlessness, the Nazi occupiers did not take long to answer the the Danish Underground's attempts to slow down the German war machine.

On January 7, 1944 SS soldiers stormed into a small vicarage in western Jutland and abducted Kai Munk, a popular Danish clergyman and playwright who had sermonized against the invaders and given some minor assistance to one of the numerous Danish Resistance groups. To serve as an example, Munk was summarily shot in the back of the head; his body was thrown into a ditch on a narrow country road just outside Silkeborg. (In the 1960s, traveling down that same country road, my mother and I stopped to view a bronze commemorative plaque attached to the decaying trunk that remained of an enormous old tree. There, she told me the story of Kai Munk, a Danish patriot.)

On June 26, 1944, in response to increased acts of sabotage committed by the resistance, the Schalburg Corps, a group of Danish Nazis, vandalized Tivoli Gardens, the popular amusement park in the center of Copenhagen. They firebombed the concert hall and the dance pavilion (the Nazis were apparently outraged by the patrons' jitterbug dance style—a distinctly non-Aryan performance). They uprooted newly planted trees and smashed windows. Then, for good measure, they moved on to the Royal Copenhagen Porcelain Factory, which they burned to the ground. What were these Danish Nazis thinking? What twisted minds they must have had to make them believe that firebombing beloved Tivoli Gardens and destroying a porcelain factory would further their cause. Anyway, what was their cause? Inge was never able to understand what these Danish Nazis were all about.

The following day many Danish businesses, including all 10,000 workers at Burmeister and Wain went on strike. At night Danes ignored the curfew and lit bonfires on the streets of Copenhagen. To restore order, German soldiers fired their machine guns indiscriminately into the crowds, killing a dozen civilians. The Schalburg Corps went into action again, firebombing a Copenhagen sports pavilion. (Again, what was wrong with these people?)

The attempted roundup of the Danish Jews, the murder of Kai Munk, the firebombing of Tivoli Gardens, the confinement of King Christian X at his summer palace—all these and other atrocities served not to cow the Danes into submission as Adolf Hitler had hoped, but to energize opposition to German rule. It seemed that Hitler possessed an almost pathological capacity for shooting himself in the foot, again and again enraging the once-compliant Danes.

During the general strike, for the first time since the beginning of the war, there were food shortages. At Amtssyghuset, where Inge had served as a student nurse, milk was handed out to families with children. Schools distributed hard-to-find tins of food to the needy. In the shops, bread was now being sold for blackmarket prices, though many shopkeepers, serving their customers through the back door, would allow unlimited credit, or even hand out food for free. People had to help one another out in these hard times.

Inge was beginning to feel increasingly uneasy working at Burmeister and Wain. Sabotage efforts on the part of the Danish Resistance were stepping up. It seemed likely that it was only a matter of time before the shipyard would again be targeted. The war was turning against Germany, and Hitler's defeat appeared inevitable. But instead of relaxing their grip on tiny Denmark, the Germans only turned up the heat on their "protectorate." More burdensome restrictions. More arbitrary stops of people who were simply attempting to go about their business. Showing increasing contempt for Danish citizens, German soldiers would point their guns at you as they demanded to see your *Ausweiss*. The Gestapo was now in total control of Copenhagen Harbor. There were SS soldiers, usually traveling in pairs, to be seen on every street. What would their next step be? Nazi depravity seemed to have no limits. Reprisals were swift and without mercy or justice. The German occupiers were now destroying any house from which they believed that sniper fire had issued. Any house suspected of having served as a meeting place for resistance groups was immediately blown up.

Finally heeding the advice of her parents, Inge decided to seek employment at a firm that had nothing to do with supporting the German war effort. She applied for a position at a goldsmith's shop in Hillerød, about twelve miles north of Copenhagen and a safe distance away from the shipyard. The firm paid considerably less than Burmeister and Wain, but as they manufactured nothing of any military importance (assorted flatware, spoons, candlesticks, jewelry, watches, various specialty items), they were not likely to be targeted by either the Royal Air Force or the Danish Resistance.

Inge had been working for her new employer for about a week as a bookkeeper in charge of the payroll when a small, but vexing problem came up. After paying the workers their weekly salary, Inge found an extra ten kroner remaining in the cash register. As many times as she tried to reconcile the figures in her account book, she kept coming up with the same result: there was always ten kroner too much left in the till. Had she made a mistake? None of the workers had complained that his pay was insufficient. Inge went to Hr. Hansen, her boss, and explained the discrepancy to him. Hr. Hansen smiled.

"I put that extra ten kroner in the cash register," he admitted. "It was a test. If you had pocketed those ten kroner, I would have known that you were dishonest, and I would have fired you. Congratulations."

Mother told me this story many times over the course of the years, often when she was opening her mail using the bronze letter opener that had been presented to her when she left Hr. Hansen's shop to go to America. It was one of her favorite recollections, along with her stories of growing up on Klostergaarden.

Anyway, back to the occupation. In June 1944, in response to increasing unrest on the part of ordinary Danish citizens, the Germans shut off Copenhagen's electricity, gas, and water. There was no telephone service. There were no newspapers—except for hastily mimeographed underground leaflets. The Danish State Radio was shut down. German soldiers had been transferred from the front lines to deal with the uprisings in Denmark, which seriously impacted Hitler's war effort. Panzer tank divisions surrounded the city, preventing only a select few from entering or leaving. The Germans seemed bent on starving Copenhagen's 700,000 citizens into submission. It was a war of nerves. But it soon backfired on the Germans. A second general strike was called. The formerly placid Danes rioted. Despite the nightly curfew, daring young men were defying the German occupiers by digging up the cobbled streets and paving stones, which they used to erect barricades designed to halt the advance of German tanks. Portraits and effigies of Adolf Hitler were burned. German soldiers and Danish collaborators were attacked. A thousand bonfires were lit throughout the city. German armored cars rumbled through the streets, firing wildly upon the enraged crowds. Soldiers shot people who failed to comply quickly enough with their orders to disperse, and left the bodies where they lay. Clearly, no part of Copenhagen was safe anymore. But Inge realized that getting out of the city under such conditions would be extremely difficult. Some people managed to escape through the sewers. There were no trains or busses. No taxis. No private cars. And for Inge, making the journey back to Falster on foot or by bicycle was out of the question. German sentries were posted at intervals along all the main roads. ("*Ausweiss, bitte.*") Better to stay put and wait for the unrest to die down.

On July 3, 1944 the general strike was called off after the Germans agreed to scale back their restrictions. The electricity, water, and gas were turned back on. People were once again allowed to enter and leave the city.

But it was only a temporary respite. Despite the mutual attempt at accommodation, the violence continued. Acts of sabotage and revenge were committed by both sides in the conflict. Nearly every day the sound of an explosion would be heard; the sirens of fire trucks blared as they sped to the latest conflagration. By now it was a rare street in Copenhagen that did not have at least one building that had been bombed out or that had walls pocked-marked with machine-gun bullets. Nazi-owned shops were vandalized and set afire. A large cinema in the center of Copenhagen was blown up by the traitorous Schalburg Corps. The Royal Yacht Club near Langelenie was blown up by the same group to target upperclass Danes. A theater that had shown a film disrespecting Adolf Hitler was firebombed. Around the same time, Members of the Danish Resistance blew up a factory that manufactured rifles according to German specifications. The Danish Petroleum Company, which supplied oil and gas to the German army, was blown up; the resulting fire could be seen all over Copenhagen, raging for days.

Early in 1945 another crisis arose. German refugees whose homes had been destroyed by Allied air strikes now began streaming into Denmark, putting an additional strain on the economy. These refugees had no respect for their Danish hosts. They would barge into shops and, with the support of the German police, simply take what they wanted from the shelves. They were a wretched lot, some of them suffering from wounds they had received during the Allied attacks on Germany. Many were seriously ill, spreading disease in crowded refugee camps scattered throughout Copenhagen. Sleeping on the ground in partially bombed-out factories or warehouses, or squatting in the shells of abandoned row houses, scores of these German refugees were dying every day. Schools in Copenhagen were requisitioned to house this flood of people. There were too many corpses for the German soldiers to deal with, so they were left where they lay, or dragged into basements for someone else to dispose of. If there was any consolation for the Danes it was that conditions in Germany must be absolutely horrible to have caused this mass exodus. Many years later when the subject of refugees came up on the TV evening news, Ella Buus told my mother and me that she could never have survived as a refugee (*flygtningen*). She declared that she would have just lain down by the side of the road and waited to die.

Shortly before noon on March 21, 1945, Inge and her co-workers at Hr. Hansen's shop were startled by the heart-stopping wail of the air-raid siren. As they headed for the nearest shelter, a squadron of planes came from the east (they had flown low over the fields of Jutland, waved on by numerous farmworkers who had spotted them). The tight formation buzzed by at high speed just above the rooftops of Copenhagen. Looking up in the clear blue sky that morning, Inge could easily make out the white-blue-and-red Royal Air Force roundels on the undersides of the planes' wings. Her first thought was that they were having another go at Burmeister and Wain. But the planes were not headed for the shipyard.

Their target this time was the Gestapo headquarters housed in the Shell House (formerly the headquarters of the Shell Oil Company) in the center of Copenhagen. Braving heavy antiaircraft flack from the Germans, RAF Mosquitos dropped their bombs precisely into the bottom two floors of the infamous building, hoping that Danish Resistance fighters, imprisoned in the sixth-floor attic and subjected to the most brutal of tortures (thumbscrews, broken fingers, beatings with whips and canes, branding with red-hot pokers, being strung from the ceiling by one's ankles), might be able to flee in the resulting confusion. The raid achieved its objective. Twenty-six prisoners managed to make their escape from the bombed-out building, while 200 Germans and Danish collaborators perished. Gestapo records listing the names of suspected Resistance fighters were destroyed. Unfortunately, some of the RAF bombs went astray, demolishing the Jeanne d'Arc School, a Catholic school for children in nearby Fredericksberg. Eighty-three children and twenty nuns lost their lives. Nevertheless, the mission was considered a success.

But such aerial bombardments, however massive, however successful, were not going to drive the Germans out of Denmark. Hitler had already faced major reversals in the prosecution of the war. The attempted siege of Stalingrad from August 1942 to February 1943 had been a disaster, resulting in the surrender of the entire German Sixth Army; more recently, German forces had been overwhelmed by the Normandy invasion in June 1944. The Nazi regime seemed determined to dig in and fight on to the bitter end. Who knew what a cornered German army was capable of? It would take many more boots on the ground before this particular phase of the war was over. And help was on the way.

The Yanks were coming.

# ARMY DAYS

One Yank in particular was facing a personal dilemma. Robert (Bob) Peterson had begun working for the naval architectural firm of Gibbs & Cox in 1938. Contracted out to the Federal Shipbuilding and Dry Dock Company in Kearney, New Jersey, he was employed initially in the mold loft, where molds and patterns were made from which ships were constructed. A quick learner, he was soon advanced to the position of junior draftsman in the hull structural division.

When the United States declared war on Germany on December 11, 1942, young men of draft age eagerly volunteered or else they were drafted to serve in the armed forces. Those draft-age men not entering the army were subjected to disapproving looks and disparaging remarks when they appeared in public. Bob Peterson wanted to join up, but was told at his local draft board that this was not possible, since he was employed by Federal Shipyard in an essential war effort. He was now working on the hull design of the LSTs (Landing Ship Tanks). These were shallow-draft vessels capable of landing troops and heavy equipment on a beach. (Picture an oversized dumpster with propellers on the back. The fact that these ungainly vessels could actually sail was a testament to the shipyard.) There was a pressing need for thousands of these LSTs. Federal Shipyard was building them with all deliberate haste, and they would prove to be a decisive factor in the successful Allied landings at Normandy Beach on D-Day, June 6, 1944. Bob Peterson endured the taunts of the unenlightened as best as he could. But even after a lengthy explanation, some people simply thought that he was shirking his military service. Bob was greatly relieved on May 13, 1943 when he finally received his much-anticipated draft notice. His service record reveals that his military training took some ten months, commencing on May 20 when he began active duty at Fort Dix, New Jersey. He began basic training at the Aberdeen Proving Ground in Maryland on July 1. After completing basic training, he moved on to technical training from August 4 to October 9, then underwent cadre military training until November 6. He began field training on November 27, and was assigned the rank of corporal. On February 20, 1944 he was transferred to the Second Provisional Headquarters in Jackson, Mississippi, where he was assigned to the 3164th Artillery and Fire Control Company.

Whew! This is only a brief summary of Bob Peterson's military training. Forget whatever you've seen in the movies depicting a rushed six weeks of basic training. It wasn't just about being able to do push-ups and sit-ups, slog around with a fifty-pound pack on your back, and fire a rifle. These were no mere grunts the army was turning out; they were well-trained fighting men, possessing highly specialized skills. Among other things, Bob learned how to fire and repair a "Long-Ton" 155 millimeter gun (it was over fifteen feet long), and to drive and repair an M-4 tank.

On March 31, 1944, battle-ready Bob Peterson arrived at his port of embarkation in Miles Standish, Boston. His commanding officer was General George Patton (whom Bob never saw). He boarded the troop ship

Wakefield (the former passenger liner Manhattan) on April 12. Leaving Boston Harbor on April 17, he arrived at Liverpool, England on April 20. He was stationed for a time at Artillery Park Number 5 in Toddington, then was billeted in Toddington Manor, a stately country house dating back to Elizabethan times. He remained there until until December 14, when he was sent to Ashchuch. (In one of his rare reflections on his days in the army, Bob mused that if had not been for his coming down with the measles, which delayed his sailing to France for some two weeks, he would have been thrown into the thick of the fighting at the Battle of the Bulge.) Leaving Ashchurch on December 15, Bob drove an M-4 tank to his port of embarkation in Portland. On December 17 he guided the tank onto an LST. Ironically, this was the very same LST that he had been working on in the hull design department at the Federal Shipyard in Kearny, New Jersey, a year and a half earlier. His LST arrived in Le Havre, France on December 18, disgorging men, tanks, and heavy artillery onto the beach. By now, the furious tank battles in the Ardennes Forest had been raging for two days. The Germans, despite their setback in the war, were still dangerous. In violation of the Geneva Convention, they were routinely massacring captured Allied prisoners. Would Hitler's desperate attempt at a breakout in the Ardennes succeed? Because of the deep snow, it took Bob's M-4 tank until December 23 to cover the fifty miles to Forges les Eaux, north-east of Rouen, France. Two men were required to drive such a tank. The observer, peering out through the open hatch, gave instructions to the driver, who sat down below and could not see where he was steering the tank. Corporal Peterson was seated in the open hatch, calling out directions. Unfortunately, the tank skidded off the snow-covered road and ended up in a ditch. During the crash, Bob slammed his chin against the rim of the open hatch, receiving a nasty cut.

By now, the Battle of the Bulge was fast nearing its conclusion. The foul, cloudy weather—the so-called Hitler weather—that had made it possible for the Germans to advance without serious opposition had finally cleared, allowing Allied aircraft to dominate the Ardennes battlefield. There was no longer a need for Allied tanks to advance to the battlefield. A photo taken in Forges les Eaux at this time shows Bob with a big gash on his chin and several other soldiers standing in the snow in front of a row of now-unneeded tanks.

The winter of 1944-45 was one of the coldest in a hundred years. GIs learned to stuff newspapers under their clothes to serve as insulation. They filled their wet socks with stones and put them on top of a stove to dry them. Of course they had to keep watch over their drying socks lest someone looking for a pair with fewer holes was waiting to swipe them.

For the rest of his life, Bob never complained about the heat.

On December 29, Bob arrived by truck in Rethel, France, not far from the German border. The Battle of the Bulge was over, but hostilities continued. Early one morning in their barracks, Corporal Peterson and his fellow soldiers were awakened by the drone of a low-flying aircraft. Before anyone had time to scramble to safety, a German plane strafed the building they were in. Bullets pierced the entire roof from one end to the other. Fortunately, the German pilot steered an absolutely straight course, following the centerline of the building. The GI's beds were arranged on either side of the centerline, leaving a narrow corridor in the middle of the floor. No one was injured in the attack.

Some of the French had a conflicted attitude toward the presence of American GIs on French soil. They particularly resented GIs consorting with French women. GIs were instructed by their commanding officers to always walk the streets in pairs, and to maintain a discreet distance from any doorway in which a potential assassin might be lurking. In later years Bob would speak of several American soldiers who had died horribly after imbibing Calvados in a French bar. The liquor had been laced with wood alcohol. It was a strange way of showing gratitude for the sacrifices American troops had made in liberating France.

The war was winding down, but mop-up operations continued. On January 24 Corporal Peterson was sent on what his official military record calls "detached service" to the village of Wermerville, about twelve miles from Reims. "Detached service" is a military term for a soldier who is sent on a secret mission apart from his assigned unit. What he did there, I do not know, for his military record supplies only dates and places. He was next sent on a "contact reconnaissance" operation in Luxembourg on February 9. Bob and his fellow soldiers were brought into the country on a glider, towed behind an airplane. Years later, he described the eerie sensation when the glider was detached from its escort plane and drifted in total silence (except for the sound of the rushing air) to a landing on a distant field. Their mission was to monitor German troop movements. Retreating German panzer tank units were still operating in Luxembourg at the time, so it was very likely that Bob and his fellow soldiers were sent in to keep tabs on them and provide coordinates so Allied planes could drop bombs to neutralize these remnants, or at the very least, hasten their retreat to German soil. On the completion of the mission, Bob was promoted to technical sergeant. He never told me how he eventually made his way out of Luxembourg, but I have been able to piece together some of his movements from pictures taken at the time. There is a shot of him emerging from the hatch of an American tank. Another picture shows him perching atop a disabled German tank, its gun blown off in one of the last tank battles of the war. In a third picture, Bob strikes the pose of a battle-hardened soldier as he stands, with a cigar clenched firmly in his mouth, an ammunition belt slung casually over his shoulder, a second belt fastened about his waist, and cradling an artillery shell in his left arm—the same 155-millimeter shell he had fired in battle from a Long-Ton gun, which was capable of hitting a target seven miles away.

The war was now over. German General Jodl surrendered to Supreme Allied Commander Dwight Eisenhower at Reims, France on May 7, 1945. As revealed in several photographs, Bob was in Reims in March, but did not witness the historic surrender. (Nor did he ever see any of the performers sent under the auspices of the USO to entertain the troops: Bob Hope, the Maguire Sisters, the Andrew Sisters, Bing Crosby. They must have visited a different battlefront.) On May 25, 1945 he returned to Rethel, France, and was then sent on detached service to Strasbourg on June 5. On July 1, while inspecting a captured German tank, he accidentally knocked over a magnesium flare gun. The blinding explosion when the gun hit the floor of the tank sent a shower of flaming magnesium particles ricocheting around the sides of the confined space. A tiny fragment of the burning metal entered Bob's left eye. Brought to the 1778th General Hospital in Strasbourg, he feared that he had lost sight in the injured eye. A week or two later when his bandages came off both, he and his doctors were surprised to find that his vision was unimpaired. An X-ray revealed that the burning metal fragment had penetrated Bob's cornea, passed through the vitreous humor, pierced the retina, and lodged in the bone of his eye socket. The hot metal had completely and perfectly sealed the wound as it passed through his eye. Ever resourceful, Bob stole the X-ray of his eye from the doctor's office in case the wound should ever cause him trouble. Years later Bob's ophthalmologist asked him if he had ever had surgery on his left eye. The doctor shook his head when Bob told his story. There was no way that such delicate eye surgery could have been performed back in 1945. It was truly a miracle.

Soon after recovering from his wound, Bob was transferred to St. Dizier, France. He left St. Dizier on September 28, 1945, stayed briefly in Luxembourg on his way to Belgium, where he remained for only a day.

He stopped in Holland on September 29, and arrived in Germany on the same day. On leave, he chose to go to Denmark. A group photo taken of Bob and his unit in November shows them posing in front of Fredericksborg Castle in Copenhagen.

And all during this long and circuitous journey across Europe, Sergeant Bob Peterson had not the faintest inkling that he was on his way to the most important rendezvous of his life.

# MAY I HAVE THIS DANCE?

Bob was on a ten-day leave in Copenhagen when he spotted an announcement pasted up on a storefront window inviting GIs and British soldiers to a dance. When Bob and a couple of his comrades got there, the dance floor was already crowded. There were more men than women. Bob might have asked any one of the girls in the hall to be his partner, but he chose a red-haired beauty with an engaging smile. She spoke flawless English, with perhaps the merest trace of a British accent. Bob doubted at first that she was Danish, for all of the English-speaking Danes he had encountered thus far spoke English with a distinctive Danish accent. Inge assured him that she was, indeed, Danish.

"I'm Inge Buus," his dance partner said.

"Buus?" Bob knew that name. Only the day before he had purchased a commemorative plaque featuring the Danish flag. It had been sold to him in a shop bearing the name Buus. Were they related?

They were not. But the coincidence kept the pair talking for far longer than they might otherwise have. Inge explained the meaning of the inscription on the plaque Bob had purchased: *Danmark er Danske, og Sproget er Vort* (Denmark is Danish, and the Language is Ours). This somewhat cryptic slogan was actually a subtle dig at the German occupiers, outright expressions of Danish nationalism having been forbidden for the past five years. The pair soon discovered another coincidence: they had both worked at a shipyard. When Inge mentioned Burmeister and Wain, Bob was already familiar with the name of the largest shipbuilder in Denmark. Bob described his work on the LSTs at the Federal Shipyard in Kearney, New Jersey, the landing ships without which the Normandy invasion would likely have been impossible.

The lonely GIs and British soldiers in the hall easily outnumbered the girls, but Bob, now a sergeant who was used to ordering his men about, would have easily rebuffed all attempts to cut in. There was a fair amount of tension in the hall: the handful of Danish men present resented the fact that Danish women were taking up with these uniformed foreign soldiers; they resented this almost as much as their women consorting with German soldiers during the war. The pair kept on talking through several more dances. The rising volume of voices in the hall made conversation difficult. Bob and Inge likely went out for coffee, and agreed to meet the following day. It was a whirlwind courtship. With only a few days remaining of his leave, Bob went to meet Inge's parents at Ourepgaard in Nykøbing Falster. Though he spoke not a single word of Danish, his friendly and engaging manner quickly won over Inge's parents and her younger sister, Anna Lise. Her older brother, Knud, was working as an interpreter in Germany at the time, and didn't get to meet his future brother-in-law until twenty years later.

Presumably, Inge and Bob shared some more lunches and dinners, attended a movie or two (no more of those tiresome German films), and perhaps spent a night or two in a hotel. I never asked Inge how she how she could have made up her mind to marry a man she had known for less than a week, and there are unfortunately no photographs from these critical days to shed any light on what took place. Fifty years later, Inge's aunt Stinne would express her continuing astonishment in a video recorded by one of her sons how her young niece had gone off to America with a man she barely knew.

With his leave up, Bob returned to his duties in Germany. Though the war was over, there was still much work to be done. Tanks, Long-Ton guns, assorted armaments and ammunition had to be inventoried, removed from the many battlefields, and either destroyed or shipped back to the States. There were German prisoners who would have to be quartered and processed. On March 10, 1946 Bob sailed from Bremerhaven, Germany. He arrived in the U.S.A on March 23. On March 26 he was debriefed in Fort Dix, New Jersey and was discharged from the army on March 27.

# THE WICKER BASKET

Inge Buus had plenty of time to think over her decision to start a new life in America with a man who was practically a complete stranger. I assume that there was a steady stream of letters to keep the flames of the relationship alive. Unfortunately, none of those letters have survived. Inge was never much of a saver. For a long while, I suspected that the reason she had for marrying this GI after no more than a week's acquaintance was that she had become pregnant, so I never pressed her on what had precipitated this whirlwind courtship. It was not until after my father died and I went through the records from his army days and studied the dates on the backs of some old photos, that I discovered that Inge could not possibly have been pregnant. (Anyway, with her training as a nurse, she would have known how to avoid such an outcome.) It turned out that I was about a year off in my earlier calculations. My mother did not become pregnant until she had been in the States for five months. By then, she and her GI were happily married. All Inge ever told me of her momentous decision to emigrate was that if she found that she did not like her new life in the States, she always had the option to return to Denmark.

So the question remains: what prompted my mother to leave her homeland and go off to a foreign land with a man she had known for no more than a week? She got along well with her parents and siblings; she had plenty of friends; her prospects were good; she liked living in Copenhagen. As I researched the economic conditions in Denmark in the aftermath of the war, I came upon a possible answer. My mother's wages as a bookkeeper at a small goldsmith's shop could hardly have compared to what she was earning at Burmeister and Wain, which employed some 10,000 workers under the German occupation. The Danish economy after the war was once again plunged into a depression. Most businesses, including the formerly busy shipyard, were laying people off. Good-paying jobs were hard to come by. Denmark had become a dreary, suffocating country. But imagine making a new start in America with an ambitious and resourceful GI (who had no doubt embellished his prospects). The Statue of Liberty, the Empire State Building, the can-do spirit of the *Andy Hardy* movies— all these and other iconic images of America must have captured Inge's imagination. The choice was between leading a humdrum, predictable life in Denmark, or taking a chance on beginning a new life in the land of opportunity. And no doubt, love played a considerable part in this equation.

In September 1946, which gave her more that ten months to change her mind if she had been so inclined, Inge packed all of her treasured possessions into a large wicker basket. Her clothes, several pillows knitted by herself and her mother, a photo album, several books, her last Danish composition booklet, a silverware set her parents had bought for her as a wedding gift, a silver perpetual calendar given to her by Knud, the bronze letter opener presented to her on her last day at her job in hr. Hansen's shop, a handheld silver mirror and two silver hairbrushes, and, carefully rolled up, a large oil painting, a second gift from her parents, which depicted a scene from nineteenth-century rural Denmark (a church, some peasant houses, a cluster of farm buildings)—all of these went into the sturdy wicker basket. Why a wicker basket? Mother told me on more than one occasion how there was a shortage of suitcases at the time, with displaced people moving hither and yon, and German refugees heading back to their war-ravaged homeland.

Many years later, Mother would later describe her last meeting with her maternal grandfather. Ole Peter Petersen Lise, who had been born in 1869. He explained how each day of his life, since he had begun working on his father's farm at the age of 14, was indistinguishable from all the others: getting up before daybreak to feed the animals, milking the cows, sowing seeds, walking the fields to see how the crops were coming up. He made a sweeping motion with his upraised hand and emitted a whistling sound to indicate how swiftly his long life had passed. He died in November 1947, the same month that I was born.

On September 25 Inge said good-bye to her parents, brother, and sister and boarded the Swedish passenger liner, the M.S. Gripsholm, in Copenhagen Harbor, the scene of so many wartime bombings. It was a calm, sunny voyage that took about seven days. A series of photos show Inge and two or three girlfriends her own age that she had met onboard enjoying themselves up on deck. (Inge easily made friends.) In the evenings they would go dancing or see a movie. On October 2 the Gripsholm entered New York Harbor. Everyone crowded over to the port side of the ship to catch a glimpse of the Statue of Liberty. Soon after, as the ship cruised up the Hudson River, they went to the starboard side, where one of the deck stewards pointed out the Empire State building. The ship docked at Pier 86, where Inge was met by her future husband and his parents, Robert and Mildred. (Bob would later express his regret that he had not gone back to Denmark to bring Inge to America, but after a four years' absence from his job during the war, a month's vacation might seem to be pushing his luck.) Inge's wicker basket barely fit into the trunk of of the the large black Oldsmobile. They made their way to Robert and Mildred's apartment at 177 Van Nostrand Avenue in Jersey City. The rooms were small. The kitchen had a worn linoleum floor. Fortunately, Bob's younger sister, Velma, who had occupied the tiny bedroom after Bob went off to war in 1942, had by now moved into her own apartment. Bob had repeatedly encouraged his parents to find more spacious lodgings, but they explained that they had remained in the cramped apartment for fear that if they relocated to a different location, their son, who had been fighting his way across Europe for the past four years, would be unable to find them when he returned home. Inge and Bob settled into the tiny bedroom. They were married in a civil ceremony on October 8, 1946 at 4:15 P.M. Bob's parents attended the ceremony. The witnesses were Bob's sister, Velma, and Bob's best friend, Scotty Cheeseman.

If the thought ever crossed Inge's mind that it was something of a comedown to move into her in-laws' dingy apartment after having grown up on a large farm with cooks and servants, she never let on. And this arrangement was to drag on for the next two years. Apartments in Jersey City were in short supply, what with millions of GIs returning from Europe at the same time and looking for a decent place to live. So Bob and Inge would simply have to put up with the cramped quarters. Whatever the outcome, Inge still had her wicker basket close at hand. Because of the limited space in her in-laws' home, she found it convenient to keep her spare clothes in the basket. So a return to Denmark was only a boat-ticket away. Considering the disparate backgrounds of the two families, Inge Buus could be considered to have married down, but that was never a factor in her decision whether or not to remain in America. She was not concerned with the family tree, only with the most recent branch, her dashing GI.

Soon after their marriage, the happy couple honeymooned at Niagara Falls. Photos taken on that October day show that the weather was ideal. Bob, gazing nonchalantly up into the sunny sky, was still sporting the little Errol Flynn style mustache that he had grown in the army in order to make him look older. Inge, sitting on a large rock at the water's edge and smiling at the camera, was the very picture of the happy bride. Whenever anyone asked, Bob would say that his bride was from Copenhagen. Her actual birthplace of Stubberup was hard to pronounce, and further elaboration when Bob mentioned the island of Falster only drew blank stares. In any case, Inge had been living in Copenhagen when Bob met her, so she became the girl from Copenhagen.

The apartment on Van Nostrand Avenue grew even more confining with the arrival of a baby in November 1947. A crib, a baby carriage, and other essentials had to be squeezed in beside my parents' bed. There was a record snowfall that winter, so my baptism had to be postponed for a month. After my birth, my father, an eminently practical man, declared that the family budget could not afford another child. So I would have no siblings. My mother, who always had a head for figures, reluctantly concurred.

# BACK TO DENMARK

My mother brought me to Denmark in April 1948 when I was just five months old. Not yet a citizen, Inge needed her husband's permission to bring me out of the country. I was issued my very own passport containing my baby picture and my mother's signature. (I was two feet and two inches tall.) Of course, I remember nothing of the trip. We made the crossing aboard the same ship, the Gripsholm, that had brought Inge to America. My mother later told me that we saw a whale spouting in the distance. For my part, I had a rubber duck that I tossed overboard somewhere in the middle of the Atlantic Ocean.

Inge was eager to show off her newborn son to her family. I began crying when she handed me over to Anni, one of her younger cousins, but I stopped as soon as I heard my mother's reassuring voice. Photos in one of Inge's albums show the family doting over me. Knøs, the family dog, was now old and infirm and nearly blind, But he greeted Inge with excited wags of his little tail. Lars Buus had also had his reversals. The photos show that he was now walking with a cane. By now the large farm of Ourepgaard was but a memory. Shortly after Inge had left for America, Lars was inspecting a crumbling retaining wall. Unexpectedly, the wall toppled over, pinning and crushing his right leg. His doctors had first wanted to remove the leg, But Lars overruled them. How was a one-legged farmer going to get around on his fields? With his horseback riding days behind him, Lars sold Ourepgaard and bought a smaller farm called Herringløse, also on the island of Falster.

We stayed at Herringløse for a little over three months before returning to the States, once again aboard the Gripsholm. It would be only the first of many trips to Denmark that my mother and I would make, and I would get considerably more out of these subsequent trips

Having had no luck finding their own apartment, Inge and Bob were still living in their cramped quarters at Van Nostrand Avenue. But Bob, drawing on his days in the army, was resourceful. He bribed the superintendent of an apartment complex on nearby Hudson Boulevard fifty dollars to put him at the head of the line as apartments became available. It was only a matter of weeks before an opening finally turned up.

In December 1948 Inge and Bob settled into their own apartment at 2159 Hudson Boulevard. Though it contained only a single bedroom, the rooms were spacious. The oak floors in the living room and bedroom were covered by area carpets (rather dingy and well-worn, but providing me sufficient cushioning for romping about on my knees as I played with my toy cars.) The bathroom and kitchen had tile floors (I can still picture the small gray hexagons—though I did not learn until some years later that they were called hexagons). There was a dumbwaiter in the entrance hall, upon which residents would place their garbage bags, lowering them by means of a drawstring into the basement where unseen persons would dispose of them. There was plenty of room in the hall for my three-feet-long toy box, which provided a convenient place to sit when you were putting on or taking off your boots. From the living room window there was not much of a view, only of the apartments on the opposite side of the U-shaped complex, so the Venetian blinds were generally kept closed. The bedroom had a view across the Hudson River of New York City. At night the winged red horse representing Mobil Gas dominated the skyline.

One of my earliest memories of my father was of him sitting in the living room smoking a cigarette. (Chesterfield was his favorite brand.) He had mastered the art of blowing a perfect smoke ring, which would rise above his head, slowly expanding and then dissipating into the air. Fascinating. The army, in conjunction with the cigarette companies, had handed out free cigarettes to the soldiers, thus addicting many of them to to this unhealthy habit. My mother had smoked for a short while, but stopped after becoming nauseated when she became pregnant with me. My father wanted to quit also, but he was unable to give up the habit. One night we were on our way downstairs to sit on a bench on Hudson Boulevard and watch the passing traffic. (There were only three networks on TV at the time, and more often than not there was nothing worth viewing.) My father was carrying me on his shoulder with a cigarette dangling from his lips. He had just opened the front door of the apartment building when a sudden gust of wind blew a cigarette ash into his eye. We hurried back upstairs, where my father washed his eye out with water. This second assault on his vision motivated him to give up smoking for once and all. During his withdrawal period, he developed a rash on his fingers for several weeks, but he never touched another cigarette.

My father continued his employment with Gibbs & Cox, now at their main office on 21 West Street, which overlooked the Hudson River in lower Manhattan. In 1947 he began design work on the S.S. United States. The work was top secret, as the sleek and luxurious passenger liner was being built to serve a dual purpose: in the event of a new conflict (the Soviet Union, our former ally, was now our sworn enemy), the ship could be quickly refitted to carry as many as 14,000 soldiers. Its top speed was a matter of national security. No reporters or photographers were allowed to enter the dry-dock construction site in Newport News, Virginia. All blueprints at 21 West Street had to be put under lock and key when they were not being worked on. Any employee passing information on the secret project to the press would immediately be fired. Newspapers at the time speculated that the S.S. United States could do 32 knots. But they were only guessing.

Bob's boss, William Francis Gibbs, was by all accounts something of a character. My father described him vividly as sporting a battered brown fedora and steel-rimmed glasses. He would wear his old gray overcoat even on a summer day. He kept an eye on the drafting tables below him from his glass-walled office (known as the Glass Menagerie), which had a dramatic view of the ships sailing up and down the Hudson River. Gibbs was too cheap to foot the bill for air-conditioning, so his workers sweated over their drafting boards during the hot summer months, which was a slow and tedious process in those days with the draftsmen still having to dip pens into an inkwell. Gibbs would periodically descend from his Glass Menagerie to the drafting-room floor and steal up behind his employees to see what they were working on—and woe to anyone who was not working full speed on Gibbs' baby, the S.S. United States. The 990-foot-long vessel was launched on July 3, 1952 from Pier 86 (now the permanent home of the Intrepid Sea Air and Space Museum). It attained an average speed of over 35 knots on its first trans-Atlantic crossing, reaching England in a mere three-and-a-half days, as opposed to the week or more a cruise ship such as the Gripsholm took. The S.S. United States' top speed was actually more than 40 knots; it was the fastest ship in the world. During its heyday it carried such celebrities as former President Harry Truman and his daughter, Margaret, John Wayne, the Kennedy family, Marilyn Monroe, Salvador Dali, Bob Hope, and Kim Novak.

My father was saddened when the S.S. United States was mothballed for lack of congressional funding in 1970. (The aircraft carrier was now the navy's ship of choice.)

# DOILIES

I couldn't have been much older than three when Mother and I chanced to meet in the hallway the elderly widow who lived in the apartment next to us. Mrs. Stuyvesant had white hair. She wore a long black dress that brushed the tops of her sturdy black shoes. She invited us in for a visit. Her apartment was smaller than ours, but the white, wall-to-wall carpets were luxurious, with a thick pile. The back of a desk, a nearby shelf, and the top of the TV were crowded with framed photographs and porcelain figurines. Even though it was the middle of the day, the lights had to be kept on, as the living room had no window—the apartment's sole window being in the bedroom. I don't recall if we were offered refreshments. Mrs. Stuyvesant turned the TV on for me while she and my mother chatted. I settled down into a large, plush armchair, the back of which was covered with a white-lace doily to protect the fabric from oily hair. The arms of the chair were protected from dirty hands by elongated doilies. All of the chairs in the living room were similarly decorated with white-lace doilies. I have no recollection of what Mrs. Stuyvesant and my mother talked about. Presumably, they discussed their respective life histories. I'm certain that Mrs. Stuyvesant would have been fascinated by my mother's story. Would that I could go back in time and listen in on their conversation.

# TREE

I was perhaps four years old when my mother brought me on a visit to her girlfriend, Nicole, a native of Belgium, who, like Inge, had married a GI and emigrated to America. Nicole had two sons, Eddie and Ray, who were about the same age as I was. We played a game of pin-the-tail-on-the-donkey, at which I failed miserably. Blindfolded and spun around, I was lucky if I could come anywhere near the large poster mounted on the wall. Unbeknownst to me, the brothers had rubbed the donkey's hindquarters with a white crayon, so that you could feel, if not see, where to place the donkey's tail. Eddie and Ray proposed another simple game, which involved counting. I don't recall how I fared on this task, but when we got home my mother was disappointed with me. It seemed that throughout the game I had repeatedly pronounced the number "three" as "tree."

"It's "three," my mother admonished me, leaning forward and exaggeratedly placing her tongue on her upper incisors. "Three."

I quickly corrected myself. But where had I gotten the notion that the number "three" was pronounced "tree?"

It was not until several years later that I hit upon the answer. Apparently my trip to Denmark when I was but five months old had made an impression on me after all. There is no "th" sound in Danish. The number "three" is an explosive "*tre*," which must have sounded to my ear like the word "tree." In 1955, when Mother and I made our second trip to Denmark, my grandfather would coach me in Danish. "*En, to, tre, fire, fem,*" I would chant, and Morfar (mother's father) would encourage me to continue, "*seks, syv, otte, ni, ti.*" Obviously he must have coached me in much the same way when I was a baby, and I had retained at least one Danish word, however imperfectly. Learning Danish would later come easily for me, no doubt due to my early exposure to the language.

# SNOW

Early one winter morning my mother bundled me up in my warmest clothes and brought me downstairs. I sensed from the outset that I was in for a special treat, and sure enough, as we emerged from the front door of the apartment building, I saw that the landscape had been magically transformed during the night. The ground was everywhere carpeted with a glistening layer of white. The low-cropped privet hedges that bordered the front walk were similarly capped with white. What was it?

"It's snow," my mother told me.

Nearby, a man with a broad shovel was busy scraping the snow off the sidewalk. I scooped up a handful of the stuff in my brand-new, red leather mittens. It took me several attempts to learn how to pack the snow together between my cupped hands to make it stick together in a round little ball.

Two of my playmates, Elaine and Jimmy, now came out of the apartment building with their mother. They were similarly entranced by the sight of this endless white covering. The three of us assumed that this addition to the landscape would be permanent. Our young minds buzzed with the many possibilities of what we would be able to do with such a substance.

"It's not as good as clay," I opined as my friends joined me in scooping up handfuls of snow. "But there's a lot of it." Within minutes we were throwing snowballs at each another, more often than not missing the target.

After a half-hour or so of play our mothers decided that it was time for us to go back in. I scooped up a final handful of snow and followed after my mother.

"You can't bring all that snow upstairs," she said. "It's going to melt."

*Melt?* "But it's only a handful."

My mother quickly yielded to my protestations and allowed me to carry my frosty little treasure upstairs to our apartment. She brought me into the bathroom.

"Put it in the sink," she told me.

I did as I was instructed, still not comprehending the problem. Perhaps my mother was not as wise as I had thought.

I stood over the sink and watched my snowball slowly begin to shrink away, trickling drop by drop down the drain. After ten minutes, there was nothing left of it.

So much for snow.

# THE MAN IN THE MOON

My father was driving us somewhere in our secondhand De Soto. I don't recall where we were going. Perhaps we were simply taking a drive around the city to pass the time. People did that in those days. With only three television stations that broadcast nothing but test patterns for a considerable portion of the day, it was not as if you had to rush home to catch your favorite program. The sun was just setting. Shadows were lengthening, giving the streets a mysterious quality as the lights in the buildings began to come on. We drove past a succession of chemical holding pools, various shades of green by day, but an inky black now in the fading light. The acrid smell that they gave off, however, was undiminished, and Mother quickly rolled up her window in anticipation of the foul air. I was taking all of this in, turning my head left and right to catch the view down each side street we passed. Suddenly, behind us, I spotted up in the sky a dusky orange ball. It had a crude, patchy face on it. My father made a turn and the orb disappeared, only to reappear in a different direction. I giggled as I went from window to window trying to guess where the orb would next appear. Its movements were unpredictable. It seemed to be hiding behind the buildings and then suddenly popping out in an effort to catch me unawares.

"He keeps following us," I said as I again caught sight of the apparition through the back window.

"It's only the moon," my mother said.

*The moon,* I thought, not fully grasping the concept. "But he's following us."

"It's not following us. It goes around the earth up in outer space."

Earth, moon, outer space. I had a vague understanding of other worlds. Recently, we had seen Eddie Fisher on TV singing *Lady of Spain.* The set, bathed in a subdued light, had an otherworldly, haunting appearance. The buildings did not quite look real. The barren landscape was unfamiliar. Stars could be seen twinkling in a sky that resembled no night sky I had ever seen. Spain, I decided, must be another planet up in outer space. Like this moon thing.

# ECHOES OF THE PAST

I was not allowed to enter the bedroom when my mother was using her new sunlamp. I had only a brief glimpse of her wearing her green bathing suit and sunglasses as she stretched out on the bed beneath the brilliant lamp. The sunlamp was a tall, standup affair with a bronze hood that could be tilted in the appropriate direction. My mother used the device for several months. Looking back, I wonder why her doctor didn't simply prescribe some vitamin D tablets, for vitamin D supplements had been around since the mid-twenties. Maybe the doctor calculated that he could get more money by selling my mother a sunlamp that he could get for prescribing inexpensive vitamin D tablets.

Around the same time, Mother began missing her family back in Denmark. She would often begin crying after receiving a letter from her mother. Noticing her tears one day after he came home from work, my father said, "Those letters will have to stop if they upset you so much." But they never stopped. While Father could be a hard man, he was not unreasonable. He would encourage his wife to make a trip to Denmark any time she felt like it, and he would prove to be unstinting in paying her fare. Curiously, however, Mother did not begin saving her mother's monthly letters and aerograms until 1957.

Mother told me that after they were married, Bob would sometimes awaken from his sleep, murmuring incoherently and drenched in sweat, having dreamed about the war. But he would never tell her the details of his nightmares. In fact, he rarely spoke of what he had experienced in the war, though it had obviously affected him deeply.

# NONCHALANT

If I had to write about my father's childhood, I would be hard-pressed to come up with a single relevant detail. His mother, Mildred, once told me that he had been born a "blue baby" and had to be placed in the oven to warm him up. Happily, he had the right number of fingers and toes. Other than that, I know virtually nothing of his early background until he started working in the mold loft at Federal Shipyard in Kearney, New Jersey. He did once confess to me that his father would steal up behind him when he was sitting at the kitchen table and flick his ears with a cocked finger. Hardly an endearing image of a father-son relationship. Unlike my mother, who often spoke to me in glowing terms of her childhood, my father almost never spoke of his. Nor did he leave a family album of photos taken during his formative years. After a small baby picture, he turns up at the age of perhaps twelve in a couple of photos taken on a road trip the family made to Florida, his father driving a secondhand Model T Ford. He looks bored and uncomfortable, posing for the picture on a hot summer day wearing a black tie similar to the one his father has on. I remember him complaining of the mosquitos and horseflies in Florida. You could have found the same pests at the Jersey Shore—no need for an eighteen-hundred-mile round trip. There is a single picture of him in his 1938 high-school yearbook. From his yearbook I know a few of the bare facts of his seventeenth year. After graduation, he would be heading off to New York University. He had served on the senior yearbook staff (the *Scroll*) and the finance committee; he was in the science club, the mathematics club, and the nature hiking club. The one-word description of him is "nonchalant." Bob was popular with his fellow students. His yearbook contains 64 signatures from girls in his senior class, and 77 signatures from boys. Quite the charmer.

Apparently, high-school yearbooks were not part of the tradition in Denmark during the thirties. Mother saved a photo of her high-school graduating class, a photo of her tennis team, and a photo of her nursing-school classmates. I'm certain that she would have saved a yearbook if she had one. It was not like the *Ausweiss* card that she disposed of because it reminded her of an unhappy period in her life. Did my father not have a happy childhood? I wonder.

# BOY RESCUED FROM
# WATER-FILLED SANDBOX

There was a playground a few blocks away from our apartment building equipped with swings, teeter-totters, and a sandbox. My mother got my tricycle out of the basement storage room so I could peddle to our destination. On this particular winter day it had been raining heavily overnight. The sandbox had at least a foot of water in it. A little girl and her mother turned up at the playground about the same time as my mother and I arrived. I had met the little girl previously. Her name was Eva. While my mother and her friend sat chatting on a nearby bench, I began showing off, racing my tricycle around the sandbox and pulling back on the handlebars in an imperfect imitation of a wheelie. Keeping my eyes on Eva and not looking where I was going, I sped over the rim of the sandbox and plunged headlong into the freezing water. Without a moment's hesitation, my mother jumped in after me and pulled me out. Not far from the sandbox was a caretaker's station. My mother brought me there, shivering violently in my soaking wet clothes. After I shed my clothes, the caretaker wrapped me up in a blanket and sat me down beside a hot pot-bellied stove. My mother, also dripping wet, left the caretaker in charge of me while she hastened back to Hudson Boulevard. She returned perhaps an hour later with a change of clothes for me. Now nice and warm from sitting beside the stove, I put on my dry clothes and, mounting my tricycle, peddled back to our apartment building.

# GRAPES

I suppose my mother told me where we were going as she combed my hair and made sure that I looked presentable. If she did, it failed to register with me. In any case, before we had gone more than two or three blocks from our apartment on Hudson Boulevard, I realized that we were not following one of our usual routes. Normally, I would lead the way, with Mother lagging a few steps behind me as we headed for the grocery store, a doctor's appointment, or for my grandparents' apartment on Van Nostrand Avenue. Today, however, Mother held my hand to ensure that I did not wander off. We walked for a long while through a neighborhood that was unfamiliar to me. My new shoes began to pinch. At last we came to an apartment building that looked not unlike our own. We climbed a flight of narrow wooden stairs and proceeded to a door at the end of a long hallway. A woman greeted us effusively. She spoke my name. She looked familiar, but I was not clear who she was and I clung closely to my mother.

"You remember Eva," Mother said as we entered the apartment. It was a bit larger than our own apartment, with both a living room and a dining room. My mother's friend led us into the kitchen. And there was Eva, trying to conceal herself behind the kitchen table. We were a little shy at first, not having seen each other since the sandbox incidence. She had just celebrated her fifth birthday. I would be five the following month. I admired her Mickey Mouse wristwatch (a birthday present), and she noticed my new shoes. (My old pair had been ruined when I fell into the sandbox.) We concluded our reintroduction in halting phrases interspersed with long intervals of silence. Then, moving into the dining room, we began to play a rudimentary game of hide-and-seek. Circling slowly about the dining-room table, we would attempt to conceal our faces behind the chairs, giggling sheepishly every time our eyes met amid the forest of legs, and bursting into nervous laughter when we happened to emerge together on the same side of the table.

All traces of shyness had vanished by the time Eva's mother called us into the kitchen for refreshments. We chatted easily now, and, indeed, were so taken with each other that we had to be reminded about the ice cream that was melting in our dishes. More than once our chatter became so effusive that our mothers saw fit to hush us up, obliging Eva and me to confine ourselves to matters that could be conveyed by subtle looks and gestures. We each had a slice of chocolate cake and sampled a few of the home-baked cookies that her mother set down before us. Then, weary of being under adult scrutiny, we provisioned ourselves with a bowl of red grapes and went off into the living room.

There, making ourselves comfortable on the sofa, we exchanged childhood confidences (she aspired to be a ballerina; I wanted to pilot a spaceship to Mars), and were astonished by the similarity of our likes and dislikes (we were both avid fans of Laurel and Hardy; but were positively bored by the Three Stooges—those stupid pokes in the eyes). Extending her left arm for my inspection, Eva displayed a scratch on her wrist that she had received the day before from some playground bully, whereupon I, speaking through clenched teeth, vowed to avenge her. As Eva cheered me on, I demonstrated with a series of karate chops what I would do when I caught up with the cowardly rogue. I was just beginning to get the better of this make-believe foe when our mothers called out from the kitchen and asked what was going on.

Eva and I turned to each other and grinned broadly. We sat in a giggly silence for a while. Then Eva picked up the bowl of grapes and motioned for me to follow her. We lingered briefly in the dining room, and then, still able to hear our mothers' voices in the kitchen, we continued on into the bedroom, tiptoeing across the wooden floor.

"I sleep on a bed," Eva said proudly as she patted her bed, "not in a crib."

I lied and said that I slept on a bed, too. (Though I had recently overheard my parents speaking about getting a bed for me, as I was clearly outgrowing my crib.) There was a faint smell of perfume in the air. An alarm clock on the bureau ticked steadily away. Nudging me in the side, Eva directed my attention to a pile of clothes that had been thrown over the arms of a nearby chair, and we both chuckled softly at the complicated array of hooks and fasteners that protruded from her mother's girdle. We moved on past a dressing table cluttered with an assortment of bottles, combs, and hairbrushes. We made faces in the mirror, then, with the bowl of grapes between us, we sat down cross-legged on a shag rug at the foot of the bed. With an impish look in her eyes, Eva popped a grape into her mouth, making it appear and disappear several times between her puckered lips before, fluttering her eyelashes, she swallowed it with a faintly audible gulp.

I don't recall who started it, but by and by after we had consumed our fill, one of us discovered that the succulent grapes, if squeezed in just the right way, could be made to deliver a tiny squirt of juice. Taking turns, we would each pick out a promising specimen from the bowl, hold it up to the other's face as if making an offering, and then squeeze violently, the victim squealing with pretended surprise when the trickle of liquid found its mark. The game continued in this fashion until it occurred to me that I could improve my aim considerably by holding the grape directly over Eva's head as I squeezed. This I did, whereupon Eva countered by taking two or three grapes at once and mashing them into a pulp on top of my head.

Our playful little duel escalated by leaps and bounds, and we grew more inventive with each exchange as in some Laurel and Hardy routine (perhaps we were imitating them). When Eva crushed a grape inside my shirt pocket, I slipped one down the front of her overalls, letting it tumble down to her stomach before I ruptured it. For the handful of grapes Eva stuffed inside my trousers, I retaliated with two handfuls, applying them front and back, wherever I could gain entrance. The final stage of the game saw us rolling together on the floor, laughing and shrieking as we struggled for possession of the remaining grapes. We were aware, briefly, of the sound of approaching footsteps, and then, still convulsed with laughter and unable to control ourselves, we were forcible separated and borne away by our respective mothers.

I can still picture Eva, her hair damp and matted, standing in the middle of the room and trying not to giggle as her mother smacked her on the bottom and took away the bowl of grapes. We were kept apart for the remainder of the visit. Mother took me into the bathroom for a quick grooming while Eva was sent off to change her clothes. It was time to go. My last glimpse of Eva came as Mother led me down the hall. Slipping past her own mother, a barefoot Eva darted out onto the landing to see me off, and, leaning over the banister, she continued to call out to me even as I descended the stairs.

Mother didn't scold me as we made our way home. In fact, I never once heard her raise her voice in anger. She never lost her temper, but would calmly explain what it was that I had done wrong. Back in our apartment, she combed what remained of some grape skins from my hair and gave my head a brisk rubbing with a towel. While she went out into the kitchen to get supper ready, I stayed in the living room and waited in front of the TV for the *Early Show* to begin, enjoying the *Syncopated Clock* theme that preceded the featured movie. Absentmindedly reaching into my shirt pocket, I discovered a handful of grapes that had managed to survive the afternoon's activities more-or-less intact. I contemplated the bruised and pitiful little cluster. Then, emitting a weary sigh, I sat down crosslegged on the floor and, twisting them off the stems one at the time, began to eat the flabby but still succulent grapes. I never saw Eva again.

# PAINTING

One day on a shopping trip in Journal Square—this was in 1952—my mother chanced to spot a greenback blowing along the sidewalk. She picked it up and was surprised to find herself holding a twenty-dollar bill in her hand. She looked around but there was no one to lay claim to the money. Back home, my mother wondered what to do with her windfall. In the 1950s twenty dollars was a lot of money. She might spend it on groceries, but then it would be gone and become nothing but a memory. Mother had always had an artistic bent—sewing, knitting, and crocheting. At the age of nine she had painted a watercolor picture of Mickey Mouse and Minnie Mouse. That was it. She would spend the twenty dollars on a set of oil paints. Her first effort was an impressionistic rendering of a typical Danish marsh: a tangle of bullrushes and tall grasses in the foreground, a placid body of water in the middle distance, a stand of trees on the far shore, a clear blue sky above. The painting was done on a large canvas, nearly as large as the 34-inch wide by 26-inch tall painting that Mother had brought with her from Denmark in her wicker basket. Unfortunately, there was not enough room in the apartment to display a second large painting. Or perhaps the real reason was that my parents' budget could not be stretched to cover the cost of the large frame that would have been required. I was never clear on this point. Many years later Mother told me how, when it came to framing the large oil painting she had brought with her from Denmark, they had only been able to afford a skinny gold frame. The proprietor of the craft store they had gone to thought that the skimpy frame they had selected did not do justice to such a fine painting (signed by C. Rasmussen), so he threw in at no additional cost a white inlay to make the frame appear wider. Over the years, Mother made no mention of her own painting, and I never thought to ask her about it. The last time I remember seeing her painting was in the communal storage room in the basement of our apartment building. My father propped the unframed painting atop some other items for which there was no room upstairs.

"This will be my albatross," he said disdainfully, giving the painting a final glance before he led me out of the basement.

I did not know what an albatross was, or what my father's gloomy declaration implied.

As I said, my father could be a hard man. I have no idea what became of Mother's painting. It did not survive our eventual move from Jersey City, when there would have been plenty of room to hang it up in our new house.

My mother, however, without any encouragement, persevered in her painting, though on a more modest scale. Her next painting, which still exists, was a twelve-inch-by-ten-inch rendition of her maternal grandfather's (Ole Peter Petersen Lise's) house in Stubberup, Falster—her birthplace. It, too, was an impressionistic composition: a snow-covered road and fields, a couple of pollarded trees and a rustic fence leading up to a cozy farmhouse and several outbuildings. The sky had a few streaks of blue above, a luminous golden sunrise below. To my eye, her painting compares favorably with those of Vincent Van Gogh. Where did my mother learn this impressionistic technique? Over the years, she did a few more paintings in this same style. Everyone who has seen my mother's paintings has been impressed with them. I recently looked through several introductory books that my mother had on painting. No mention whatsoever of Van Gogh. No examples of his paintings. Where did Mother's sophisticated style come from? What would she have accomplished if she had received a few words of encouragement?

# ROBINSON CRUSOE

My expectations were high when Mother brought me to Journal Square for a showing of *Robinson Crusoe,* the first movie in color that I had ever seen. The big screen had me shifting my head from side to side to take everything in. And the brilliant colors made the celluloid images come alive as they never had before on our Capehart TV at home (equipped with wooden doors that could be closed over the screen when you were not watching anything). Color! If a wave had splashed out of the screen into the movie theater, I would have been prepared for it. But after ten minutes or so the novelty of color began to wear thin. *Robinson Crusoe* turned out to be a bit of a disappointment. It was dull. Though the film was in color, it simply didn't measure up to the black-and-white episodes of *Flash Gordon* I had seen of TV, which had a dramatic scene or a crisis every few minutes. There was nothing much going on that I could see. Just this one man alone on an apparently uninhabited island, finding shelter in a cave, wandering around, building a stockade, hunting, planting crops. There was a dog, but the dog died. Though I was too young to appreciate it at the time, all of this was mere prologue. The hero's travails were only just beginning. My memory of *Robinson Crusoe,* is vague, not so much due to a failure of memory, but because I never saw the entire picture. What I had seen so far was a yawn: more traipsing about the island, harvesting the grain planted in the spring. Ho, hum. It wasn't until the movie was nearly halfway through that I got the feeling that something was finally going to happen. Walking along a pristine beach beneath his makeshift parasol, the hero spots a footprint in the wet sand. A single footprint. He places his own foot over the impression in the sand and realizes that this footprint is far larger than his own. There was barely time for poor Robinson to react when my mother gasped and grabbed my hand, hastily leading me up the aisle and out of the theater. It wasn't because she thought something was coming up that might upset *me* that she left; it was because she sensed that whatever was coming up would upset *her.* At the time I did not understand how the mere sight of a footprint in the sand could possibly upset anyone. At the age of seven, I was not old enough to pick up on the subtle foreshadowing that had alerted my mother to the arrival of cannibals on the island. Some years later, I teasingly reminded Mother of the incident.

"We never saw anything like that in the movies in Denmark," she said.

I suppose not. There were no cannibals in the *Andy Hardy* movies, or in the musicals she had enjoyed in her youth. Still, as I think back on her reaction to a footprint in the sand, I find it hard to reconcile her distress over something so innocuous with what she had experienced during the years of the German occupation of Denmark. She had seen a woman plunge to her death on the sidewalk right in front of her. She had daily contact with helmeted German soldiers armed with machine guns. Nazi tanks had menaced the streets of Copenhagen. On her way to work she would pass by buildings that had been blown up either by Germans or by the Danish Resistance. It was not uncommon for a squad of German soldiers to jump off the back of a truck and machinegun a dozen innocent civilians in a random act of reprisal. And yet, with all this going on, Inge Buus chose to remain in Copenhagen. She had seen death. She had seen the worst that mankind had to offer. Clearly, she was no shrinking violet. Except, apparently, when it came to a scary movie like *Robinson Crusoe*. It was not until years later on a TV rerun that I finally got to see Robinson Crusoe sail away from the island with his man Friday.

And that was not the only time that Mother fled from a movie theater because she was alarmed by what was taking place on the screen. Shortly after we had left Jersey City and moved into our newly completed home on Huyler Road, we went to see a movie in the local theater in Somerville. It was a science-fiction film, dealing with some strange goings-on in a nuclear facility located in a remote Western desert. In the opening scene a man burst forth from the facility, only to collapse in the desert sand. As he struggled to crawl away, a closeup showed his face swollen and distorted with enormous pustules. Mother abruptly stood up.

"We're leaving," she said. It was barely ten minutes into the film. Father and I reluctantly followed her out of the theater. I wonder now, more than a half-century after the fact, what it was that had set her off. Was it her lack of exposure to such gory films back in Denmark, or was it because such scenes reminded her in some way of trying times during the German occupation?

Father had just gotten home from work one day in 1962 when Mother announced that after supper we would be going to see a movie called *Dr. No.* She showed us the advertisement of the first James Bond film that she had circled in the local paper. Obviously, she had read up on the film and knew that it contained graphic scenes of violence. She related to us some of the plot and background of the picture that she had gleaned from a review. Recalling her previous reaction to violent films, my father and I were somewhat taken aback by her cheerful description of this one. But we were game to go. As expected, there was a lot of shooting. The body count mounted steadily. But Mother did not flinch a single time, even when a large tarantula crawled up Sean Connery's shoulder as he lay in bed. Somehow, she had overcome her aversion to violent and scary American films.

# OFF TO SCHOOL

I remember my very first day in school. Mother was getting me ready for the afternoon session, kindergarten being only a half-day affair. She combed my hair, patting down a stubborn cowlick.

"Will you be coming in with me?" I naively asked, presuming that my mother would be seated in class at the desk beside me.

"I'll bring you into the classroom," she told me, satisfying my fears for the time being.

Number 24 School was only a short walk down Hudson Boulevard from our apartment building. My first sight of the imposing red-brick structure with its tall windows did not reassure me. Children were crying when we got to the classroom. I began crying, too, when my mother left, although she had promised to meet me at noon when the class was over.

Mrs. Kearney, the kindergarten teacher, quickly captured the attention of her wailing pupils. She cut a formidable, commanding figure, which at the same time had a calming effect on us. I was further reassured by her resemblance to Mrs. Stuyvesant. Clearly, they were of the same generation. Like Mrs. Stuyvesant, her white hair was done up into a tight bun. She wore a black dress that descended to her ankles. A black shawl and a pair of stout black shoes completed her outfit.

The classwork was not demanding. With six pupils sitting at each of several large tables, we mostly played games, or made crayon drawings. There was a sandbox and a slide in the back of the room. Mrs. Kearney would instruct us in printing in capitals the letters of the alphabet.

"You're letters are too skinny," she admonished plump Anthony. "Make them fat, like you."

Picking up a small book, Mrs. Kearney would read to us from Grimm's Fairy Tales. "Humpty Dumpty sat on a wall. Humpty Dumpty had a great fall. And all the king's horses and all the king's men couldn't put Humpty together again."

I remember after this recitation making a crayon drawing of Humpty Dumpty sitting on a wall before his famous fall.

Not long after I began attending Mrs. Kearney's class, she summoned me to up to her desk and questioned me about my middle name, which was my mother's maiden name, Buus. I didn't even know that I had a middle name.

"Is it Bus?" she asked.

I had no idea, so I had to bring Mother to the classroom to clarify this little puzzle. Mrs. Kearney was surprised to learn that my mother, who spoke English with no obvious trace of an accent, had come from a foreign country.

Another day, as fall approached, I had hung my new blue jacket on a hook in the classroom cloakroom. After class I went to fetch my jacket, but it was nowhere to be found. My mother was waiting for me, as usual, out in front of the school.

"Where's your jacket?" she asked.

I shrugged. "Someone must have taken it."

My mother took me by the hand and brought me back up to the classroom. Mrs. Kearney was still seated at her desk, taking care of some paperwork. My mother explained the problem, and the three of us went into the cloakroom. Just as I had said, there was no sign of my jacket, only a row of bare coat-hooks and a single item, Mrs Kearney's cape, which was hanging on the hook closest to the cloakroom door. With a sweep of her arm, Mrs. Kearney removed her voluminous black cape from the hook. Underneath was my little blue jacket.

The following term I began attending the morning session of Mrs. Kearney's kindergarten class. I was now one of the older boys and felt superior to the kids arriving for the afternoon session. We were still working our way through *Grimm's Fairy Tales* ("Hickory dickery dock, the mouse ran up the clock"), but our printed script now included both uppercase and lowercase letters.

Arriving at home in time for lunch, I would watch *Fun at One*. Then there was *Howdy Doody* with Buffalo Bob Smith and his silent partner Clarabell the Clown entertaining the kids in the Peanut Gallery. It was the golden age for children's television. Later on Buster Crabbe playing Flash Gordon would do battle with Ming the Merciless (a subtle take on the Yellow Peril, although the implication was lost on me at the time), and Flash's love interest, Dale Arden, would have to be rescued innumerable times. William Bendix starred as the hapless Riley in *The Life of Riley*. A young Betty White had a variety show in which she would display her childish ignorance of the world in a running series of non-sequiturs. *The Early Show* would come on at four o'clock, introduced by its theme music, *The Syncopated Clock*. While I watched the featured movie, often a Western, my mother would be busy in the kitchen fixing supper. One day, as I was viewing one of my afternoon shows, I happened to break open a plastic whistle and found a pea-sized plastic ball inside. For some reason, I stuck the little ball up my nose. Whoops!

"It went up my nose," I cried out.

Emerging from the kitchen, my mother knew exactly what to do. She quickly produced a tissue and handed it to me.

"Blow," she said, and the plastic ball came out in the tissue. And so I learned not to stick small objects up my nose.

There was an Easter pageant in school that year. As I was playing the part of a rabbit, my mother made a rabbit suit for me. The other rabbits all had floppy ears that hung limply over the sides of their heads. But my mother reinforced my long ears with wire coat hangers, making me a standout among all the other rabbits.

# THE HOMESTEADERS

In 1952, my parents purchased an undeveloped plot of land in rural Branchburg, New Jersey. It was about three-quarters of an acre and heavily wooded. There was no Levittown in those days, so anyone buying a lot would be left to his own devices to clear the land and build a house on it. We began driving out to Branchburg on Friday evenings, camping out in a crude plywood shed that my father had constructed. It would be dark by the time we arrived at our building site. For light, we relied on oil-filled lanterns, hung on a convenient tree branch or nailed to a two-by-four in our shed. We slept on cots, crawling into sleeping bags when the nights grew cold. I would cuddle up with Smokey the Bear. Our toilet consisted of an eighteen-inch tall wooden barrel into which a metal pail had been inserted. Father would empty the pail into a small pit he had dug in an out-of-the-way place. After consuming during the course of the day the cereal and sandwiches Mother had packed for us, we would heat our supper, usually Chef Boyardee Beef Ravioli and some baked beans, on a Sterno Stove, a small metal stove into which you placed a can containing a flammable gel (Sterno Canned Heat). You lit the gel with a match and the resulting flame would warm whatever was set on top of the stove. To stop the flame, you would carefully replace the lid on the can of Sterno, which could be reused several times. (A few years later, after our house was finished, we referred to the cozy grove of trees in which we had once prepared and eaten our meals as "the old kitchen.")

The first order of business was to make a clearing on the heavily forested lot so that our car, a maroon De Soto, could be pulled safely off the road, which was only a rough gravel road at the time. That would be our first driveway (dirt, no gravel). My father used an ax and a bowsaw to fell whatever trees that were in the way. The remaining stumps were left to rot away. I had a little hatchet that I used to cut down a sapling or two. My mother would help drag fallen trees and branches to a growing pile at the back of the lot where they would later be burned. (Just try nowadays making a bonfire of a huge pile of tree trunks and branches on your property.) Mother was not averse to rolling up her sleeves and pitching in anywhere help was needed. I never once heard her utter a cross word, either in English or in Danish, no matter how frustrating the task at hand might be. In fact, she dissuaded me from repeating the mild oaths that Father would use when he hit his finger with a hammer or experienced some other mishap.

Sunday evening, after working on the lot for two exhausting days, we would pack up our things and head back to Hudson Boulevard. It would be getting dark by the time we reached the outskirts of Jersey City, and the neon signs above the various businesses along the way would begin to come on as we proceeded. I was pleased that I could spell and read the sign for IPANA with no hesitation. But farther on, my inability to pronounce PEPSODENT brought tears of frustration to my eyes. It would take a couple more trips before I was able to master all of the signs.

Thinking back on those days, it strikes me that my parents were not unlike the pioneers who settled the early American West. They were true homesteaders. We had neither running water nor electricity. There was no government to assist us. You had to rely on yourself and your neighbors to get by. Our next-door neighbor was Frank Wachino, who was employed with my father at Gibbs & Cox. He had the clever idea to build his one-car garage before he began working on his house. He and his younger brother, Joe, with help from my father and mother, soon had the garage completed. We then began sleeping in Frank's garage instead of the makeshift shed my father had constructed. And by this time we no longer had to bring water along with us in heavy jerry cans filled in our apartment on Hudson Boulevard and laboriously carried down the stairs to the car; we now had a source of fresh drinking water on Huyler Road. Arnold and Katy Ouin, émigrés from Estonia, had purchased a lot at the end of the road. Their first order of business was to have a well dug—the first one on Huyler Road—and they supplied the other two families with all the water they could use. Arnold was a husky fellow. I remember seeing him carry a twenty-foot-long joist on his shoulder. One winter his car skidded on snow-covered Huyler Road and turned over, landing on its roof. Unhurt, Arnold pushed the car upright and continued on his way into work.

Camping out in the wild and building your house from the ground up—nothing like this could possibly take place today. You would not be allowed to live on your property with no toilet facilities, no running water, no electricity, not even a roof over your head. In the present day you would be required to have an occupancy permit. A building inspector would come snooping around and sign off on every single step of your construction before you would be permitted to take up residence in your own house. The government is looking after you. Or is it? Back then, we got along just fine on our own. These were happy times, perhaps among the happiest in our lives. Unfortunately, the days of the rugged individualist are over. Self-reliance is now considered a reactionary term. Like it or not, Big Brother is looking over your shoulder, but its not you that he's looking out for.

The work on our house proceeded steadily. A man named Gullner came with his bulldozer and excavated for the foundation. (Several years afterward we learned that he had been shot to death in a suspicious hunting accident.) A man named Block poured the concrete foundation. My father and mother would do all the rest of the work themselves. They laid the cinderblocks, using a taught string to keep them aligned. Before cementing over the top row of blocks, they filling the hollow centers with crumpled-up newspapers and empty cans of Eslinger beer—whose surfaces were covered with obscure facts and statistics that I always enjoyed reading (the number of times a second that a hummingbird beat its wings, the maximum speed of a cheetah, the amount of time it took light from the sun to reach the earth). Falling back on his experience as a design engineer at Gibbs & Cox, Father had drawn up detailed plans for the house. (Fortunately, old man Gibbs never caught him working at the drafting table on his dream house.) He ordered the necessary materials at a nearby lumberyard. I remember the day when a large flat-bed truck arrived and delivered an enormous pile of lumber. It contained all the rafters, joists, two-by-fours, floorboards, and plywood that were to go into our house. During the week, all this lumber sat out in the open under a large canvas tarpaulin. Someone could easily have driven in with a pickup truck and made off with whatever he wanted. But no one ever did. It was a simpler, more neighborly time in the early 1950s. All that ever went missing from our pile of building materials were two jerry cans and a hundred-foot tape measure, and my father blamed himself for leaving them in a too-obvious spot.

Father spent his summer vacations working on the house, which greatly speeded up the process of construction. Once the floor planks were laid, it would not do to leave the unfinished house exposed to the elements. One morning, my parents got up soon after sunrise to put up the end walls of the house, massive constructions of two-by-fours that included both the first-floor framing and the gable end of the attic, which my father had assembled the day before. They had to complete this demanding work while the air was still, for once the wind kicked up my mother would have been unable to steady the unwieldy structures. She held the frameworks in place by means of a conjoined couple of two-by-fours that had been nailed to the middle of each structure. Expertly wielding his hammer, my father quickly secured the first and then the second framework to the sill. The following day would see the framework for the front and back walls go up. Nailing guns did not exist in those days, nor did Teco Plates, which now makes joining two pieces of wood together a breeze. As we had no electricity, a power saw was obviously impossible. All of the cutting had to be done with a handsaw. Father's right hand became visibly swollen from sawing and nailing the roof rafters into place. At the end of an exhausting day, he would take a bath in a rusty old oil drum filled with water carried now from Arnold and Katy Ouins' well. Father showed me how to hammer a nail and saw a two-by-four by sighting with one eye along the blade. But mostly all I did at the time was to use a hammer to straighten out bent nails (struggling to obey Mother's admonition not to swear when the hammer missed its target and connected instead with my finger.) Four-by-eight sheets of plywood soon covered the roof. How my father managed to get them up there by himself, was a sight to behold. My mother would steady the heavy sheets from the bottom while my father manhandled them up a rickety, 24-foot-long aluminum ladder. The plywood was then covered with tarpaper, over which my father nailed down asbestos shingles. With the roof completed, work could now begin on the interior of the house: Sheetrock, windows, doors, woodwork. We were now able to move out of Frank's garage and sleep in our own house on weekends. (Occupancy permits were not required back in the fifties.)

There is a sad story associated with Frank's brother, Joe. At the age of eighteen he had gone off to war. He entered the fray at Anzio in central Italy, which saw some of the bloodiest fighting of World War II. He never spoke about his experiences. In fact, he did not speak very much at all. Even to a young boy such as myself, he seemed just a bit *too* quiet. I recall him studiously and silently painting the woodwork in his and his older brother's house. We got along very well. When I started learning to use a typewriter, Joe instructed me how to position my fingers on the middle row of the keyboard so I would be able to touch-type. But despite his ability to function in such domestic situations, Joe was not well. One day, back in his apartment in Jersey City, his inner demons finally got the better of him. He apparently started a fight with someone, and in a fit of rage wound up putting his fist through the glass window of a basement door. He was subsequently hospitalized and would remain in the hospital under medication for the remainder of his life. The treatment he received had only limited success, while it calmed him down, Joe was never able to return to the house that he and his brother had built together on Huyler Road.

An interesting history comes to my mind associated with the plot of land that we settled on. We were told that in the previous century, there had been a racetrack covering the rear of the property and extending through several of the adjoining ones. The remnants of a raised berm that had marked the outer perimeter of the track could still be seen in our backyard. Standing on the berm, one could easily imagine a crowd of people gathered on the same spot a hundred years ago to watch a horserace. Some of the big old trees that remained around the berm had very likely provided shade for these long-dead spectators, just as they provided shade for my parents and me when we consumed our lunches.

# OF ANT LIONS AND THE EMPTY CHURCH

Although Mother was never one to engage in idle chitchat, she had a knack for striking up a conversation with total strangers. After attending a sermon at the Methodist church across the street from our apartment building on Hudson Boulevard, she became friendly with the pastor and his wife. Mother and I would often visit their home, which was adjacent to the church, and I would play with their two sons, Richard and David. My parents brought me on a regular basis to Pastor Booth's Sunday sermons, where, clad in a formal black suit, he seemed to become a different person than the friendly man sporting a flannel shirt that I had spoken to during the week. Once, Richard procured the key to his father's normally locked church and allowed me to slip in with him to view the empty pews and climb up to the pulpit from which his father delivered his Sunday sermons. The high-ceilinged room was eerily silent except for the ticking of a nearby pendulum clock. We did not remain for more than a few minutes in the church, both of us sensing that we were intruders in God's house. We stole silently out, and Richard locked the door behind him, thus restoring the sense of mystery that our clandestine entry had temporarily suspended. Of course, when I told Mother at lunchtime how Richard and I had spent the morning, I omitted any mention of our little adventure in the church.

One particular Christmas celebration in the Methodist church stands out in my mind. Earlier in the year I had shown Pastor Booth a cupful of sand that I had brought from Huyler Road. It was no ordinary sand. I had carefully dug it up in a dry area beneath the overhang of our soon-to-be completed house. There was a funnel-shaped depression in the center of the cup; it was a carefully constructed trap, at the bottom of which lurked an ant lion waiting patiently for its next meal. The body of the ant lion was concealed beneath the sand, but its black, pincerlike jaws were just barely visible. Careful not to shake the cup, I dropped an ant I had brought along into the funnel of sand. As the ant reached the bottom of the little pit, the ant lion's jaws immediately seized it and pulled it down out of sight.

Pastor Booth was amused by this little miracle. And I had the distinct feeling that he regarded my mother and me as his special favorites among his congregation. So I was more than a little perplexed when he seemed to be snubbing my parents and me at the Christmas service that year. As Pastor Booth called out the names of his parishioners, the head of each household would step forward from the pews to accept a small gift: a bag of oranges or apples, a box of cookies, an assortment of candy; it was the thought that counted. After five minutes or so, it became apparent to me that most of those assembled today had by now received their Christmas presents. As what had been a large pile of gifts on the table at the front of the room continued to dwindle, my consternation mounted. Had Pastor Booth forgotten us? I repeatedly glanced over at my parents, but they did not seem to share my concern. And then the pastor called out the name Peterson. My father rose and advanced to the front of the room to accept a bag of oranges from the smiling pastor. I breathed a sigh of relief as my father sat down beside me. At the time I did not understand the concept of alphabetical order. The Peterson family had not been ignored or forgotten after all.

First grade represented a great leap forward from kindergarten. I missed the afternoon television shows, but I enjoyed being in school more than I did sitting at home before the TV set. The class lasted for the full day, and my mother no longer had to bring me to and from school. I was now big enough to walk the three or four blocks on my own, carrying a smart leather briefcase containing a pen-and-pencil set and a ruler. The desks in the first grade class were anchored to the wooden floor on immovable metal tracks. There was a round hole at the back right-hand side of the desk (an inkwell), which we kids decided was intended as a speedy way of putting a pencil into your desk without having to go to the bother of lifting the hinged lid. We were now beginning to learn addition and subtraction. Our reading selections were more advanced, too. We were given copies of *My Weekly Reader*. Our teacher, Miss Cavendar, read to us the poem *Trees*, by Joyce Kilmer. One day she asked the class what our favorite day of the week was. I immediately raised my hand and answered, "The days you have to go to school."

Second grade passed in a whirlwind of expectations. I was excited to be learning to write in an adult, cursive hand, but I was even more excited to contemplate a move into our newly completed house in Branchburg, where I would be attending a new school, and on top of that my mother was planning on bringing me with her on her upcoming trip to Denmark. We would be traveling not by ship this time, but by airplane. Think of that! Though I would be leaving school before the end of the term, my second grade teacher, Mrs. Muller, was almost as enthusiastic about my upcoming trip as I was. "I wish I could shrink myself and go along in your pocket," she declared.

# THE HIGH AND THE MIGHTY

Speaking of flying, there was a heat wave in the summer of 1954. Our apartment on Hudson Boulevard had no air conditioning; opening the windows and turning on our small, oscillating fan offered scant relief. So on an especially oppressive afternoon we would board a bus to nearby Journal Square to take in a movie and cool off in the air-conditioned theater. One movie I remember was *The High And The Mighty*, staring John Wayne as an aging airline pilot. I had a bit of trouble following the convoluted (for a seven-year-old) story line. I understood that something had gone wrong with the airplane's engines, and the plane was no longer able to maintain its altitude. This was not a good thing when you're flying over the ocean. As the apparently doomed aircraft continued to lose altitude, sinking closer and closer to the water, the passengers were ordered to surrender their luggage so it could be cast overboard to lighten the load. Somehow I got the impression that in spite of this desperate measure the airplane had finally plunged into the sea, where it continued to forge ahead like a submarine, only to finally rise from the depths as it neared the airport. Of course, these scenes did nothing to inspire confidence in me regarding the plane trip that my mother and I were planning to take the following year.

It was still sweltering hot outside when we emerged from the air-conditioned theater, so my parents immediately decided to turn around and go back inside. Seeing the movie a second time cleared up most of my earlier misconceptions about the ill-fated flight. It hadn't "ditched" into the sea after all, remaining perilously but constantly above the waves. Leaving the theater, holding my mother's hand on my left and my father's hand on my right, I squinted into the late-afternoon sunlight in imitation of John Wayne, my new hero.

# DENMARK 1955

In 1955 we left Jersey City for good and moved into our new house on Huyler Road. The interior was not yet finished. There was painting to be completed. Rolls of linoleum were waiting to be glued down in the kitchen and bathroom. The oak flooring in the living room, dining room, and bedrooms still had to be installed, leaving us to trod carefully across the rough floorboards and avoid the stacks of oak planks awaiting my father's hammer. We had not been in the house for more than a month or so when my mother and I went off on our second trip to Denmark. It was to be one of many that we would make together. This time we made the journey by air, leaving Idlewild Airport on a Scandinavian Airlines System four-engine propeller-driven Douglas DC 6-B. (SAS would not begin flying jet aircraft until 1960, when it introduced the Douglas DC-8 on its trans-Atlantic route). While we waited for a long time on the runway, the captain's voice came over the intercom. (It was definitely not John Wayne's voice, unless John Wayne had suddenly acquired a foreign accent.) He announced that the flight was scheduled to take about sixteen hours, less if we had favorable tail winds. Because of the jet stream, flights traveling from New York to Europe took less time than those going in the opposite direction. At the front of the cabin, smiling reassuringly through her entire delivery, a stewardess demonstrated how to use a life vest in the event of an emergency landing over water. After putting it over your head, you inflated it by jerking on these two cords. If that failed you would pull out this tube and inflate the life vest with your own breath. (Shades of *The High And The Mighty*. Better pay attention.) Then, remove your eyeglasses, cross your arms over your face and put your head down between your knees. But not to worry. Such an emergency was extremely unlikely. And SAS had a perfect safety record.

The propeller nearest to the body of the plane began to turn first, joined momentarily by the one farther out on the wing. It took the engines several minutes to rev up to full power. The propellers would run faster and faster only to slow down again. Sitting directly behind the wing, I could see daylight through the wing flaps as they were alternately flexed up and down. (Not a reassuring sight.) At last the plane began to taxi forward, rapidly picking up speed as it approached the end of the runway. Suddenly we were airborne. My mother was almost as impressed by the novelty of our first flight as I was. With the plane rapidly gaining altitude, we both experienced the tug of gravity on our arms as we experimentally lifted them above the armrests. The New York City skyline shrank away below us under a setting sun. A stewardess passed out small bags of peanuts. (This was before the discovery of peanut allergies.) There were no onboard movies in these days, so you had to amuse yourself with a book or magazine or by looking out the window. Gazing down below at the tops of the clouds, still illuminated by the dying rays of the sun, I imagined strange masses of land, rugged islands with massive promontories. It was hard to believe that these solid-looking structures were composed of nothing but tiny droplets of water.

The air in the cabin was stale, smelling of cigarette smoke. Both my mother and I could feel our noses getting dry. There was no fresh air to be had. The constant hum of the airplane's engines was another minor annoyance. But the main thing was that we were on our way to Denmark.

A stewardess, nimbly wielding two plastic trays down the narrow aisle, served us our supper: rubbery chicken, some nondescript vegetables, a baked potato, a small glass of orange juice. (Or was the entrée some kind of fish? The meals we had on this and our successive flights now all seem to merge together, no single one of them being particularly memorable.) As I recall, neither my mother nor I had much of an appetite. After the trays were collected, it was time for lights out. The stewardess distributed pillows and blankets. I could not sleep. I lifted the window shade and peered out into the night. The stars seemed to shine with an unusual brilliance. Was it because that, flying at thirty-nine thousand feet as the pilot had informed us, we were closer to them? I pointed out to my mother a formation of stars that looked like an elephant.

Morning burst upon us with bright shafts of sunlight streaming through the windows. We were served with cereal and milk—much better fare than last night's disappointing meal, whatever it was. The captain pointed out to us the southern tip of Greenland. There was the Greenland ice sheet. We could see Icebergs floating in the green water. I wouldn't have wanted to go down there. Farther on, we passed over Ireland. It was, indeed, a verdant, emerald-green island. Soon we were flying over Jutland. Although my mother had never seen Jutland by air, she did not need the captain's commentary to tell her what we were looking at. The spit of land up to the north, barely visible through the scattered clouds, was Skagen. The meandering channel of water to the south of it was the Limfjord. Hastening down the narrow aisle with her tray, the stewardess used a pair of tongs to pass out hot towels, which Mother and I draped over our faces. Soon we were descending toward Copenhagen Airport. Buildings began to grow larger and larger. Boats could be seen in the harbor below. Seagulls seemed to be scattering out of the way, some of them flying backwards in an optical illusion. And suddenly the plane touched down. There was a single bump, the squeal of tires. Some of the passengers applauded the pinpoint landing. The plane taxied over to the awaiting hangar and we disembarked row by row, a smiling stewardess bidding us good-bye.

After we retrieved our suitcases from the revolving carousel. Jenny, the wife of my mother's cousin, Helge, found us in the crowd and drove us to her home. I had expected to be taken immediately to my grandparents' farm, so I was a bit taken aback when Jenny brought us to an ordinary red-brick house. Where was the farm Mother had spoken of? Jenny and Helge had two children, Søren and Dorit, a boy and a girl. I didn't realize until I was looking through one of Mother's photo albums to research this memoir that I had actually met Dorit back in 1948, when we were both four months old. A photo shows Dorit and me sitting on a blanket in the garden at Herringløse. Søren would be born the following year. While my mother reminisced indoors with Jenny, I was sent out in the backyard to play with Søren and Dorit. Still no sign of anything that looked like a farm. No barns. Not a cow in sight. It was just a smallish, nondescript backyard. I had no idea what the children were urging me to do.

"*Sige yo!*" said Søren.

"*Sige nej!*" said Dorit.

In the end, I sided with Søren. "*Yo!*" I said decisively, without the faintest notion of what I was answering to.

I never discovered what my declaration had committed me to do, for shortly after I said "*Yo,*" my mother and I were taken off in a taxi to my grandparents' farm in Paarup, far to the north on the island of Zealand.

Here at last were the barns and haystacks I had expected to see. The farm, my mother told me, was smaller and less modern that the one my grandparents had previously occupied in Herringløs. There was an outhouse—a wooden privy with a metal bucket beneath the seat, which my grandfather would periodically empty, depositing its contents into a large cistern that contained the waste from the cattle and horses. This did not discomfort me in the least. After my experiences on Huyler Road, I was used to roughing it. Having a roof over your head while you did your business was actually a step up for me from squatting on an upended barrel out in the open. To save a trip to the outhouse, I would urinate upon rising in the morning in a porcelain chamberpot held by my mother. No problem. Better than going outside and urinating against a tree.

Incidentally, Danish toilet paper was made of much more durable material than our soft American toilet paper. It was light brown, and you could write on it without tearing it, if you were so inclined. But I had no qualms about using this heavy-duty toilet paper. Back home, using our makeshift toilet, I had employed, in a pinch, torn-off strips from a magazine. No problem there, either.

The first night, my mother took a bath in a large wooden tub in a washroom just off the kitchen. Her parents, Lars and Ella, peered in through the half-open door, cooing and murmuring with delight as my embarrassed mother covered her breasts with her hands. They had no doubt not seen their daughter in the altogether since she was a little girl at Klostergaarden.

I soon learned to call my grandparents "Mormor (mother's mother)" and "Morfar (mother's father)." Morfar wasted no time in bringing me up to speed in Danish.

"*En, to, tre, fire, fem,*" he would declaim, resuming the lessons that I presume he had begun when I was but five months old. I quickly began to pronounce "*tre*" with a proper Danish accent, sounding nothing at all like "tree."

Speaking of lessons, my mother had brought along to Denmark several textbooks that I would be using in the next term so I would not fall behind in my schooling. We would not be returning to the States until the middle of November, which meant that I would be missing not only the end of second grade, but also the start of third grade. So every afternoon Mother would sit down with me to go over my textbooks from home. This did not take long. I was more interested in learning to speak Danish. Every day I would master another phrase or two. By now I was beginning to read the language, too, learning the words by studying *Anders And* (Donald Duck) comic books. And of course Morfar continued to instruct me. One day at lunch, seeing me place a chocolate wafer on my open-faced sandwich to make the standard black rye bread more palatable, Morfar jokingly admonished me, "*Det er baby mad. Spise mandfolk mad* (That's baby food. Eat manly food)."

My grandparents owned a large Airedale terrier named "Muff." If I squatted down on my haunches beside him our heads would be almost on the same level. Instead of a ball, Muff had a coconut to play with. He was able to open his jaws just wide enough to get a grip on the coconut and carry it around with him. Muff was a farm dog, accustomed to roaming about on his own or following after Morfar as he surveyed the fields. Nevertheless, he was allowed inside the house, and would stretch out at his favorite spot on the living-room floor. One day the two of us were outside. Muff was following me around, occasionally looking up at me with a quizzical twist of his shaggy head. Suddenly I felt a couple of raindrops. Nothing to be concerned about. But Muff had felt the drops, too. We were over by one of the barns. Gently, Muff seized my right hand in his jaws. (I did say that he was a big dog.) He began to lead me across the cobblestone courtyard to the house. I remember asking Muff what he wanted to do—as if he could understand me. He brought me to the door of the farmhouse. I knew that one had to pass through two doors to get into the living room. The first door led to a mudroom. Muff could open the interior mudroom door by pushing down on the door handle with his paws. But the outer door had a round knob, which was impossible for Muff to turn. Sometimes Mormor would leave the outer door ajar so Muff could get into the living room on his own. But that was not the case today. I opened the outer door, then the inner one. Muff trotted inside and promptly plopped down on his usual spot on the living-room floor. Shortly afterward, a heavy downpour began. Smart dog, dry and content, his tail thumping on the rug.

I found farm life to be an endless source of fascination. I was allowed to feed the chickens. I collected the eggs on several occasions. The mildly protesting pecks of the hens did not deter me as they had my mother. I sort of adopted a newly born calf that I dubbed "*Lille Kalv,*" and for a couple of years afterward I carried a picture of it in my wallet. One morning, well before sunrise, Morfar awakened me and brought me out to stall where a prize sow was giving birth to a litter of squealing piglets. Mother chose not to accompany us. She had of course witnessed the same event more than once when she was a little girl growing up on Klostergaarden.

I turned out to be no better than my mother had been when it came to milking a cow. Morfar demonstrated the technique to me, but I never succeeded in getting a single drop of milk to flow, probably because, afraid of hurting the cow, I wasn't pulling hard enough on its teats. Morfar often brought me along on a horse-drawn wagon to the nearby town when he had a delivery of milk to make. It was stored in large aluminum cylinders that clinked together as the wagon moved along the road. My one and only attempt to ride a horse came as Morfar invited me to climb up onto the back of one of his workhorses. This I did, with considerably difficulty as the horse was very high and I was very small. Morfar led the horse for a few steps before I hopped off. Unlike my mother, I was apparently not cut out for horsemanship. But perhaps Mother's horse back in the thirties had been a more suitable steed for riding bareback, not like the broad-backed workhorse I had mounted.

One afternoon when we were all gathered in the living room, Morfar began to say something about his right leg. My mother had to explain to me how his leg had been badly injured at Ourepgaard when a stone wall fell on him. He encouraged me to pinch his thigh as hard as I could. This I did, gently at first, then with increasing pressure as Morfar urged me to continue.

"*Jeg kan ikke mærke det,*" he said, and, indeed, showed no sign whatsoever of feeling any pain.

Mormor clearly did not approve of this spectacle. "*Far, holde op med det,*" she said, shaking her head.

Morfar's leg did not trouble him very much any more, though when he made his daily rounds of the farm he often walked with a cane, which he would use to swing at the occasional dandelion showing its head in the fields, deftly decapitating the invasive yellow flower with a single swift blow.

Mother's brother, Knud, also had a predilection for using a walking stick, but in his case the stick was a found branch from a tree, to be used as a hiking aid. Thrusting the long stick ahead of him, he would propel himself forward in long strides. Lean and fit, he was a fast walker. Some days, with me struggling to keep up, we would walk together into town, where Knud would stride into the bakery and purchase some chocolate éclairs or a loaf of French bread for the family's afternoon snack.

One day as we started off on our brisk walk, Knud's walking stick snapped in two. He would have to find another stick. Unfortunately, there were not a lot of suitable tree branches to be found on a farm.

"I know where there are some good walking sticks," I said brightly, momentarily forgetting the fact that the sticks I had in mind lay in some woods on the other side of the Atlantic Ocean.

Mother's sister, Anna Lise, was engaged to Verner Pilgaard, who worked as an airplane mechanic at Copenhagen Airport. Noticing that he was an inch or two shorter than his intended, I remarked to my mother with childish candor, "He's a little man." Fortunately, I had spoken in a whispered voice, otherwise everyone, whether or not they spoke English, would have been able to understand the phrase, "little man."

At times, I could be something of a scamp. One day when my mother was going out on some errand she told Mormor that if I should have to use the outhouse (which was on the other side of a tall fence that had a locking gate), I would say to her, "I have to go to the bathroom," whereupon Mormor was to go out with me and unlatch the gate. Soon after Mother left, I cried out, "I have to go to the bathroom." Unsuspecting my intentions, Mormor led me to the gate. As soon as we were on the other side, I ran back through the gate and latched it shut, returning by myself to the house. My simpleminded ruse, however, was unsuccessful, for Mormor returned to the house only moments after I did, laughing at my innocent prank.

Another time, Mormor and my mother had just laid out on the dining-room table several dishes of food, among them a plateful of sliced Bologna, which was to serve as lunchmeat for the whole family. I picked one slice off the plate and made quick work of it. A second slice went down just as easily. Soon the plate was bare except for a single slice. Of course I knew that the almost empty plate would be quickly discovered, but I had a plan in the back of my mind. Muff was squatting beside me on the dining-room floor, watching my every move. He was big enough to have stood up with his paws on the edge of the table and picked something off. Should I give him the last slice of Bologna? No, I wanted it all for myself, and promptly polished it off. I feigned ignorance when the others began to file into the room. Mormor immediately spotted the empty plate.

"It must have been Muff," I said. But it was obvious as I crouched guiltily in a corner who had actually committed the act. Muff had never done anything like this before.

There was a subsequent occasion—I don't recall what I had done this time. But apparently it was serious enough for me to find it necessary to hide myself on a hill on the edge of the farm. Mother called out to me in a loud, firm voice, "If you don't come down from there, I'll give you the spanking of your life." I promptly came down from my hiding place, glad that there was no one around who could understand what my mother had said. But there would be no spanking today. Mother never spanked me. Her mere disapproval was enough to make me fall into line. (Actual spankings, performed only on rare occasions, were left up to my father.)

Mother and I made a trip by ourselves to Copenhagen. It was a long trip, about an hour and a half by bus and train. We toured Fredericksborg Castle. My father had visited the castle with some of his army buddies a few days before he met my mother in 1946. A photo shows Sergeant Bob Peterson and about twenty other GIs posing in front of the castle. It was lavishly furnished. In the bedrooms were four-poster beds that could be closed off at night with heavy draperies to keep the sleepers warm. Some antique upholstered chairs were roped off so no contemporary visitors would be tempted to sit on them. Most of the ceilings were decorated with intricately carved wood or elaborate paintings depicting hunting scenes and idyllic forests. There were paintings and tapestries in every room, hanging so closely together that there was hardly any open wall space to be seen. You could easily lose your way wandering through this seemingly endless succession of rooms. It would take a full day to take in even a fraction of this vast collection. There were hundreds of portraits of kings and queens, dukes and earls. Who were all these people? After a while all the faces began to look alike. The one painting that sticks out in my mind was a clever *trompe l'oeil*. It had a particular appeal to a child's whimsey. Set in a narrow hallway so that you had to approach it from the side, you saw a man's face from one direction; approach it from the other direction and you saw the face of a beautiful woman. The two portraits were painted on a series of triangular ribs. Viewing the painting straight on, all you saw was a fractured jumble of the two sliced-up portraits.

Another day we took a bus to Kronborg Castle in Helsingør. After seeing Fredericksborg, my expectations for Kronborg, a far more famous castle, were running high. There were cannons positioned on the battlements. Cool. One's first view of Kronborg could not fail to impress: massive stone walls surmounted by three copper spires rising to the sky. Anyone attempting to attack the castle would have faced a succession of obstacles. First there was a steep earthen berm that the enemy would have had to scale under a barrage of arrows. There was a moat. A drawbridge. Then came at least two massive, iron-studded doors. The castle looked absolutely impregnable. What wonders lay inside?

Unfortunately, the interior of the castle was something of a letdown for me. Instead of the elaborately carved ceilings at Fredericksborg, there were bare wooden beams. True, there were ceiling murals in a few of the rooms, but they did not seem to go with what was below them: a cluster of chairs set about a small table squeezed into a corner of a vast hall and looking totally lost. You might have fitted four people at such a table. Not much of a banquet. There were some paintings and tapestries, but they were dominated by the bare white walls that surrounded them. It did not strike me as a palace fit for a king.

We concluded our tour with a visit to the gift shop, where Mother bought me a small lead replica of Kronborg (which I would place at the bottom of a fish tank a few years later and watch my goldfish swimming over the spires and battlements of the castle). Then, presumably, we took the afternoon bus back to Paarup.

Or did we? In the course of writing this memoir I have used a number of sources to jog my memory and fill in some of the blank spots in Mother's story: old photographs, 35 millimeter slides, postcards and letters, ticket stubs, maps, travel guides and brochures, old newspaper clippings, historical accounts of occupied Denmark. I called my mother's sister, Anna Lise, who had just turned ninety-three at the time, and asked a her a few questions to help flesh out my narrative concerning the years of occupation. Unfortunately, she was unable to help me. Her memory was failing. Sadly, between what Mother told me about those five terrible years and my readings of contemporary accounts of the period, I now knew far more about the German occupation of Denmark than Anna Lise did.

An additional source of information was the series of passports my mother and I accumulated over the years. From these I can verify with absolute certainty the dates on which we had departed for Denmark and returned to the United States. Our joint 1955 passport, however, presents me with something of a mystery. Between the visa stamps documenting our arrival at Kastrup Airport on August 20, and our departure on November 9, there are four additional visas. They show that on September 8, we went from Helsingør, Denmark to Hälsingborg, Sweden, returning to Helsingør, on the very same day. Kronborg Castle is in Helsingør, not far from the ferry that would have carried us to Sweden, a short distance across the Ørsund. So Mother must have taken me aboard the ferry to Sweden after our visit to Kronborg.

I have a distinct recollection of my mother bringing me to this red-brick house. I am certain that we walked there; it was situated on a hill. A man answered the door. Who he was, I have not the faintest idea. As far as I know, none of my mother's relatives ever lived in Sweden. I remember sitting in a rather dark parlor while my mother and this man chatted out in the kitchen. We may or may not have been offered some refreshments. In any case, we did not stay for very long. So who was this man? Was he an old flame of my mother's? Or do I just have a suspicious nature? (My assumption that my mother had to get married to an American GI that she barely knew due to a pregnancy turned out to be totally false.)

I believe that we made only the one excursion to Copenhagen on our 1955 trip (apart from our final trip to Copenhagen Airport when we were on our way home). Tivoli would have been a logical place for my mother to bring a seven-year-old. There were rides and amusements for children. There were miniature antique cars, which I distinctly recall seeing on subsequent visits to Denmark. But I never took a ride on these cars when I was seven. I would have remembered this paradise for kids probably even more clearly than I remember my visit to Fredericksborg and Kronborg. Obviously, mother realized that a trip to Copenhagen was simply too exhausting for both of us: an hour-and-a-half-long ride by bus and train, a couple of hours to see the sights, including lunch, then another hour-and-a-half-long trip back to Paarup. So our future excursions would be confined thereafter to the vicinity of Paarup. We made several visits to the nearby harbor of Gilleleje, viewing the fishing boats and walking on the beach, from which you could see Sweden.

One day, my mother's young cousin, Anni, and her husband, Vilhelm, came to visit the family in Paarup. About twenty years old by now, Anni was the girl in whose arms I had begun to cry at the age of five months when my mother handed me off to her. Anni's husband hailed from Germany. I remember him blowing a puff of smoke from his pipe over the top of my windup toy tank as it advanced across a tabletop. Later, half a dozen of us piled into Vilhelm's Volvo and took a ride to a nearby point of interest. I sat up front on Anni's lap. It was not a long drive. I remember the car pulling into a gravel parking lot surrounded by tall trees. We mounted a nearby hill. I vaguely remember peering up at a slender tower constructed of large stone blocks. It had been built in commemoration of something or other. But in commemoration of what? I had no idea. Perhaps my mother explained it, but the significance eluded me. It was not something memorable, like Fredericksborg or Kronborg: it was just a stack of stone blocks on a hilltop.

No doubt we made several more such excursions, but nothing sticks out in my mind. I would just be guessing if I attempted to name places in Northern Zealand that we might have visited. I do, however, clearly remember celebrating my eighth birthday in Paarup. Mormor offered me a plate of sliced Bologna—all I could eat. In the way of presents, I received a plaster tyrannosaurus rex and a box of Lego bricks. These would have been among some of the earliest Lego bricks produced. Unfortunately, I did not save the box they came in, which would have made the plastic bricks a collector's item. The remaining bricks sat for many years in a plastic bag on a closet shelf in my mother's bedroom, untouched for well over half a century. The dinosaur still squats at the back of my desk, a daily reminder of my long-ago birthday. The little model of Kronborg Castle, rescued many years ago from the bottom of the fish tank, nestles somewhat incongruously beside it.

So our trip was fast nearing its conclusion. A few days after I turned eight, we packed our bags and returned by train to Copenhagen. We stayed overnight with Helge and Jenny. Helge, knowing that it had just been my birthday, made me a present of a plastic cuckoo clock—actually a little bank into which you could deposit your coins. Press a lever on the top, and the coins dropped down inside, simultaneous with the emergence from the front door of a yellow cuckoo.

I could now understand a good deal of what Søren and Dorit were saying to me. Spreading his arms out in imitation of an airplane about to take off, Søren exclaimed, "*Og saa, oppe i loftet* (And so, up into the air)." Morfar's coaching and my reading of Anders And had paid off.

The following day we took off from Kastrup Airport on what was supposed to be a routine flight. There would be a stopover in Gander, Newfoundland for refueling since the Douglas DC 6-B did not have sufficient fuel on the eastbound flight to reach Idlewild Airport. As we neared North America our pilot announced over the intercom that there was a minor problem with one of the engines. Nothing to be concerned about. However, we would be putting down at the airport in Gander until this minor problem could be corrected.

In Gander Airport, I had my first glimpse of a Canadian Royal Mountie (wide-brimmed hat, bright red uniform). Mother and I were led to a hotel room to await the repairs. The hotel complex was still under construction. There were as yet no sidewalks. We trod carefully upon wooden planks that had been laid over the muddy ground. Mother stretched out on the hotel bed and promptly fell asleep. I remained awake, thumbing through the comic book she had bought for me in the gift shop. After a couple of hours an announcement came over the intercom. We were instructed to proceed back to the airplane, which was now ready to take off. Mother slept soundly through the announcement. I awakened her and told her that the plane was ready and we had to leave. At the age of eight I was looking after my mother.

# ECONOMY

All through the fifties and sixties the household budget had to be stretched to make ends meet. There were loans to be settled, creditors to be paid. These came first. Keeping track of expenditures naturally fell to my mother. Reflecting her background as a bookkeeper back in Denmark, Mother kept an account book listing every grocery bill, phone bill, and electricity bill; she dutifully recorded all of our expenditures on gas, clothing, shoes, postage stamps, even a mere five cents spent on a newspaper. Mother did the wash using a scrub board, hanging it outside on a clothesline to dry. But as the weather would not always cooperate, we acquired a secondhand wringer: place the wet item between the two rollers, turn the crank, and the water would be squeezed out. Mother economized further by making her own clothes. She knitted sweaters for Father and me. She made a rug for the side of her bed using her old nylon stockings. (Nothing went to waste.) In our fenced-in backyard garden we grew tomatoes, carrots, peas, watermelons, pumpkins, and sunflowers (to be used for feeding the birds). Mother showed me how to peel off the inner membrane of the pea pod so the entire pod could be eaten along with the peas—a trick she had learned as a child at Klostergaarden. Having a well that might have run dry during a drought, we collected rainwater in a fifty-gallon garbage can, and also saved our dishwater for the garden. As a substitute for ice cream, Mother froze fruit juice in plastic forms to make ice pops. We had milk and eggs delivered by a local farmer at a cheaper price than could be had in the grocery store. On Sunday nights, Mother would make pancakes for supper—a tradition that continued for many years. I would carefully fold up the square of aluminum foil Mother had used to wrap my sandwich for my school lunch so it could be reused the following day. (To this day I continue to reuse aluminum foil, plastic bags, and Saran Wrap.) Father did his part, too, in managing our expenses. Instead of bringing me to a barber, he bought a hair clipper and cut my hair as I sat in the backyard on a bench he had made from some leftover lumber.

# CHRISTMAS

For as long as I can remember, we followed the Danish tradition of opening our presents on Christmas Eve instead of on Christmas morning. (Which effectively precluded in my mind any belief in Santa Claus, as it was difficult to imagine how the red-suited gentleman could manage to steal into the living room without being observed in broad daylight on December 24 and place his gifts under the tree.) After supper, the three of us would gather about the Christmas tree, with Mother performing the honors of passing out the gifts. We carefully removed the wrapping paper, which would be rolled up and saved to be reused the following Christmas. Once in a while, I would decide to leave one of my presents unopened until Christmas morning, thus bridging the gap between the two traditions.

Every year when I was little, Anna Lise would send me a Danish Christmas calendar. Properly set up, it would unfold to form a house or some other structure with twenty-five windows. You would open a window each morning to reveal a Christmas-related scene: a candle, a reindeer, a *Jul nisse* (Christmas elf). The final window would invariably open to reveal a smiling Santa Claus. One of the more elaborate of these calendars was in the form of a castle with a spiral ramp leading down from a crenelated tower. When you placed a small red racing car at the top of the ramp it would wend its way down (vanishing a couple of times behind the walls of the tower) and emerge at the bottom of the ramp. The castle is long-gone, but I still have the little red racing car.

When we moved to Huyler Road we had plenty of space to put up a full-sized Christmas tree in the living room. With the tree firmly secured in a water-filled metal basin in front of the picture window, Mother would open the wicker basket that she kept at the foot of her bed and bring out a burlap Christmas blanket. The unfinished blanket had been a gift from her mother. Such blankets were used to decorate the bases of innumerable Christmas trees in Denmark. Mother had sewn red and green threads to outline the whimsical *Jul nisser* that decorated the perimeter of the blanket. She had also stitched the year in which she had completed the blanket: 1956. In later years, the novelty of a full-sized Christmas tree having worn off, we would set a small artificial tree atop a dough box, with Mother's blanket underneath. We decorated the little tree with a string of fairy lights, stuck some Danish flags in among the branches, along with two paper drums, which symbolized the actual drums that guests would beat as they marched around the Christmas tree singing traditional Christmas carols. We also stuck in among the branches some red-spotted mushrooms (*flu svampe*). I'm certain that Mother explained to me the significance of decorating the tree with these colorful mushrooms, but I've forgotten what the story was.

Getting back to that dough box for a minute. Mother always called it a dough box, but is that really what it was? The four-legged box was made by the Ethan Allen Company. It had a hinged top and a front rack in which Mother stored her cookbooks and several magazines. Inside, there was plenty of room for Mother's yarn, more cookbooks, and our Retina camera. There was a small brass handle at either side of the dough box, which would pinch your fingers when you tried to lift the thing. Moving the heavy box from one room to another was a struggle. We also had an Ethan Allen cobbler's bench. I can see how the cobbler's bench, with its multiple drawers and bi-level construction would have been a convenient workbench for a shoemaker, but as for the dough box, I find it hard to imagine anyone storing dough for later use in such a large wooden container. But I'm sure that Mother had it right. She must have heard it called a dough box in the store that sold it to her, and no doubt there was an explanation as to how this box was used in an earlier time. It would have been out of character for Mother to have gotten something like that wrong.

No Christmas could be complete without some fresh-baked butter cookies, and Mother and I would make them together, decorating them with red and green and chocolate sprinkles. As our own cookies usually did not last very long, we would augment them with a tin or two of imported Royal Dansk Butter Cookies.

Some years ago, Anna Lise and Verner sent us a *Jul moder* and *Jul fader* that had been fashioned by a local artisan. Sporting festive red caps, the pair perch upon a length of driftwood that came from Tranum Strand. Mother and I would hang them up every Christmas from the ceiling in a corner of the family room at Castlewood Drive. It became a yearly tradition in our home, along with me trundling the bulky dough box from the dining room into the family room, setting the little Christmas tree on top of Mother's festive burlap blanket, and baking those delicious butter cookies.

# A NEW SCHOOL

Back on Huyler Road after our 1955 trip to Denmark, my mother and I admired the oak floors in the living room, dining room, and bedrooms. Wielding a hammer, my father had nailed them down in our absence so we would not have to listen to the incessant hammering. He had also glued down linoleum floors in the kitchen and bathroom. He had painted the living-room walls a stately shade of blue; the dining room was a delicate rose color.

A day or two after our return to Huyler Road, Mother enrolled me in Branchburg Elementary School. As she did not have the use of the car this morning, we had to take a two-mile walk. My new school soon turned out to be something of a disappointment. The class in third grade was divided into three sections based upon one's presumed abilities. I was arbitrarily assigned to the intermediate group, though I knew that I belonged in the advanced group. I was not tested or given any kind of formal evaluation. In second grade, back in Jersey City, I had mastered the art of cursive handwriting. But now in third grade the class was still printing their letters. And so must I. My teacher, Mrs. Moore, expressly forbid me from showing off my cursive writing skills. The class would learn cursive handwriting in the fourth grade, not before. It would simply not do for each student to proceed at his or her own pace (apart from the three groups). I had also mastered addition and subtraction in the second grade, but here we were sent out into the playground to gather pebbles, which we would line up on our desks to do our sums. Ho hum. True, we were now moving on to multiplication and division, but this was also to be mastered by counting the rows of pebbles. Obviously, I had missed nothing by taking a couple of months off from school. I was actually far ahead of my peers. I had been abroad. None of my classmates had even flown on an airplane. I had visited castles dating back to the Middle Ages. I had lived on a farm. I was able to speak at least the rudiments of a foreign language. But all of this knowledge counted for nothing. I doubt that Mrs. Moore appreciated how advanced I really was. She might have asked my to share my experiences in Denmark with the class. But she never did. Which was odd, because the advanced group, in their separate weekly sessions, was currently focused on the theme of traveling to foreign lands.

There was just one limited area in which I lagged behind my peers. The class had learned how to hyphenate words before I started school. (The text books my mother had brought along for me to study in Denmark made no mention of hyphenation.) There was a simple trick to this task: you only had to look up the designated word in a dictionary, which showed you exactly where to place the hyphens. Absolutely no thought required. Why you would ever need to hyphenate a word, I do not know. I have never in my life felt the need to hyphenate. You can simply place the word that won't fit on the next line, no need to chop it into pieces. But that was the lesson. Mrs. Moore never bothered to tell me that all you needed to do to complete this simpleminded task was to crack open a dictionary and copy the hyphenation. So I struggled on my own to guess where the hyphens should go, and failed miserably at the task, which caused me no end of embarrassment when Mrs. More returned our test papers and made us read our scores out loud for the whole class to hear. I had never before, back in Number 24 School in Jersey City, achieved less than top marks. ("P, P, P, U," I remember stammering in Mrs. Moore's class as I read the marks she had made in red ink on the top of my test paper.) The purpose of this exercise was apparently to get us accustomed to consulting a dictionary. But it was still a pointless task. And I remain perplexed to this day as to why Mrs. Moore did not draw me aside (as she should have done) after my first failing test result and clue me in on what the class had covered in the two months before my arrival. It would have taken only a moment of her valuable time.

Now that I think of it, Mrs. Moore never made us read any other of our test results out loud in class, on which I always scored well. I can't say for certain whether or not she had engaged in this practice before I entered her class, but I suspect that she had designed this reading aloud of our hyphenation test results as a special torment for me, to put me in my place, to make me feel stupid. And my classmates, hearing me read out my disastrous results certainly thought that I was stupid, for I was the only one in the class to receive a failing grade on this task. (Even the "stupid" group excelled in this exercise.) What earthly reason did Mrs. Moore have for handing back our test papers and then making us read aloud our marks? Obviously, having graded our papers, she had already written down our scores, so this step was totally unnecessary. Too young at the time to realize what was being done to me, I will now in retrospect charitably call Mrs. Moore a mean-spirited individual. For some reason she had developed a personal animosity for me. To be fair, however, other students in the class had an entirely favorable impression of her. In an unguarded moment, one of the girls slipped up and addressed her as "Mom."

Mother quickly fell into the role of chauffeur for Father and me. Arising before six A.M. in the morning, she would accompany Bob to the railroad station in Somerville, where he would board the express train to New York City. Mother would then drive home and have the use of the car for the remainder of the day. I would walk to the school-bus stop in the morning (it was all downhill). But after school my mother would usually pick me up at the bottom of the hill, giving me more time to to enjoy my afternoon snack before supper. Around six o' clock Mother would drive to the Somerville train station and pick up Father and our next-door neighbor, Frank. On alternate mornings Bob and Frank would share a ride to the station in Frank's car, giving Mother a rest from the daily commute.

Getting back to my schooldays. Another of my pet peeves with my third grade class was with our reading material. Our main work of fiction concerned an orphaned young boy by the name of Tom Hastings (a poor, pale copy of *Tom Sawyer*, which would have been a far superior book to read.) This Tom was on his way to a new home with his aunt in the West. The description of a stagecoach driven by a character called Lightning Jim, who was whipping his horses and speeding along a narrow canyon road with two wheels of the coach hanging over the edge of a precipice struck me as completely ridiculous. "What's the hurry?" I asked in class. "Why does he need to whip his horses? My grandfather never used a whip on *his* horse when he drove his wagon into town." The writer of this rubbish obviously didn't know what he was talking about. But there was nothing to be gained by bringing up such objections. Mrs. Moore simply shook her head at me and moved on to other matters. What did I know? Did Mrs. Moore resent my somewhat smart-alecky criticism of Lightening Jim? Here I was, after having missed two months of school, putting on airs about how much I knew. I was an upstart. Perhaps Mrs. Moore resented my having traveled abroad, a luxury that she would probably never be able to afford on her modest (at the time) teacher's salary. I doubt if she had ever ventured farther from Branchburg than the

Jersey Shore. (Mrs. Moore was a far cry from my second grade teacher, Mrs. Muller, who, upon learning of my upcoming trip to Denmark, wished that she could magically shrink herself to fit into my shirt pocket and go along with me.) Can it be that Mrs. Moore was jealous of this eight-year-old upstart?

A final word about Mrs. Moore's division of her class into three sections—a practice that I have never before or since witnessed. (Apparently, Mrs. Moore had never heard of "late bloomers.") Being labeled at a young age as "smart" or "stupid" can be a self-fulfilling prophesy. All of the kids in the bottom group knew that they were the "stupid" ones. How many kids' lives, I wonder, were ruined by Mrs. Moore's ignorant teaching methods? If memory serves me, I don't recall any of my classmates assigned to the "stupid" group moving on to college.

Looking back now on those days, I realize that we had settled in a rural area that was only just beginning to build up. There was no doubt a shortage of qualified individuals for the teaching profession to draw from among the predominantly rustic population. ("We'll take what we can get.") It requires no stretch of the imagination to speculate that the caliber of the teachers in Branchburg Elementary School was nowhere near as high as it was in Number 24 School back in Jersey City, where there would have been intense competition from a large pool of candidates for every teaching position. While my parents may have found the Promised Land, I was far from content with my new environment.

However trying a day in school I might have had, I could always renew myself in my sanctuary on Huyler Road. So what was the use of complaining to Mother when I got home? Oftentimes, she would have a dish of warm pudding waiting for me (its surface overlaid with a piece of wax paper so it would not form a skin), and any lingering cares that I might have would melt away as I enjoyed my pudding.

Perhaps the main reason I never complained to my parents about my disappointment with my new school was that I feared that it would have sounded as if I was criticizing them for having taken me out of the more advanced school system in Jersey City and enrolling me in an obviously inferior rural system. Also in the back of my mind was the thought that if Mother had not brought me to Denmark when she did, causing me to miss the first two months of third grade, I would have been up to speed on the hyphenation test. After finishing a school day back in Jersey City I would excitedly describe to my mother all the significant things I had done and learned in class—not so here in Branchburg. Even when she asked me how my day had gone I told her nothing of my experiences with my nemesis, Mrs. Moore. I had no doubt that I would eventually overcome whatever deficiencies my new school presented. At home during this time, I was avidly reading the stories of Hans Christian Anderson, two volumes of which, translated into English, had been sent to me by my Danish grandparents. At the age of ten I was reading Melville's *Moby Dick*, which I pulled out of my parents' bookcase while I spent an enjoyable two weeks recuperating from the measles. My parents had a small, but well-stocked library. A set of volumes published by the *Literary Guild* featured such classics as *David Copperfield*, *War and Peace*, and *The Brothers Karamazov*. The Fine Editions Press, with titles stamped in gold, included *The Adventures of Tom Sawyer*, *The Adventures of Huckleberry Finn*, a collection of stories by Edgar Allen Poe, and other masterpieces. (The books I found in my parents' library, compared with the mediocre works we were reading in school, makes a good case for homeschooling.) I always enjoyed being sick, for then I could stay home from school, remain in bed all day and read whatever I wanted to. In the morning before it was time to get ready for school, I would force the proffered thermometer as firmly as I could under my tongue in the vain hope that this would serve to raise my temperature enough to get me off from school for another day. Naturally, my mother would dote on me during my illness, bringing me bowls of chicken-noodle soup. She had a wonderful bedside manner. During my summer vacation, Mother would bring me to the library in nearby Somerville, where I would select a stack of books to peruse in my spare hours. My favorite authors at the time were Jules Verne and H.G. Wells. Whatever we were reading now in school paled by comparison with the works of these masters.

"I can't move my legs," I told my mother one morning when I didn't feel like getting up and going to school. And I truly believed that my legs wouldn't move, so strong was my desire to stay home. (I don't recall what unpleasantness awaited me in school on this particular day. Perhaps I was anticipating yet another reading of our scores on the weekly hyphenation test.) Mother instantly saw through my simpleminded stratagem.

"I'll give you five minutes to get dressed and come out for breakfast," she said.

Earlier thoughts of my mother calling a doctor to make a house call and examine me quickly dissipated, and within moments my legs were fully functional. After breakfast, I walked the half-mile to the school-bus stop with no difficulty. Did I learn anything important in school that day? I doubt it. I'd have learned more by staying in bed and having another go at *The Adventures of Tom Sawyer*, or perhaps browsing through *The New World Family Encyclopedia* that my parents had just bought.

I considered third grade a total waste of time. We were going over material that I had already mastered in the second grade back in Jersey City. It was not until fourth grade that we finally got around to learning cursive handwriting. But having been discouraged from using cursive writing for an entire year, the quality of my script was not up to what it had formerly been. My letters, once well-formed and eminently legible, were now crabbed and difficult to decipher. To this day I find myself resorting to printing things in capital letters—a far slower process than cursive script, but at least the words are legible. Thanks a lot, teachers. Now that I think back on what Mother told me about her early schooldays, I can see that there was a huge disparity in our respective educations. In the third grade she was already beginning to study English and German. There was no language instruction in my school. While my mother was memorizing multiplication and division tables, I was sent out into the playground to gather pebbles to be used as a counting device. No contest. As a result, my mother was always good at math; I was not.

I had enjoyed going to Number 24 School in Jersey City. I wrote earlier how Miss Cavendar, my first grade teacher, once asked the class what our favorite day of the week was. "The days you have to go to school," I replied. On my final report card Mrs. Cavendar entered a comment: "Glenn is a credit to his class." But things were different in Branchburg Elementary. Unlike my mother, who expressed not a single word of criticism about any of her teachers, I did not get along with several of mine. In my new school, I preferred holidays and summer vacations. Schooldays were no longer my favorite days of the week. Out of school, I could spend my time reading books that interested me, and, although there were no castles to visit, my parents would bring me to interesting places. We frequently took the train into New York City to tour the American Museum of Natural History. Shunning the noisy cafeteria there, we would stroll across Central Park and have our lunch in the Metropolitan Museum of Art (where I would one day have my first bottle of Heineken). We attended a special exhibition of paintings by Jean DuBuffet at the Guggenheim Museum with its unique spiral staircase. Summer vacations brought us to Cape May, New Jersey; Bar Harbor, Maine, where I had my first taste of lobster; Sturbridge Village, Massachusetts, where I learned about eighteenth-century America; in Boston Harbor, Massachusetts, visiting Old Ironsides, we ran into George Maharis, one of the stars of *Route Sixty-Six*. (They were filming an episode in Boston at the time.) He said hello to my mother as he headed for the ship's gangplank.

When we were not driving to some interesting destination, I enjoyed stretching out on my bed with a favorite book propped up on my chest. Though my parents certainly did not disapprove of my reading, they objected to my being cooped up in the house all day, and encouraged me to take my book outside and get some sun. Mother was constantly telling me how good the sun was for me. It would strengthen your bones, she explained. She should know. So I would grudgingly take off my shirt to get the maximum benefit from the sun and sit in a chair with my book in my lap. As soon as Mother told me that I had been out in the sun long enough, I would put my shirt on and go back inside, resuming my reading on my bed. In addition to books from the library, I worked my way through more of the volumes in the living-room bookcase: Dostoyevsky's *Crime and Punishment* and Fielding's *The History of Tom Jones*. Mother was also an avid reader. Preferring works of history and biography, she enjoyed Margaret Mitchel's *Gone With the Wind*, Pearl Buck's *The Living Reed*, as well as mysteries by Agatha Christie. She was a fan of James Michener, beginning with his epic *Hawaii*, and looked forward to each of his subsequent novels. On one of our trips to Denmark, she found a Danish translation of *Hawaii* and presented it to her father.

In school, our literary selections had moved up a couple of notches. In seventh grade, copies of Howard Pile's *Men of Iron* were distributed to the class. I remember reading the day's selection during the bus ride into school. It was not something so gripping that it would keep you up reading late into the night. The novel was all right, but I still much preferred the selections I found in my parents' bookcase or those that I culled from the Somerville Library.

# MUFF

Every boy should have a dog for a companion and in 1956 my parents bought a dog for me. We named him "Muff," after the airedale terrier my Danish grandparents had. Our Muff was a mongrel, but he was a handsome dog. I don't remember where we got him. From the very start he was wild and difficult to control. He would bark and tug furiously at the chain on his dog-run. One day I set down a flattened ice-cream container for him to lick clean. When he had finished, I attempted to remove the container, only to have the dog bite my extended hand, drawing copious amounts of blood. That was the last straw for this vicious Muff. The next day Mother brought him to the dog pound. She returned home with the story that a farmer who needed a dog had given her five dollars for Muff, and she presented me with the bill. Nine years old at the time, I was inclined to believe her (at least I wanted to). Some years later, I concluded that she had made the story up to spare my feelings, and the dog had likely been put to sleep. I never asked her what the truth was.

My parents quickly found another dog for me. After some research on which breed would make the ideal pet, my parents brought me to the house of a dog-breeder who specialized in Boston terriers. We carried a blanket with us into the house, which impressed the dog breeder, who stated flatly that she would not sell one of her dogs to someone she considered unsuitable. So we made our selection: not one of the dogs with two black eyes, which sold for a premium, but a cute little puppy with one black and one white eye. Our new dog had a pedigree. Born on December 16, 1957, her parents were Dee Whiz (N253776) and Wee Patty (N209217). The woman placed the puppy on the blanket that I had laid across my lap. As I gently stroked the dog, the woman handed us a booklet on the care of Boston terriers. She explained to us that a Boston terrier would either grow up to be calm or excitable, depending on how the dog was treated. We wrapped her up in the blanket and brought her out to the car. She would also be called "Muff." (My best friend, Jamison, called her "Muff the Second.")

At home we had a bed ready for her, right beside my own bed. But Muff didn't stay in her own bed that night, or most nights, for that matter. Soon after I turned out the light, she got up and began pawing at the side of my bed. I picked her up and brought her into bed with me. She was used to cuddling up with her litter mates, and sleeping by herself obviously did not appeal to her. She would henceforth only sleep in her own bed when I was away or attending school.

Muff proved to be not as clever as her original namesake. Her main trick was a simple one. If you placed her up on a chair and gently tossed her ball to her, she would return the ball, butting it with her nose. She displayed some intelligence, too, when my parents and I tried to fool her by not taking our usual places when we sat down to watch TV. Muff would become distressed, nudging us in the sides with her nose until we assumed our proper places. Unlike my grandparents' airedale, this Muff could not be allowed to roam about on her own. My father had constructed a dog-run, a long wire cable strung from the back door of the house to a distant tree. We would hook Muff onto the dog-run with a length of chain attached to her collar. One day, before she could be secured to the dog run, she took off into the backyard with the chain still attached to her collar and disappeared into the dense woods behind our property. My father and I searched the woods, but there was no sign of her. We called out; there was no response—Muff would bark only on rare occasions. As night fell, we suspended our search. Then, early the next morning, a strange dog appeared by the back step, barking loudly and persistently. It would bark at us, then turn around and look back as if it wanted us to follow. My father and I took the hint and began to pursue the dog. Perhaps half a mile into the woods sat a forlorn-looking Muff, her chain hopelessly wrapped around some bushes. We brought her home and gave her something to eat and drink. We never saw the strange dog again.

# HAVE YOU HAD YOUR IRON TODAY?

By the late 1950s my parents had become aware of the need for vitamin supplements—especially my mother, who had learned the hard way what the lack of vitamin D could do to you. We began taking a daily regimen of supplements. Every morning we would tap out our vitamin pills from three bottles. The large pills were colored a patriotic red, white, and blue. While my mother and I would gulp down our pills one by one with a glass of water, my father would simply place his pills in the palm of his hand, toss back his head, and pop all three pills at once into his mouth. No water. No gagging. I did not understand how he could do this, or why. Was it a way of showing off? Some macho thing? Then we went to see a movie set during the Korean War. It was called *Pork Chop Hill.* U.S. troops have orders to take this obscure hill in Korea at all costs, despite the fact that the war is nearly over. The enemy, manning machine-gun nests at the top of the hill, occupy an almost unassailable position, mowing down wave after wave of advancing American soldiers. The commanding officer, played by Gregory Peck, is taking a break with an enlisted man who had earlier balked at this suicidal assault. Suddenly, Gregory Peck reaches into a pocket and pulls something out, holding it in the palm of his hand.

"Have you had your iron today?" he asks, and, tossing back his head, swallows the pill.

So that was where my father had picked up this habit—from his army training.

It was obvious to me that seeing this film had moved my father. As we drove out of the parking lot, he wondered what the men who had served in this suicidal mission thought of the movie. When we got back home, my mother asked former Sergeant Bob Peterson if he had killed anyone in the war.

My father shrugged. "We never knew if we hit anything," he replied. "We were supplied with coordinates to fire upon. But the targets were miles away, far out of sight. Some of our mortar shells must have hit what they were supposed to. Did we kill some Germans? I assume so. After all, they lost the war."

# STONY BROOK SCHOOL

Seventh grade ushered in another change of venue. Only this time it was the school that moved, not I. Over the summer, I had watched the Stony Brook Middle School being built from the ground up. The new school was much closer to home than my old school. I no longer had to get up early, hike half a mile, and catch a bus; I could ride my bike into school in a mere ten minutes. This mode of transportation went well through the fall. Then came winter. It was exhausting trying to peddle through the snow-covered trail. One day, with a bitterly cold wind blowing in my face, my eyes began to tear, and froze shut. I had to stop and thaw them out with my gloved hands. I don't recall what we studied in class that day; it's only the journey that sticks in my mind. (Just as in *Tristram Shandy*, where the ultimate destination becomes little more than an afterthought.) I recall also the following spring when we kids would stop on our way home and pick the wild strawberries that grew in a patch along the bike trail. We would eat them on the spot.

There were a couple of teachers in Stony Brook that I took a distinct disliking to. Mr. Snyder, my seventh grade history teacher, was also a football coach. He suggested an extra-credit paper to the class. I completed my paper and turned it in several days later at the end of class. No one else had taken the trouble to undertake this optional assignment. I waited patiently for a few moments, as Mr. Snyder was busy talking to one of his football players. Finally getting his attention, I handed him my paper. He barely glanced at it, placed it on the side of his desk, and then resumed talking to the football player. The only word of acknowledgment was a mumbled, "Thanks." I never heard from him what he thought of my paper. Why had he even bothered suggesting this assignment to the class? I suspect that it was this incident that soured me permanently on sports, even though I had previously enjoyed playing football in the backyard with my friends. So the twig is bent. Looking back, I wonder if in my schooling I just happened to encounter a run of mediocre or indifferent teachers. My mother never mentioned to me when she reminisced on her schooldays back in Denmark any teachers that she did not get along with. She had nothing but praise for her teachers. Was it me? I don't think so. Stony Brook School was, to be sure, a rural school, drawing therefore upon a limited pool of talent. I suspect that few really qualified teachers would want to settle in the sticks and work for a lower wage than they could get in some big city.

I had a definite facility for learning a foreign language, but, unfortunately, there were no foreign language courses offered in Stony Brook, unlike my mother's elementary school in Nykøbing Falster, which offered instruction in English and German starting at the age of eight or nine. Realizing the shortcoming of my school, my parents sent me to a private French tutor to give me a head start when I entered high school. There were just six of us in the class. We met once a week for an hour. After two years I had a pretty decent French accent. Yes, I know that it would have made sense for me to have studied German, which my mother would have been able to help me with. But there were no private tutors in rural Branchburg teaching German. So French it was.

Apart from *Men of Iron* and *Great Expectations*, none of the other novels that I must have studied in English class during this period comes to mind. They were either too boring to stand out or not bad enough to be memorable. Meanwhile, I continued to work my way through the volumes in my parents' bookcase: Dana's *Two Years Before the Mast*, Thor Heyerdahl's *Kon-Tiki*, Peter Freuchen's *Book of the Seven Seas*. (Incidentally, Peter Freuchen, an old salt, was born in Nykøbing Falster, which was no doubt an added incentive for my mother to buy his book.) For some reason I always enjoyed reading tales set on the high seas. Is it possible that it stemmed from a dim and distant memory of my week-long voyage aboard the Gripsholm when I was just five months old? And this memory was reinforced over the years every time Mother told me about the spouting whale we had seen in the middle of the Atlantic Ocean. ("There she blows.") Also, my parents had a professional photographer take a picture of me in a sailor's suit when I was about a year old. So the twig is bent.

It's a mystery to me why we weren't exposed in school to Boris Pasternak's *Dr. Zhivago*, perhaps the greatest literary work of the twentieth century—which my mother purchased in 1958 for our home library. Such an omission makes a good case for home schooling.

I remember my eighth grade teacher having the class write a paper after he had read to us an editorial published many years ago in the *Boston Sun*: "Yes, Virginia, There is a Santa Clause." But this assignment was given to the class as a punishment for us having been noisy during the teacher's absence. Mr. Federici had a predilection for giving out writing assignments as a punishment. "Yours not to reason why," he was fond of saying. "Yours but to do or die." He did not ask for volunteers when he assigned classroom tasks; he simple announced who would be doing what. One week, he selected me for the duty of taking ice-cream orders for the class. I was already an assistant projectionist on a permanent basis, so obviously I was not averse to playing my part in the classroom workforce. But to spend my lunchtime taking orders and fetching ice cream from the lunchroom struck me as an unreasonable imposition. I was a slow eater: there was no way that I would be able to take the orders, go to the lunchroom, pick up the orders, and have time left to eat the meal my mother had packed for me in my blue metal lunchbox: a sandwich, two or three slices of carrot, a chocolate-chip cookie, and a thermos bottle of milk. So I handed over to one of the girls in the class my assigned task for the week. She was delighted to take over for me, for she had a boyfriend in the lunchroom. (Had Mr. Federici deigned to ask for volunteers, she would have eagerly raised her hand.) Returning to the classroom, Mr. Federici blew his stack when he saw me sitting at my desk enjoying my sandwich and milk when I should have been in the lunchroom collecting ice cream for the class. I protested feebly that I had never once ordered ice cream for myself, and in any case the ice-cream orders had been taken care of.

Mr. Federici exploded. "One thousand words, Peterson: "Accepting the Responsibilities of a Democracy." There was an audible gasp in the classroom. A thousand words was a lot to write in addition to your usual schoolwork. And I would have to complete this task every week until Mr. Federici told me that I could stop.

I composed the required essay (fearful of what my fate would be if I had stood up for myself and flatly refused) and completed more of these essays over the course of the next several weeks, but I always included a subtle dig at my teacher, whom I considered a fool. My theme remained the same throughout the series of essays: this class was not a democracy, and all tyrants should be opposed. I likened school to a prison, complete with sadistic guards, arbitrary rules, and unjust punishments. I very much doubt if Mr. Federici ever took the trouble to read my papers, for he never commented on their content. (And given his vengeful nature, would not such a contrary attitude have set him off again?)

One day after school, my mother asked me how my day had gone. I replied, somewhat intemperately, but without bringing up my unjust punishment, that I considered school little better than a prison. Mother was taken aback, and I quickly amended my remarks. My mother had gotten along with all of her teachers, bare none, even those who had so unreasonably forced her to write with her non-dominant right hand. But I doubt that she had ever encountered any teacher with such a fiery temperament as Mr. Federici. Perhaps some of the fault was mine. If I had simply complied with my teacher's assignment to take the ice-cream orders for a week, I would have avoided the whole unpleasant incident. My mother would have done so. But I was not my mother. There was something in me that would not allow me to take things lying down.

It was not long after this episode that Mr. Federici exploded again, this time over a girl who had spoken out of turn in class. Seizing a heavy dictionary from the rear of his desk, Mr. Federici hurled the book at the head of the offending student and then stormed out of the classroom. Fortunately, his wild throw missed his intended target and landed harmlessly in the aisle. (Imagine what could have happened if he had actually struck her.) We kids resolved thereafter to treat Mr. Federici with kid gloves.

Despite such outbursts, however, there was a softer side to Mr. Federici. Once, in an unguarded moment, he declared that his favorite piece of music was *Greensleeves*, an old English melody of unknown authorship that dated back to the Middle Ages. Still, despite this revelation of a sensitive soul, Mr. Federici was obviously not cut out to be a teacher.

Fortunately, I would not have to put up with such goings-on for much longer. I would soon be moving on to high school, which would hopefully present me with more challenging and more interesting subjects, and at the same time I was contemplating another trip to Denmark.

# DENMARK 1961

The flight across the pond aboard a Douglas DC-8 jet plane now took only a little over seven hours—less than half the time our 1955 flight had taken. From a guidebook picked out of a rack in Kastrup Airport, mother selected a nearby hotel. We were able to walk there, with me now big enough now to carry the heaviest of the suitcases. We checked in. We had barely placed our suitcases on the bed when my mother decided that she did not like this hotel. It was not located in a particularly nice neighborhood. The carpets were worn and the room had a seedy look to it. Mother consulted the guidebook again. We picked up our suitcases and headed back downstairs. My mother explained to the desk clerk that a relative had offered us a place to stay. Catching a taxi, we headed for a more posh hotel in central Copenhagen.

Tivoli Gardens was only a block or two away from our new hotel. We headed there as soon as we had finished unpacking. Music in the air, fountains, winding walks shaded by trees. There were formal flower gardens, a Chinese pagoda, peddle-powered boats moving around a lake. Mother shunned the formidable-looking roller coaster as well as the bumper cars that were subjecting their riders a considerable shaking. There were miniature classic cars for children to ride, but I was now too big now to get onboard. In any case, I was more interested in the slot machines, pulling repeatedly on the one-armed bandit and getting away with a couple of 25 øre *spillemærker* (play tokens) as a souvenir. (There was no one around at this time to stop a fourteen-year-old from playing the slot machines.) We wound our way through a funhouse maze in which distorting mirrors made you appear alternately tall or short, your head expanded to enormous proportions, or shrunken into a tiny remnant that would have appealed to a headhunter. Another amusement consisted of a simple stone basin filled with water. There was a glistening ten-kroner coin at the bottom of the basin. A sign said that if you could reach into the basin and grab the coin, it was yours to keep. A simple enough task. Piece of cake. I rolled up my sleeve and plunged my right hand into the water, only to be met with a powerful electric shock that caused me to quickly withdraw my hand. I tried again and again, but each time my hand would be paralyzed by the electric current. As hard as I tried, I could simply not move my fingers to seize the coin at the bottom of the basin. It was an impossible task. My mother had the good sense not to attempt it.

That evening we had supper in the Nimb Restaurant, an exotic, Moorish-style building replete with stately minarets. When we came out, the whole amusement park was lit up. The Chinese pagoda, impressive enough by day, took on a magical quality when illuminated at night. The fountains glowed with ever-changing colors. A firework display began. We headed back to the hotel and watched the remainder of the fireworks from our bedroom window.

The following day we visited Kronborg Castle. I got more out of this visit than I had on the previous one. Mother told me how Kronborg had been constructed here on the shore so a toll could be extracted from any ship attempting to pass by in the narrow Øresund—especially ships flying the Swedish flag, Denmark's long-standing enemy. (She had no doubt explained some of this to me on our first visit, but I was either too young for the information to register or I had simply forgotten.) In the early seventeenth century, the castle had been gutted by a fire that left only the walls standing. It was subsequently restored to its former glory by King Christian IV, who was responsible for building many of the castles in Denmark. In 1658 Kronborg was captured by the Swedes and occupied for two years. The Swedes ransacked the castle, removing most of the opulent interiors and taking them back to Sweden, which accounted for the mostly bare walls and ceilings. After the enemy was repulsed, the castle served as a military barracks until the 1920s. Toward the end of our visit, we descended into the extensive network of tunnels that had been hewn out of the white limestone rock forming the foundation of the castle. At the end of one of these chambers sat a larger-than-life sculptured figure, apparently asleep, with his muscular arms crossed upon his chest. He wore a Viking helmet; his shield waited in readiness beside his chair; his sword lay across his lap. Mother explained to me that this was Holger Danske, a mythological figure who, it was said, would awaken from his slumber if the safety of Denmark was ever threatened and spring to her defense. A rumor had it that during World War II Holger Danske had blinked an eye and then went back to sleep.

We caught a flight from Kastrup Airport to Tirstrup Airport in Aalborg the following day aboard an old propellor-driven plane, which looked just like the one featured in *The High and the Mighty*. After everyone was seated, the stewardess requested that some of the passengers seated on one side of the plane move to the other side so there would be a more equal distribution of weight. (Hopefully we would not be asked to part with our luggage.) The wing flaps flexed up and down several times, then the plane began to taxi down the runway, and suddenly we were airborne. Half an hour later we put down in Jutland. Trundling our suitcases, we boarded a bus bound for Silkeborg that was just about to leave.

By now, Morfar had retired from farming. He and Mormor were living in Resenbro, a small town in the lake district in central Jutland. They had a one-story redbrick house with a sizable amount of land. Neither of my grandparents drove, but they were situated on a main bus route that would take them into the nearby town of Silkeborg or into Aalborg, less than an hour's drive away. Both Morfar and Mormor were fit enough to walk or ride their bicycles into the nearby town of Resenbro to pick up a few things in the grocery store. Though the thought crossed my mind, I never did learn what had become of Muff. I did not ask. There are some questions that are better left unanswered. My grandparents now had a canary, which they had discovered fluttering about in their driveway a week or two before my mother and I arrived. How it came to be there was a mystery. Rescued from a doubtful fate, it now sat in a cage in the kitchen, chirping merrily in its new home. My grandparents had not yet chosen a name for the foundling. My cousin, Poul, had started calling the bird *Pip-Hans* (Peeping-Cock). I suggested Beila, the name of a notable 1846 comet. (I was up on my astronomy, having purchased a refracting telescope with a 2.4-inch-objective lens the previous year.) The name Beila met with my grandparents' approval. It was easy to pronounce. So Beila it was.

The convenient location of Silkeborg and its charming setting in a bucolic lake district had appealed not only to Morfar and Mormor, but their children as well. Both Anna Lise and Knud had also settled in the vicinity with their spouses and children. With the exception of Inge, the whole family was together now, only minutes away from one another, either by car or within easy walking distance.

Though Morfar had given up farming, growing and harvesting things remained in his blood. In the backyard's sandy soil, he planted long rows of strawberries and potatoes. He grew carrots, asparagus, and rhubarbs. There were several old plum trees, their trunks encrusted with blue-white lichen. Now and then, Morfar managed to catch an eel in the little brook that coursed through one side of the property. Mormor would cook the eel for our supper along with some small potatoes from the garden. The eel was very tender. A bit on the oily side. But a tasty treat.

Before our trip, Mother had shown me how to use a knife and fork in the European style, holding the fork throughout the meal in your left hand, the knife in your right hand. It was much more elegant way of eating than the American style, in which you held the fork in your right hand and clumsily switched hands when you needed to cut something. One day we were having a chicken dinner. I was proud to show off how I could wield a fork in my left hand. I sliced the potatoes and asparagus, harvested from Morfar's garden, with ease. But as I worked on the chicken, I found that my skill was unequal to the task. No matter how carefully I positioned my fork, the piece of chicken kept sliding about on my plate. It seemed that I could only slice a tiny bit of meat off the bone at the time. My knife finally slipped off the chicken and clattered upon the plate. Seeing the difficulty I was having, Mormor offered a piece of advice. Toward the end of World War I, she had been under service to a General Wolf. The general had volunteered a primer on proper dining etiquette, which Mormor never forgot.

"If it swims," the general had said, "you eat it with a knife and fork. If it walks, you eat it with a knife and fork. But if it flies, you can eat it with your fingers."

I put down my knife and fork and picked up the chicken—another facet of dining etiquette under my belt.

Mormor had lost her sense of smell in the influenza epidemic of 1918. It had been touch-and-go for a while whether or not she would survive. But survive she did, not realizing until several days after recovering that she could no longer smell anything. The loss turned out to be permanent. Mormor could not tell if a cut of meat, or any food for that matter, had gone bad. She could no longer enjoy the scent of a flower. She could not even remember what the last rose she had sniffed over forty years ago had smelled like. But she was grateful to be alive. The loss of the precious sense of smell seemed a small price to pay for the gift of life.

Mormor had two uncles who had journeyed to Russia in 1931 or 1932, expecting to share their expertise in modern farming methods with their Russian counterparts, who were going through a trying time. But after a letter or two, the brothers were never heard from again. Had they disappeared into one of Stalin's gulags? Had they been shot to death after a few short weeks on the assumption that they were spies? (Why else would anyone want to come to Russia, the paranoid Stalin must have reasoned, if not to spy?)

In retrospect, one would think that Mormor's uncles must have been exceedingly naive to have chosen to risk their lives in Stalin's Russia. But this was evidently not the case. At the time no one in the outside world really had an accurate picture of what was going on inside the Soviet Union. No one knew about the gulags, or Stalin's forced relocation of the kulaks, which resulted in the deaths of millions, mostly due to starvation. Researching the Stalin era, I learned that the outside world's knowledge of the conditions in Russia in the early thirties came almost entirely from the reports of one Walter Duranty, ace reporter on the *New York Times* who was awarded a Pulitzer Prize for his series of dispatches from Russia. His accounts on developments in the new Soviet Union were uniformly glowing. He praised the "progressive reforms" of Joseph Stalin. Sure, he wrote, the Russian people were going through tough times, but you had to break an egg to make an omelet. Unfortunately, everything Duranty wrote was cooked up to please his Soviet masters. He had a cushy job, simply retyping the propaganda that Uncle Joe handed to him to be used in his cables to the *Times*. Had he written a single dispatch exposing what was really going on, he'd have been promptly booted out of the country, and that would have likely been the end of his career. So Mormor's uncles were not naive after all; they had been duped, as had many others, by these false reports into believing that Stalin was a benevolent dictator, and that the new Soviet Union was a land of opportunity. According to Walter Duranty, communism was not something to be feared, but emulated. Mormor's uncles left no descendants. Thanks a lot, *New York Times*. Thanks a lot, *Pulitzer Prize* committee. Fake news is nothing new.

Getting back to Resenbro, Morfar would periodically use a scythe to cut the tall grass growing on a small meadow on the lower slope of his property. I tried my hand at it, but after a couple of strokes the blade of the heavy scythe would invariably dig into the ground. Once the grass had all been cut down, Morfar would call up a neighbor who owned a farm that lay across the nearby river, called the Gudenaa, which flows to Silkeborg. His farm could be seen from the front door of my grandparents' house. Hr. Rasmussen would come over and, using a long rope, bundle up a huge load of hay on his back and carry it down to the river, where he had left his rowboat. Loading up his boat, he would pole across to the far side of the river. It would take him several trips to gather up all of the hay. Sometimes he would pole his boat across the river with a couple of his cows aboard so they could feast upon the grass on the opposite shore. The cows calmly endured the crossing.

There was no shortage of things to do and explore in the vicinity of Silkeborg. In the Silkeborg Museum Mother and I saw the 2,000-year-old Tollandman, a sacrificial victim who had been strangled and thrown into a peat bog, which had fortuitously preserved his remains for future generations to see. His stomach contained a half-digested ritual meal that he had consumed shortly before his death. According to newspaper accounts at the time of the Tollandman's discovery, which Mother translated for me, one of the investigating police officers, thinking that he was witness to a recent grisly murder, was so horrified upon viewing the blackened remains that he suffered a heart attack.

Himmelbjerget (the Sky Mountain) was another nearby destination for us. Though a mere 500 feet high, it ranks as the tallest summit in Denmark. The most relaxing way to reach it was to board a boat in Silkeborg Harbor and head down the narrow Gudenaa, which soon widens into the Brasso. Our first trip was aboard the 100-year-old Hjelen, a coal-fired, paddle-wheeled steamship. It remains a favorite subject for tourists' cameras. But we realized as soon as we pulled away from the dock that we had made a mistake. The copious white smoke that poured from Hjelen's smokestack tended to blow back onto the passengers, forcing us and many others to change their seats. Henceforth, we would wait to board one of the modern, if less picturesque boats, even if the Hjelen was steaming up and ready to cast off.

The trip to Himmelbjerget proceeded along a series of tree-lined lakes. Here and there, nestled in a clearing would be an elegant summer house. The boat made several stops along the way: Hattenæs, Sejs, Svejbæk. At each stop the first mate would leap off onto the dock with rope in hand and secure the boat to a piling (it's sides worn smooth by many such maneuvers). Once in a while there would be a touch-and-go moment when it appeared as if the boat was not going to stop, and the rope, wound several times around the piling, seemed about to slip out of the first mate's hands, leaving him stranded on the dock. But somehow he always managed to hold on. Perhaps he was just putting on a little show for the tourists. There were not many people getting on or off the boat at these stops—two or three at most. Most of the passengers were headed for Himmelbjerget.

The climb up the mountain was a bit taxing for the uninitiated. It required a sturdy pair of shoes. The path's sandy soil provided little traction; one found oneself tending to slip backward with each step. Mother did surprisingly well on the slope, but I recall a couple of girls wearing flimsy sandals who could barely make any headway. Their feet kept slipping out of the sandals until they figured out that they could make better progress by walking up the slope backwards.

Once you had attained the summit, there was a red-brick tower, rising perhaps thirty feet. From this vantage point, you could gaze down at the heather-covered slopes of Himmelbjerget. Looking off in the distance you could see all the way back to Silkeborg. Following the river to the right you could make out Resenbro, but even on a clear day we were never quite able to pick out Morfar's and Mormor's house. Moving to another window, Mother pointed out to me the city of Aarhus, a major port on the eastern coast of Denmark.

Descending the sandy path was no problem, providing that you took care to hold yourself back lest you start tottering forward and gaining speed on the steep slope. At the bottom of the hill was a restaurant with some picnic tables outside. Mother and I usually ate our sandwiches there so we could enjoy the view. After lunch we would take a stroll along the shore, where I discovered, lying there just for the picking, fossilized sea urchins. They had formed, I learned later, over a hundred million years ago, when the oceans were much higher than they are today, and all of Denmark was underwater. Back in Resenbro, showing my fossils to Morfar, I remarked that there were no such fossils to be found back home in America. Morfar knowingly shook his head.

"It's only because no one has bothered to look for them," he said.

And he was right. Back home in America, I was walking home from school one day when, near the top of the hill, I spotted something by the side of the road, which was in the process of being dug up for the installation of sewerage pipes. Amid all the unearthed pieces of broken shale, I saw what looked like a clamshell, and that is exactly what it was—a clamshell made of white shale. A fossil. The fossil proved that Huyler Road, currently more than three hundred feet above sea level, had once been at the bottom of a shallow ocean. So Morfar had it right. There *were* fossils in America if only you knew where to look for them.

But in Denmark there were fossils to be found in many places. A railroad track ran past the back of my grandparents' property. The tracks rested upon a bed of stones that had been dredged up along the coast. One day, upon seeing the fossil sea urchin I had found on the banks of the Julsø, which flows past Himmelbjerget, my uncle Knud proposed a friendly competition to see who could find the greater number of fossils amid all the stones along the railroad tracks. (He was obviously familiar with the terrain.) As it turned out, we collected no fossils that day, but Knud found a flint spearpoint, which he gave to me.

Knud and his wife Elly had two children, Poul and Rita. During the time I was in Denmark, Poul persisted in calling Beila "*Pip-Hans*". Everyone else used the name I had chosen. Okay. No reason the bird couldn't have two names. Perhaps young Poul resented being upstaged by this interloper from America.

Mother's sister, Anna Lise, and her husband, Verner, also had two children, Erik and Peter. Sometimes, seeing my cousins, I regretted that I did not have a brother or a sister to share my life with. But then I would have had to share the affections of my parents with a sibling. It was a double-edged sword: sibling companionship or sibling rivalry. Take your pick.

Erik and Peter were small enough for me to give them rides in a wheelbarrow, or even upon my shoulders. I made paper airplanes for all of the boys, which they would launch from the veranda in the rear of my grandparents' house. Rita was not interested in paper airplanes, no matter how well they flew; she preferred listening to the *Top Tyve* (Top Twenty) on the radio, and would rush inside when it was time for her favorite program.

Morfar enjoyed smoking a daily cigar. When indulging in this pursuit, he would open the windows and close the glass-paned doors to the dining room so as to not smoke up the rest of the house. Sitting in his armchair, he would puff away while reading a book he had chosen from the nearby bookcase. When the cigar had burned down to a mere stub that was too small to handle, he would stick it into his pipe and smoke the rest of it.

In idle moments, while waiting for dinner or for guests to arrive, Morfar had the habit of twiddling his thumbs, revolving them first in one direction, then the other. It was an activity that I quickly learned to imitate, and I continue to twiddle my thumbs to this day, which relaxes me as I recall Morfar doing the same. His smoking habit, however, held no appeal to me, and I have never smoked.

Not far from Silkeborg, the monastery of Øm Kloster was of particular interest to my grandfather, who enjoyed reading about historical subjects, be they thousands or millions of years in the past. The monastery lay in ruins (sacked over a thousand years ago by plundering bandits), but the graveyard remained intact. The monks' skeletons were on display to the public, protected under glass where they had been unearthed or in a small museum located on the premises. (No doubt a far cry from how the monks had pictured their eternal rest.) A few skulls showed that some of the monks had perished after suffering terrible ax wounds. Others displayed deliberately made crosshatch cuts, known as trephination, that had exposed the surface of the brain—an operation apparently routinely performed in the Middle Ages without the benefit of pain killers or antibiotics to relieve life-threatening pressure on the brain. And many of these operations had been successful, as evidenced by the regrowth of bone over the wound. A small herb garden had been planted to show what the peace-loving monks had cultivated before their monastery was attacked and destroyed.

Hjerl Hede, about twenty miles north of Silkeborg, was another of Morfar's favorite places to visit. A reconstructed settlement depicted how people had lived two thousand years ago. There were ox-drawn carts. Pigs fed from a trough in the courtyard of a thatched-roof farm. Volunteer re-enactors clad in fur skins appropriate to the time period cooked meat on open fires, and caught fish with simple fishing lines. The open-air museum traced human progress over the years. Morfar explained to me that from the first tiny individual huts people moved into straw-roofed communal longhouses, which provided safety in numbers from from roving gangs of bandits. Stone dwellings came later, along with mills powered by water wheels, and finally windmills.

All of this was was very familiar to Morfar, who was always reading accounts of olden times. One day he presented me with a stone ax that the plow had unearthed on one of his fields. (I can't recall if it was his farm in Paarup, or at Herringløs, or one of his other farms. I am certain that he told me, but, unfortunately, I did not write it down.) When I went back home I came across an article in *Natural History Magazine* that explained how such stone axes, dating back over a thousand years, were actually copies of copper axes, fashioned by people who could not afford the far more expensive copper ones. Morfar was pleased on our next visit to Denmark to learn the full story of his stone ax. By now I was able to translate the article for him. He was pleased, too, that I had taken more than just a passing interest in his gift, and that his love for history and the natural world had rubbed off on me.

Anna Lise and Verner took my mother and me on some longer trips, too. We visited Hessel, an old farm located in central-west Jutland that overlooked the Limfjord. Morfar's brother Niels and his wife, Mette, served as caretakers on Hessel. The actual owner of the farm was an aging millionaire who, Niels Buus confided in us, was something of an eccentric—though he did not elaborate on precisely what form this eccentricity took. The old man's family had owned the place for several generations going back to the 1800s. He visited the farm only a couple of times a year, sleeping overnight in his unheated bedroom. Niels gave us a tour of the grounds. The barns, dating back to the 1700s, had thatched straw roofs; their walls were half-timbered with whitewashed stone. There was no electricity or running water on the farm. While a pond in the courtyard provided water for the animals, drinking water for the house had to be carried from a nearby spring. There were only a few cows and pigs remaining in the barns, which had obviously seen better days. Niels told us that tradition had it that the original owner of the site, probably going back in the 1300s, was a pirate who used its commanding view overlooking the Limfjord to look for ships to plunder. He also told us how in the 1700s, the *herremand*, or lord of the manor, would have a wooden sawhorse set up in the courtyard. The *herremand* had complete control over the lives of his workers, who were no better off than slaves. Should anyone fail to do his work, or steal so much as an egg, he would be dragged into the courtyard and sat up upon the dreaded horse. Heavy weights would then be tied to each of the transgressor's ankles, and he would sit there in agony until the lord of the manor decided that he had endured enough punishment.

We next drove about ten miles north to the town of Farstrup. Morfar and his brothers, Niels and Alfred, had been born there at Risgaard. It remained a working farm and, as Anna Lise and my mother could see, had been extensively remodeled since the late 1930s when Severine Buus lived there after the death of her husband, Peter. The name Risgaard was still prominently displayed on a large whitewashed boulder set out by the roadside in front of the farm. As two young children sped into the gravel driveway on their bicycles, Mother wondered if we should simply go up to the door and explain who we were. It would be interesting if we could have a look around. Anna Lise shook her head. The farm had obviously changed greatly since they had last visited their grandmother, a quarter-century ago. There would be nothing left to remind them of those long-ago days, and the alterations that had been made over the years by new owners might even prove to be upsetting, overwhelming cherished old memories. Apart from the half-timbered walls, it wasn't Risgaard any more. So we stayed out by the roadside for a while, snapped a picture or two, and then drove on.

Our next stop, now heading back in a roundabout way toward Silkeborg, was Rebild. Every year on the Fourth of July thousands of Danes gather on the several hills at Rebild to watch the firework displays set off in celebration of the American Independence Day. But there no crowds today, and I raced Erik and Peter up one of the steep hills. It was no contest.

On our next excursion we headed east toward the island of Falster, where Mother, Anna Lise, and Knud had been born and raised. We drove across the island of Funen, stopping briefly in Odense to see the birthplace of Hans Christian Anderson, a tiny cottage in a poor section of town. Driving on across Langeland, we took the ferry to Lolland, then drove on to Falster. We could not go to Falster without visiting Johanne Jorgensen, whom everyone referred to as Bedstefar's Johanne, to distinguish her from another Johanne in the family (Johanne Lise). Johanne Jørgensen had been Ole Peter Petersen Lise's cook. She had taken care of him in his declining years after his wife, Hansigne, died. Johanne told us about the winter of 1941 to 1942, which had been the coldest winter in a century. There had been a record snowfall. The snow was so deep, with windblown drifts, that it took Johanne two days before she could finally crack open the back door and get out to feed the chickens. Bedstefar's Johanne was like one of the family. Mother exchanged Christmas cards with her every year until 1991, the year before she died.

We next headed up to the southern coast of Zealand to see the so-called "Goose Tower", which was all that remained of a castle originally built in the 12th century by Valdemar I ("The Great"), of which only the Goose Tower has survived intact. Its name harkens back to Valdemar IV's defiance of the Hanseatic League's declaration of war in 1368. Placing a golden goose on top of the tower, he declared that the Hanseatic League (a union of German states) was no more threatening than a silly goose. (This Valdemar sounds like a forerunner of Donald Trump.)

We drove on to the island of Møn, famous for its chalk-white cliffs, which were composed of what remained of innumerable shells that had been laid down over countless eons when sea levels were hundreds of feet higher than they are today. The White Cliffs of Dover were formed at the same time.

Mother was the first one to find as we browsed along the beach at Møns Klint, a curious, bullet-shaped segment of stone, amber in color, which was known locally as the *djævel's torden-sten* (the devil's thunder-stone). It was actually part of the fossilized backbone of an ancient cuttlefish, and was the only remnant of the creature to have been preserved. I collected several more of these thunder stones, which I showed to Morfar when we got beck to Resenbro. He explained to me what they were.

Morfar had suggested to us that during our tour we should stop at a certain museum devoted to farming. He told us that there was a picture of his uncle, Jens, who had written the first book in Danish covering all aspects of farming. Beneath his picture was a copy of his book. Morfar was disappointed when we reported back to him that his uncle's picture and his book were no longer on display.

So our trip to Denmark was fast winding down. Mother and I would make one more pilgrimage to Himmelbjerget—this time by car, sparing us most of the arduous climb up the sandy slope. The day before our flight, we would take a final walk with Morfar in the backyard to see how the garden was growing. The plums were just getting ripe. We picked a few and brought a bag of them along with us to the airport, eating them while we waited for our flight. By our next visit, five years in the future, Beila (or *Pip-Hans*) whose joyful chirping had entertained us at breakfast every morning, would be just a memory. I would miss seeing my cousins grow up, following their progress only through Mormor's and Anna Lise's cards and letters. Their faces were already beginning to fade as I gazed down through the clouds at the vast Atlantic Ocean below us. The airports in both New York and Copenhagen had been more crowded on this trip than on the one six years ago. The waiting room was packed with foreign travelers. On the flight home, a woman from India sat in the aisle seat beside us. She wore a sari and had a black dot between her eyes to indicate her married status. She offered Mother and me some pastries that her mother had baked. They were round balls, about an inch and a half in diameter. I bit mine in half, only to discover a coarse black hair connecting the two pieces. Sitting by the window, I was able to discreetly extract the hair from the pastry. It was not bad. A bit doughy, perhaps. Different.

# BUDDING CAPITALISTS

Not long after our return from Denmark, Father brought us to see the New York Stock Exchange, which was only a few blocks from his office. The hectic traders on the floor of the exchange (the pit), shouting orders and flashing signals with their upraised hands, could not fail to stir one's blood, but more inspiring was an old film (slightly scratchy, but in color) shown in a room off the visitors' overlook. It starred Glynis Johns and Ray Bolger. Glynis Johns portrayed an ordinary housewife who goes with some trepidation to the Big Apple to the office of a stockbroker. The broker quickly allays her fears and sets up her account. Before long she is trading stocks and booking steady profits. Ray Bolger, portraying her husband, is astonished to see how easy the process is. Of course, the film was nothing more than a blatant advertisement for the New York Stock Exchange, but it had the intended effect. My mother and I were hooked.

Soon afterward, Mother brought me to a local broker in Somerville. The film had not lied: setting up an account was a simple matter. Using most of my limited savings, I purchased two shares of AT&T. (I had wanted to buy Polaroid, but my parents objected, saying that the stock was too risky.) When the stock certificate arrived in the mail, I promptly framed it and hung it up on a wall in my bedroom—a long-term investment to be sure. Apparently not satisfied with the local broker's cramped office, Mother selected a large brokerage house in New York City. One day She took a train into the city to meet face-to-face with her broker, a woman who hailed from England. She and my mother, both ex-patriots, got along well—at lest initially.

At four o' clock on weekday afternoons, Mother and I would turn on the radio to get the closing stock quotes. AT&T up three quarters. I had made a dollar and a half. On the weekend I would scour the business section of the *New York Herald Tribune* in search of promising stocks, which I would chart on graph paper. After a year or two of watching strong gains in the other stocks I was following, my shares of AT&T began to look a bit tame to me. My mother was regularly trading stocks with her broker and making profits, just like Glynis Johns in the film. I took my AT&T certificate off the wall and brought it in to my broker, exchanging the shares, on which I had a tidy profit, for shares in Control Data and Hoffman Electronics. My new stocks soon soared.

Things were not going quite so well, however, for my mother. The first hint that her broker was not up on the daily financial news came in 1966 with the unexpected death of Walt Disney. Speaking with my mother on the telephone over a completely different matter, the broker wondered why Disney's stock had taken such a large tumble this morning. Mother had already heard the news on the radio and informed her broker of Walt Disney's death—something a competent Wall Street trader should have known about. And things would only get worse. Mother's broker began selling stocks for a quick profit, giving notice only after the fact. It soon became obvious that she was churning my mother's account. The brokerage commission in those days amounted to about seventy dollars for a hundred shares. If you eked out two or three hundred dollars on a quick trade, the broker would net a hundred forty dollars for the round trip. Quite an incentive. The broker explained that this was no longer a buy-and-hold market. You had to take a quick profit or lose it. Mother didn't accept this self-serving explanation. She had a falling-out with her broker. She asked the broker to send her certificates for the remainder of her shares so she would have control over them.

I continued to chart the rising share prices of my two stocks. Both of them rose over the top of the graph paper and I had to start my charts over with a higher price scale. Not long after I did this, however, the share prices took a hit. It was just a temporary dip, I told myself, for analysts' reports remained bullish. The sky was the limit. Unfortunately, within a month the share prices of my stocks had fallen back to what I had paid for them. They went down much faster than they had gone up. My fat profits turned into small losses. I realized now that my mother's broker had been at least partially right: this was not a buy-and-hold market, and it was wise to take your profits when you had them.

Mother, realizing the futility of being invested in stocks in a flat or declining market, would make no more trades for the next twenty years. Still believing that I could outwit the market, I persevered through several more losing trades. It was a painful lesson: investing in the stock market was a gamble; it was no better than going to an Atlantic City casino. At least when you took the bus to the casino you'd get a roll of quarters to feed the slot machines and a ticket for a free lunch.

# JE VAIS À LA BIBLIOTÈQUE

Before I get back to the main subject of this memoir, I need to get something off my chest. After experiencing a somewhat mediocre education in the rural schools in Branchburg, I had hoped that high school would be different. Somerville High School, however, did not meet with my expectations. In French class, we were divided into two groups. One group was a traditional class: intensive drills in grammar and vocabulary. The second group, into which I fell, was an experiment called the *Audio Lingual Method*. We did not plunge, as the traditional group did, directly into the study of French grammar. We were not even allowed to see anything written in French for the first six weeks of class. We repeated after the teacher simple phrases in French. We memorized a hypothetical conversation involving two people, and took turns, two by two, standing in the front of the room parroting perhaps the most insipid dialogue ever written. ("Where are you going?" "I'm going to the library." "Oh, you're going to the library. I'm going, too.")

*ALM* was based on the faulty notion that the best way to learn a language was in the same way that a young child would learn it, absorbing the intricacies of grammar and vocabulary simply by hearing the spoken word. Even when we were finally allowed to see the written word, we received no textbooks, only mimeographed handouts reflecting the *Audio Lingual Method*. It was an easy course, with little or no homework (at least initially), so no one complained. Those of us in the *ALM* group did not fully realize how we had been shortchanged until our final exam. The *ALM* students and the traditional students were assembled in the same room. The exam booklets were distributed. The traditional students received thick booklets, reflecting how much they had learned during the course of the year. We *ALM* students, by contrast, received thin booklets, reflecting how little we had learned. The utter failure of the *Audio Lingual Method* could have not have been clearer. My high school was administered by morons.

The following year all of the *ALM* students were placed in the traditional French class. We were told that no one was available to teach the *Audio Lingual Method*. (Oh, really?) We were also told after it became obvious that we were lagging behind our classmates who had been taught using the traditional method that we would soon catch up with them. (Really?) As it turned out, I was the only member of the *ALM* group to complete four years of French, all the others having dropped out along the way. It was difficult for me to explain to my parents how I went from getting an "A" in my first year of French, to scraping by with a "C" the following year. (And the teacher chose to give the *ALM* students "Cs" instead of the "Ds" we deserved. She knew that were handicapped by our wasted freshman year.) Did my parents accept my explanation? Certainly my mother did. She knew that I had an affinity for languages, seeing how quickly I had learned to speak Danish. And I should have been well along in French after two years with a private tutor. What had gone wrong? After I explained the *Audio Lingual Method* to my mother, she expressed her incredulousness how anyone could have thought that such a system was practical. In her classes in English and German, they had quickly gotten into the conjugation of verbs—past, present, and future tenses. She asked me if I was sure that we hadn't seen any written texts for the first six weeks of class. I assured her that we had not. So thanks a lot to the "educators" who dreamed up the *Audio Lingual Method*, which was no doubt subsidized by a generous government grant. In fact, as I was later to discover, *ALM* was a cheap and inferior rip-off of the *Berlitz Self-Teacher*, which also emphasized speaking drills and omitted any formal presentation of verb tenses and other aspects of grammar that could be quickly gleaned from a concise table. After thirty years, my mother could still flawlessly recite the conjugation of German verbs that she had learned in school. By contrast, I struggled with my French conjugations, which I had never been required to commit to memory. I thought back on how easily I had picked up Danish. Total immersion in a foreign language was a far cry from doing silly, repetitive drills. And so I sat there in my second year of French, bored out of my skull and unable to keep up with the students who had studied under the traditional, "old fashioned" method.

I'm not saying that I wanted high school to be over as quickly as possible. A friend of mine once told me that he wished that his high-school years would pass overnight so he could immediately begin his real life—whatever that was. But those four years would pass quickly enough on their own.

Nearly every year as the fall season began, Mother would quote a Haiku that I had written in high school: "One leaf falls, then another, soon the trees are bare."

# ACROSS THE MILES

I often wondered how my mother could bear not seeing her family back in Denmark for such long intervals. Scarcely a week passed without me seeing my American grandparents. The frequent letters (mostly aerogrammes written on thin blue paper) that Mormor sent provided only a tenuous link. She reported that Anne Lise and Verner had gone on vacation in the north of Jutland; they were contemplating building a gas station in Tranum. In other news, Mother's aunt Agnes' husband, Emile, (whom we had last seen only a few short months ago climbing a ladder to stop a leak in the roof of his house) had died of cancer. For Christmas, Mother would invariably choose cards from Hallmark's *Across the Miles* series. It would take her some time in the store to pick out the twenty or so cards she wanted to send to her relatives in Denmark, as she wanted to avoid too many duplicates. So, after exhausting the Hallmark series, she would turn to other brands, selecting those with the least mushy sayings, or blank cards, with no sayings at all.

The years 1960 and 1961 came and went. The dreary, repetitive sameness of my high-school days made them pass quickly. At least most of the teachers here were more professional than those I had encountered in Stony Brook Middle School. But whenever I happened to meet a former classmate from those days, we would fondly reminisce about our old school, particularly Mr. Federici and his legendary temper tantrums. What a character. He was one of a kind. I almost missed him. There were no interesting characters like that in Somerville High School, nothing to relieve the monotony of each day. Mother would wake me at a quarter to seven each morning. After a quick breakfast of cereal or oatmeal, I would march over half a mile down Huyler Road, lining up in invariably the same order among five or six other students to catch the yellow school bus into Somerville. The ride took ten minutes. Every morning as the bus waited with its doors closed in front of the school, the principal would be standing outside on the steps of the three-story, red-brick building, repeatedly consulting his watch (which was actually quite unnecessary, for the nine o'clock school bell would inform us when it was time to begin the school day.) Ticktock, ticktock. As the principal finally raised his hand, the school bus would disgorge it passengers, and I would make my way to my homeroom class. After roll call and the pledge of allegiance, I would move through the usual series of forty-five minute classes, each one introduced and terminated by a bell, followed by gym and lunch and another class or two. After the final bell, I would hurry to catch the bus for the ride home. If I failed to catch it, I would have to call up my mother for a lift. Dutiful son, I missed the bus only once. After a twenty-minute trip back to Huyler Road I would march half a mile up the hill. (Unless Mother was waiting for me, as she often did.) I once calculated that if all of my walks up and down Huyler Road could be laid end-to-end I would have reached California. All things considered, my daily routine was not unlike the description Mother's maternal grandfather had imparted to her of his all-too-swiftly passing years: get up early and after a quick breakfast milk the cows, feed the animals, do your chores. The only difference between our respective lives was that I had to contend with teachers and my fellow students, while my great grandfather only had to deal with animals and crops. Take your pick. Either way, a significant portion of your life is over faster than you can imagine.

Meanwhile, our lives on Huyler Road were nothing short of idyllic. My father and I had laid out a badminton court on the cleared ground situated over the septic-tank field. There was as yet no municipal sewerage, so you had to provide your own system for the disposal of bathroom waste. (I remember my father, during our final days in our apartment in Jersey City, tearing up a cement bag and flushing it down piece by piece in the toilet, saying that we would never be able to do such a thing in our new house, lest we clog up our septic tank.) Muff, although she had her own cozy little bed on the floor next to mine, still preferred to climb up into my bed and snuggle up under the covers with me.

In addition to badminton, we enjoyed using a bow and arrow in our backyard. The property, over two hundred feet deep, was big enough so an errant arrow would not end up on a neighbor's property; likewise, the shots we fired at the target with an air pistol. I became quite proficient at horseshoes. And in the winter we could amuse ourselves on a twenty-five-foot diameter skating rink. These were happy times.

On hot summer days we would sit outside in the breezeway my father had constructed. The breezeway was a popular feature of single-story houses in the fifties. After building a one-car garage, Father constructed a roof connecting the house to the garage. A concrete slab in the breezeway provided a pleasant place to sit during the summer heat. Cooling northern breezes would waft gently through the structure, almost as good as air-conditioning, which still lay for affordable personal use some years in the future. On a really sweltering day we'd retreat to the cool basement for relief. At night a wet towel placed over my chest helped me get to sleep.

During these halcyon days, Anne Lise and Verner came to visit us. We made a weekend trip to the Delaware Water Gap (where I remember a flurry of rats scurrying down a hillside strewn with garbage, apparently dumped by people who were saving on the expense of a regular trash collection); we climbed the slippery wooden walkways at Bushkill Falls; we toured Washington's Headquarters in New Hope; we roamed the trails at Bowman's Hill Wildflower Preserve; we basked in the sun at the Jersey Shore. But since I was in school at the time, I missed all of the weekday excursions: an afternoon spent sampling various brews at the New Hope Winery; Valley Forge, where General Washington and his troops camped out during a brutal winter in their fight against the Hessians; a couple of trips to New York City, with visits to the Metropolitan Museum of Art and the Playboy Club. They may have taken in a Broadway play. Damn. Another gap in my education. What did I learn in school during those two weeks? Not a clue.

By now I had two American cousins to keep track of. My father's sister, Velma, had gotten married in 1957, and had two boys, Joey and Peter, in quick succession. I remember my grandparents coming to Huyler Road one day, both of them practically in tears. They had just learned that Velma and her husband, Joe, would be moving to Pittsfield, Massachusetts, about 150 miles away as the crow flies—which was no distance at all compared to the nearly 6,000-mile move my mother had made away from her parents. Velma would visit her parents at least two or three times a year, bringing the boys along with her. I am still amazed how my mother managed to cope, seeing her parents only at five-year intervals. In some ways, Mother remained an enigma to me. I confess that I never fully understood how, after a brief acquaintance with a GI she met at a dance, she could simply pack her things into a wicker basket and sail off to America to start a life that would be radically different from the one she was used to. But somehow this implausible relationship worked out.

Mother continued with her painting. After a trip to Sturbridge Village, Massachusetts (during which we made a side trip to visit Velma and Joe), she painted from a photograph the white, steepled church in the town square, complete with a horse and carriage parked out in front. She then went on to paint from memory a church back in Denmark, including recognizable figures of herself, her mother and father, and Anna Lise approaching the stone wall that surrounded the churchyard. Mother told me on more than one occasion the name of the church, but I have forgotten it. At the 1964 New York World's Fair Mother admired the paintings of Winston Churchill, some of which were on display at an exhibition celebrating his life. (Churchill's immortal lines from World War II echoed through the halls of the exhibition hall, "We shall fight them on the beaches. We shall fight them on the landing grounds. We shall fight them in the hedgerows. Never, never surrender.") Finding himself with much time on his hands after leaving the British Admiralty in 1915, Churchill had taken up painting. His somewhat impressionistic style was not unlike my mother's, but I think that Mother was the better painter. Churchill's paintings included landscapes and many well-known buildings, but never people. While Mother never did any portraits, the human figures she included in a couple of her paintings were convincingly life-like; so too were her horses, their slender legs capturing the beauty of the animal. I speak from experience. I, too, tried my hand at painting, but confined my efforts to landscapes. My renditions of trees and clouds and farm buildings in the distance were quite good. But I never mastered the human form. I could not have painted a horse and carriage. Mother once suggested to me that I do a painting of Muff. I never did, favoring the camera as my artistic medium.

Incidentally, on our visit to Velma and Joe in Pittsfield, Massachusetts, I discovered that I had something in common with Uncle Joe. We were both avid stock-market investors. Joe was impressed with my purchase of shares in Control Data, which had not yet tanked in the general market correction. Joe, who would shortly buy a house trailer and travel out West visiting abandoned towns and remote Indian villages, owned shares of Winnebago (which would also plummet).

# CALL ME ISHMAEL

In 1960 my grandparents moved from their apartment in Jersey City to a single-family home in Avenel, New Jersey. The move greatly pleased Mildred, who could now gaze out over her own backyard instead of staring at the next apartment block as she labored at the kitchen sink. Soon after the move, my grandfather purchased an outboard motor that could be attached to the stern of a rowboat. He would take us Mildred's Boat Rentals in the town of Morgan, just off Raritan Bay, where we could rent a boat for the day. I think he chose this particular establishment because of the name "Mildred." How could his wife resist going out in a boat from a place called Mildred's? In the calm inland waterway of nearby Cheesequake Creek, Grandpa taught me how to row a boat, how to feather the oars so as to avoid making an ineffective splash. Venturing out into the deep waters of Raritan Bay, he showed me how to navigate, using a distant landmark off the stern of the boat, so that when rowing you did not have to be constantly looking over your shoulder to see if you were still on course.

Mother accompanied us only on only a couple of these excursions. She didn't mind when we were paddling around in the calm waters of Cheesequake Creek, but when we ventured out into he the choppy waters of the open bay, it was another story. Grandpa's wife, Mildred, did not like the rolling ocean waves of Raritan Bay any more than my mother did, but she went along simply to please her husband, who could be quite insistent.

While Father and I were out in the boat with Grandpa, Mother would work at home on her needlepoint, fashioning attractive floral-themed covers for pillows, or making her own clothes using paper patterns. In a corner of her bedroom she kept a clothes dummy upon which she would stitch together her creations. She also made a nice little winter coat for Muff.

Motoring across Raritan Bay to Staten Island, we would pull the boat onshore, anchoring it just out of reach of the waves. With sandpipers skittering ahead of us, we would spend an hour or two exploring the beach, looking for interesting shells along the way, pausing by the occasional tidal pool to see what the crabs were finding to eat. (Which reminded us to go back to the boat and have our sandwiches.) Now and then we would come across an overturned horseshoe crab, struggling feebly in the sand and attempting with repeated pokes of its long tail to right itself. (Totally useless as a weapon, the fierce-looking tail was of little use in restoring the crab to an upright position.) Lifting the animal carefully by the rim of its carapace, we would place it back into the water, where it would be safe from the marauding seagulls which could eviscerate a helpless crab in a matter of minutes.

When Father and I got back home I would show Mother the little treasures I had picked up at the Jersey Shore. I never did find any fossils, but I would often bring back a live specimen: a clutch of horseshoe-crab eggs, which I would hatch out in my salt-water aquarium, or a hermit crab, for which I would have to return to the shore to find a larger moon shell for it to inhabit as it grew. Fortunately, there was no need to keep running back to the shore for food; the hermit crab was content with strips of Danish ham.

Mildred was relieved to be able to stay home when we men set off on a longer voyage, sailing across Raritan Bay and motoring through the Arthur Kill Van Kull waterway to climb aboard the wreck of an old wooden cargo ship under the Outerbridge Crossing. Sunken up to its gunwales, the ship was now host to clumps of beach grass and other weeds that were invading the slowly decomposing deck. We took care not to disturb the occasional bird's nest.

Grandpa did not care much for fishing. He complained that when he took his brother, Walter, and his brother-in-law, George, out in a boat, all they wanted to do was sit in one spot and wait for a fish to bite, agreeing to move on only after they had not received a nibble for an hour or so. Grandpa hated sitting in one spot. He had no patience, preferring to motor about from one place to another. He seemed to have a preference for deep water, as opposed to the placid channels of the inland water way. Out on the often choppy open waters of Raritan Bay I could easily imagine myself in a longboat on the high seas, in pursuit of the great white whale.

At the time, I did not fully appreciate the danger we were in as we motored across the bay, where the swell from a passing oil tanker could have easily have swamped our fifteen-foot-long rowboat. I wore a life vest, but all the others had was a cushion stuffed with kapok fibers, which the man renting the boats assured us would keep everyone afloat. Grandfather had the sense not to venture out into the bay unless the waters were calm. On a windy day we would confine our sailing to Cheesequake Creek. Out on the bay, Grandpa would expertly steer us away from the wake of passing tankers. He had learned his boating skills from his father, Peter Peterson, who, after serving in the U.S navy during the Civil War (off the coast of Japan of all places), became a fisherman. Owning his own boat, he set out lobster traps along the shores of the Arthur Kill Van Kull between New Jersey and Staten Island, and earned a decent living. Unfortunately, he took to drink. His favorite haunt was a bar in Jersey City. His fishing boat, beached on the shore in Bayonne, fell into disrepair. But he was a tough old bird, using a cane in his old age to steer people out of his way as he proceeded down the sidewalk.

My grandfather's knowledge of the sea served us well. On a day that had started out with brilliant sunshine, the skies darkened as a sudden squall began to blow in from the west. We were a mile or two out on the open waters of Raritan Bay. The wind was picking up. We were racing the approaching storm. There was a flash of lightening and a rumble of thunder in the distance. Being out on the sea in a open boat was not a good place to be during a thunderstorm. Realizing that we were not making enough headway with the outboard motor, Grandpa erected a makeshift sail using a large square of plastic. (Why he had brought along this piece of plastic, I do not know. But there it was.) While Father steered the boat, Grandpa oriented his sail to catch the wind. We were moving faster than we ever had before in the little rowboat, even with the motor on full throttle. Soon we were back in the still waters of Cheesequake Creek, hastily docking the boat at Mildred's Boat Rentals and unfastening the motor. We had only driven a mile or two in the car when a torrential downpour began. Unfortunately, this episode would turn out to be the last of my seafaring days.

# ON THE BANKS OF THE OLD RARITAN

When I was in my senior year in high school my father asked me once what I wanted to do with my life. I informed him that I wanted to be a beachcomber. Not at all surprised by my flippant response, he told me that I could do whatever I wanted to do so long as I went to college and earned my sheepskin. Which I did. Thanks, Dad.

I did not realize it at the time, but looking back I can see that our move from Huyler Road to New Brunswick was equivalent to the Biblical expulsion from Eden. Father didn't want me to have to commute every day to Rutgers, where I had just been accepted. I protested, saying that a secondhand car would serve me just fine. But Father would not hear of it. He knew from his daily, hour-long commute by train to New York City how tiring such a trip could be. We would move to New Brunswick and that was that. Actually, my father expressed another, more practical reason for the move. A jetport had been proposed for the area around Huyler Road. While nothing had definitely been settled, the mimeographed maps circulated to the alarmed residents showed the houses that would likely be condemned. While Huyler Road and our house would have been spared, we would be sitting smack between two runways. Of course, a fair price would be offered for all of the affected homes, but what was a fair price for a house in the middle of a busy airport? Talk about being stuck between a rock and a hard place. New Brunswick, it was.

After our somewhat precipitous move from Huyler Road, we settled temporarily in an apartment in Piscataway. A good portion of our furniture had to be put in storage; a few pieces we had simply left behind (which would become a common practice in our subsequent moves). It became Mother's responsibility to take Muff for a walk a couple of times a day. She brought a paper towel along with her so she could drop Muff's waste into a convenient storm drain. And with Father and myself off to work or school, it was Mother who conducted the search for a permanent residence in New Brunswick. About six months into her quest she discovered a home for sale on Winthrop Road at a knock-down price. It seemed that the previous owner, a model, had painted the stuccoed bathroom walls black so that any stray reflections would not interfere with the lightning as she applied her makeup. The stark black walls of the bathroom turned off most prospective buyers. And there was an additional sticking point. The owners had it stipulated in their contract that after the sale of the house they would have the right to come back and dig up a large holly tree in the backyard (obviously of considerable sentimental value.) Fine. We can paint the bathroom walls a nice shade of beige. You're welcome to your holly tree. So the deal was finalized. As it turned out, the former owners never returned for their holly tree. They were divorced soon after the sale of the house. We also learned that the plans for the jetport back on Huyler Road had been canceled. So we could have stayed there after all, my acceptance at Rutgers notwithstanding. Father was not at all dismayed by this turn of events. He had followed what he considered the most prudent course of action. But looking back, I suspect that my father had known from the outset that there was only a remote chance that the jetport would ever be built; for how would we have been able to have received a decent price for our house if it was likely to have wound up sitting between two busy runways? I now believe that Father used (and exaggerated) this threat to soften the sting of our move. This way it could be argued that having to relocate wasn't just for my benefit. At the time, I was inclined to accept such a line of reasoning, but it is clear to me now that Father had the wanderlust in his blood, and after living in one place for ten years it was time for him to move on.

It was a short commute. After dropping Father off at the train station in New Brunswick, Mother would see me off at Rutgers. I was a biology major—biocide as my fellow students called it. And for good reason. I did well in biology (I could easily work out the first and second filial generations of a dihybrid cross), but had trouble with chemistry (moles, Avogadro's number) and calculus (the chain rule). I never did figure out what possible application calculus might have in the biological sciences. Statistics, I could see. But calculus? I would eventually change my major to psychology. No calculus or chemistry needed there. A considerable distraction during my first year of studies was my grandmother's diagnosis of pancreatic cancer.

# WINGS

Even before our move to New Brunswick it had become apparent the something was seriously wrong with Grandma. It was in the winter of 1964 to 1965, on one of her last visits to Huyler Road before we moved. An overnight snow storm had carpeted the ground. Preparing to head out the the car, Grandma fainted while struggling to put her boots on. Quickly reviving, she attributed her fainting spell to the blood rushing to her head as she bent over. But my mother and father sensed that the problem was more serious than Grandma was letting on.

Six months later, after our move to New Brunswick, Grandma confided in my mother that she was reluctant to lie down during the day lest "Daddy" catch her and make a big fuss. She would do anything to placate her man. That Halloween was an ordeal for her. She told my mother how hoards of ten-to-fifteen masked kids shouting "trick or treat" would pound on the storm door and mark the glass with crayons when she was slow to respond. Incredulous, my mother asked her if she had handed out all the candy on her own. Grandma shrugged. "Daddy" had sat in the living room as he usually did, watching the evening news. Passing out Halloween candy was her job. As weak as she was, she would not dream of asking her husband for help. Her physical condition was soon declining so rapidly that she could no longer conceal it. There was a lump in her abdomen, which she had mentioned to no one. She was admitted to the hospital for tests in November. Her doctor pronounced a diagnosis of pancreatic cancer, a terminal condition. She had at most another six months to live. As was the custom in those days, Grandma was not informed of the diagnosis. It was up to the relatives to absorb the gravity of the situation and pretend for the sake of the patient that all would soon be well.

Grandma's condition continued to worsen. Her doctor administered a series of painful injections to Mildred's abdomen. These were experimental treatments. They had no effect other than to increase Grandma's suffering. But she did not complain.

"If I could only get my strength back and get back home," she said, "I'd be the happiest woman in the world."

And she did get her wish, at least for a couple of weeks. Back home she was confined to her bed. Mother drove in every day to attend to her. Grandpa was useless. "What am I going to do when she's gone?" he wailed.

Grandma was soon taken by ambulance back to the hospital. She was rapidly losing weight. Always skinny, she now appeared skeletal. When she was still able to get out of her hospital bed, her protruding shoulder blades were impossible to miss.

"I'm getting my wings," she said, trying as best as she could to put us at ease.

Mother visited her every day in the hospital, bringing her a cup of her favorite strawberry banana yogurt, as the hospital only served plain vanilla yogurt. After work, my father would drive us all to the hospital, and we would stay until closing time. Only rarely during these visits did we see my grandfather. Most days, he was too broken up to go to the hospital, too devastated to put on a happy face. Exactly what he did during these trying times, we never knew. Shortly before Mildred's death, he began disposing of her clothes and things. A strange way of coping.

We received a call from the hospital late one afternoon in February 1966 informing us that Mildred had died. We gathered around Grandma's body, paid our respects, then drifted out into the hall. It was there that my father exploded. He always had a temper. But I had never seen him so enraged. He told his father off in no uncertain terms. I don't recall his exact words. But the gist of what he said was that his father had let his wife of forty-five years down. While Mildred lay dying in the hospital, he had thought only of himself. He hadn't been there for her in the end. It was an ugly scene.

The upshot of this confrontation was that Robert W. Peterson changed his will, disinheriting his son, Robert F. Peterson. It seems that while sitting on a boardwalk bench in Perth Amboy and feeling sorry for himself, Grandpa had met a sympathetic widow who had recently lost her husband. Within a matter of days or weeks (we never learned the full story) they were married.

It was only a few months after the marriage that Grandpa turned up at our new house on Winthrop Road sounding contrite. He didn't need to spell out the details, but obviously this hastily arranged marriage was having some difficulties. His wife, Maxine, remained in the car. My father could have invited her in, but chose not to. It was an uncomfortable situation. Grandpa struggled to express himself. He was not making much sense. He left after fifteen minutes. We never saw Maxine except for a glimpse of her siting in the car. It would be the last time we saw Grandpa alive.

He died of a heat attack in June 1967, less than fifteen months after Mildred's death. Maxine was not at home when he died. (God knows where she was.) The only witness to his death had been his dog, Tiny, a Chihuahua. A neighbor, seeing a pile of mail overflowing the mailbox, had called the police, who found Grandpa lying naked on the bedroom floor. In the funeral parlor, we could see some blue paint on Grandpa's fingernails that the undertaker had failed to brush off. Apparently he had spent the last day of his life painting the bathroom walls in an effort to please his new wife. We did not see Maxine at the funeral home, though her daughter soon turned up to claim possession of the house in Avenel for her mother. My father took Tiny to a veterinarian to be euthanized.

But this was not to be the last of people who were near and dear to me losing their lives. Not long after my grandfather's death, I learned that Jim, who had been a friend of mine from the fifth grade, had died within two years after his father's own tragic death. His father owned a farm in Somerset County. Ironically, he had toured the local schools teaching a safety course, only to be involved in a horrible tractor accident. It turned out that his tractor had toppled over on one of the steep hills of his farm. Pinned under the tractor, his lungs crushed under the considerable weight, he had no doubt died a slow and painful death. There were no cell phones in those days, and no one went to look for him until he failed to turn up for supper. (A farm can be a dangerous place, no matter how careful you might be.) My friend subsequently perished in a grain silo. As he stood at the bottom of the silo, a deluge of corn poured down on him, burying him so quickly that he had no time to flee. It must have been an excruciatingly slow death. I imagine that he thought of his father in the last few moments of his life.

# DENMARK 1966

So much for the deaths and complications back in the States. I still had an intact and prospering family in Denmark. Looking back, I can see that it was something of a schizophrenic existence, as if I were living two parallel lives. Except for a monthly letter or card, my two lives only marginally intersected. When in Denmark, I rarely thought of my life back in the States, recollections of which were only stirred up when we received a postcard from Father. Conversely, Denmark faded into the back of my mind when I was getting on with my life in America. Perhaps it was the same for Mother, her former life in Denmark reinserting itself into her consciousness only through letters from her mother, sister, and brother.

We left from Kennedy Airport in the first week of July. By now we had an established routine. Arriving well ahead of time, we would sit in our car and enjoy the sandwiches and fruit juice we had brought from home. We always parked in the same area, not far from the curving, elevated walkway that led to the International Arrivals building. I can still hear in my mind the sound of a rope, driven by the wind, beating rhythmically against a nearby metal flagpole. On some trips we would see the Air France Concorde take off on its steep ascent (intended to spare the surrounding residential neighborhoods from the loud roar of its engines). We had learned to pack light: one large suitcase and one medium-sized suitcase containing our clothes, two carry-on bags with the rest. I may have been mistaken, but I got the impression that, far from being sad to see us off, Father actually enjoyed being on his own for a month.

On this trip Mother and I spent a couple of days in Copenhagen before catching a flight to Aalborg Airport in Jutland. At Tivoli's Veriétéen we attended a performance of José Greco and his troop of Spanish flamenco dancers. The hall was not very large, so wherever you sat you were not far from the stage. The clatter of the dancers' shoes upon the wooden stage in this intimate setting was sometimes jarring. (No one could doze off during this swirling, foot-stomping performance.) I fell for a dark-haired young beauty in a tight yellow dress with blue polka dots. She could not have been more than ten feet away, and, having picked my face out in the crowd, looked directly at me as she gyrated and clapped her hands over her head.

Later that day we took a walk to Langelenie. Mother pointed out to me across Copenhagen Harbor where she used to work at the Burmeister and Wain Shipyard. The company ferry that she used to take to work was not far from the statue of the Little Mermaid. Leaving the harbor, we stopped at the Gelfion Fountain, which portrays a woman driving four stout oxen through the jets of water that stream onto their faces. Mother told me the story of the goddess Gelfion, a mythical queen of Denmark, who, after years of war ending in stalemate, had been granted by the king of Sweden the right to claim all the Swedish land that she could plow in a single day. It seemed an impossible task, but Gelfion was not without resources. Much to the consternation of the king of Sweden, she transformed her four sons into oxen, and with their help carved out a huge tract of Swedish soil, which she then flung into the Kattegat. This became the island of Zealand; it's about the same size and shape as Vänern, a large lake in Sweden, lending a measure of credence to the legend. The Swedes, though they tried repeatedly over the years, never reclaimed their lost land.

Reminders of World War II were still in evidence well into the sixties. Across from the Gelfion Fountain stood a defused German underwater mine that had been fished out of the entrance to Copenhagen Harbor after the war. Originally anchored just below the surface of the water, it was spherical, about four feet tall, and bristling with numerous studs that would explode the mine if a passing ship had the misfortune to come into contact with them. It was a double-edged sword, for German ships entering the harbor had to consult their charts for the location of these powerful mines.

Mother pointed out to me the spot not far from the fountain where King Christian X, on his daily ride through the streets of Copenhagen, had fallen from his horse and was gravely injured. His horse had bolted earlier near Amalienborg Palace, but the king had managed to rein it back. Proceeding along Langelenie, the horse had bolted again as it gathered speed while descending the slope from the Gelfion Fountain. The king attempted to control his horse, but it reared back and threw him off, causing him to strike his head on a curb. Christian X was seriously injured and had to be hospitalized. He spent a long period of recuperation at his summer palace, Sorgenfri, and never rode his horse again.

We still had another full day to take in the sights of Copenhagen. There were many venues to see that were within easy walking distance from our hotel: the Copenhagen Zoo, Rosenborg Castle, and the National Museum. Mother, however, chose to take me to a movie. The movie theatre was housed on the ground floor of Dagmarhus, the upper floors of which had served during the war as the headquarters for the SS. It was an ugly, utilitarian building that took up an entire block. Mother explained to me how, hidden in the basement of Dagmarhus, a small illegal printing press had produced pamphlets that reported on the truth about the war and the German occupation. These were the pamphlets, incidentally, that Mother chose not to save.

The movie we went to see was a light-hearted Danish comedy called *Tre Smaa Piger (Three Little Girls)*. Set at the end of the nineteenth century, it followed the developing friendship between three girls in their early twenties and three sword-carrying soldiers on leave in Copenhagen. Was it merely a coincidence, or did my mother, who had similarly dated an American soldier on leave in Copenhagen, have an affinity with the plot of the movie?

Things in Denmark had changed, to be sure, though not drastically as they had changed back home. Beila was now only a memory. Poul was nearly as tall as I was. Anna Lise and Verner no longer lived in Silkeborg. They had moved north to Tranum, where Verner operated his own gas station (Esso) and an automobile repair shop.

Mormor and Morfar were still living in Resenbro. As we sat side by side in the living room reading sections of the daily *Midtjyllands Avis*, Morfar would often turn to me and ask me a question.

*"Hvornaar var den sidst Dansk halshugning?"* was typical of his queries. ("When was the last Danish beheading?")

Of course I had no idea, but I now understood enough Danish to know what he was asking.

Mother intervened, saying that I could not possibly be expected to know such an obscure fact. Of course, if I had more thoroughly perused the section of the paper that Morfar was now reading, I would have known the answer. Morfar always liked to test me.

Anna Lise drove my mother and me to her new home in Tranum. As we crossed the Limfjord we saw rows upon rows of rusting iron crosspieces, now sitting on the shore, that the Germans had set out in the shallow waters to stop Allied boats from landing in the counter invasion that never came. They've all since been disposed of for their value as scrap metal.

The Esso station was only one of two places to buy gas in Tranum. Verner would sit before the large picture window in the living room in his stockinged feet as he waited for customers. When a car pulled up to the pumps, he would slip on a pair of wooden shoes and hasten outside. I can still hear the clatter his clogs made as he ambled across the courtyard.

Tranum, despite being what might be considered a sleepy, backwater town, had played a not inconsiderable role in the German defenses during the war. It was only a short drive from town to Jammer Bugt (Misery Bay), which the Germans believed would be a prime landing site in the event of an Allied invasion. Accordingly, they constructed a chain of defensive bunkers along the coastline. The bunkers, with massive walls of reinforced concrete, were equipped with powerful guns pointing out to sea. German soldiers would peer through slits in the thick concrete walls. The invasion of the coast of northern Jutland never materialized, but the bunkers are still there, set into the same sand dunes that would have camouflaged them from the Allies. To this day you can step into one of the bunkers and experience the same view that a German soldier would have had as he scanned the waters of Jammer Bugt for Allied ships. After a small child drowned in a bunker that had filled with rainwater, several of the bunkers were permanently sealed for safety reasons.

A German-built observation tower on Udsigten, the highest hill in Tranum, also exists, now as a popular tourist attraction. Although dense stands of spruce trees have since grown up around the tower, even to rise above it, in the 1940s it would have had a commanding, unobstructed view of the bay. One can easily imagine several German soldiers stationed atop the wooden tower, peering through their binoculars over Jammer Bugt. Lucky stiffs. They might as well have been on vacation, considering how badly the war was going for Germany by 1943.

The narrow path leading up to the tower on Udsigten was steep, with sawn-off logs placed perpendicularly to hold back the sandy slope. Though Mother was never much of a walker, every time we visited Udsigten she would make this rather arduous climb to the summit. Visiting the former German lookout was like going back in time, if not a very pleasant time.

Other signs of the German occupation in Tranum continue to exist to this day. German soldiers needed to be able to move quickly through the extensive evergreen forests in order to rush men to wherever they might be needed along the coast. Accordingly, they felled trees along what would ultimately be a network of makeshift roads. With no time to construct a proper roadbed, they put down twin tracks of pre-cast concrete slabs. Each slab was about four feet long, set precisely where the tires of a jeep would go. Necessity, as they say, is the mother of invention. But their makeshift roads did the Germans no good. The concrete slabs are still there, now mostly overgrown with heather. You have to look around to locate them, for you'll find no guidebook telling you where they are.

Our second trip to Niels Buus' farm, Hessel, was something of a downer. On our previous visit the thatched straw roofs had been intact. But over the intervening years they had seriously deteriorated. Whole sections of the roofs had rotted away. The barns now lay mostly open to the weather. You could see the blue sky through the network of roof timbers. Here and there, portions of the old stone walls were tumbling down. It could scarcely be called a working farm any more. The cows and pigs were long gone. All Niels had to tend now were a number of long-eared hares that he kept in raised hutches to keep them safe from foxes.

We had an important dinner guest on the evening of our stay. It was Elle Jensen, the millionaire owner of Hessel. Uncle Niels alerted Mother and me that our guest was more than a little old-fashioned and set in his ways. He was eccentric. Accompanied by his nurse (his wife had died some years previously), hr. Jensen was a frail, gaunt man who looked as if he had just stepped out of a time warp from the previous century. His suit was buttoned up to his high collar. In his front pocket he kept a large watch that hung from a gold chain attached to a button on his coat. (I'll bet it was a watch that he had to wind up with a key.) Why this millionaire owner of a historic farm chose not to repair the dilapidated barns is beyond me. Perhaps that was one reason why Niels called him eccentric.

Niels was something of a character in his own right, with a charming sense of humor. Before Mother and I settled into our bedroom that night (under thick goose-down comforters), Niels told us a ghost story. Hessel was haunted. According to an old legend, a distraught mother had killed her little daughter and buried her body somewhere on the grounds of the farm. Her dog had search for years for the grave sight of the unfortunate child. Now, at night, the ghost of that dog continued to roam the farm searching for the girl's body. And, indeed, there was in the present day a dog that made its daily rounds of the farm. It was Niels' dog, Gretta, who followed Mother and me about as we made our tour of the farm.

Fortunately, Hessel was eventually saved for posterity. Shortly before he died, Elle Jensen sold his farm to the Aalborg community, which at a considerable expense, restored the place to its former glory. What was hr. Jensen saving his money for? Did he expect to take it with him? Hessel is now a museum, the only surviving thatched-roofed farm in Denmark. How many people can say that they slept overnight in a haunted museum?

# THE ROAD NOT TAKEN

At Expo 67 In Montreal, Canada, now having six years of formal French language instruction under my belt, I had the occasion to practice my linguistic acumen on a French-speaking couple who seemed to have lost their way. Expo 67 was not as large as the New York World's Fair of 1964, but it was easy to become disoriented by the teeming crowds. Expecting to impress my parents with my fluency in French, I approached the pair confidently and asked if I could be of assistance. The man gave me a blank stare. I repeated my offer in a louder voice. Shaking his head in puzzlement, the man turned to his wife and said, "*Il ne parle pas français*" "*Oui*," his wife replied, "*Il parle français.*" I asked the man to please speak more slowly. It was to no avail. I could not understand what the couple was asking, where they wanted to go. The man still did not believe that I was speaking his language. So much for my six years of French. After two years of college French, I had finally overcome my *ALM* handicap. I had been able to discuss Albert Camus' *The Plague* in French class, but here in Montreal I could not carry on a simple conversation with two random speakers of the French language. Of course, the people I were trying to communicate with spoke a French Canadian dialect that was different from the classical French I had studied. Nevertheless, it was a great disappointment to me. In the back of my mind came the thought that Mother had come to America speaking English like a native. Had she, after completing her schooling, ever had to ask an English speaker to repeat himself, or to speak more slowly? That never happened. It occurs to me now that perhaps our educational backgrounds were not strictly comparable. In Denmark, students attend school for six days a week, and for longer hours. Vacations are shorter. A student graduating from a Danish high school (which lasts for six years) has the equivalent of what would be at least two additional years in an American college. So was my mother's schooling in foreign languages clearly superior to mine or was she simply a better student than I? Perhaps it was a little of both. Not long after the incident at Expo 67, Mother told me that she had begun her study of English and German in the third grade. So she had actually studied English for five or six years longer than I had pursued my formal study of French. Denmark was a tiny country of less than four million people, she explained. The Danes would have found it difficult to function in the wider world if they were unable to understand foreign languages. Americans, when they venture abroad, are thus used to hearing everyone speak English, so what is the use of foreign languages being taught here at home? Thanks a lot, American schools.

Looking back, I can see plainly that I would have been better off if I had studied German instead of French. Had there been a private tutor in Branchburg offering instruction in German, I most certainly would have enrolled. After all, Mother could have coached me in German. I might have wound up speaking fluent German, not my halting French.

In any case, I did take a semester of German during summer school in my final year at Rutgers. (Perhaps it was a belated attempt to correct my earlier mistake.) During my first week, as the class was drilled in German phrases, the teacher singled me out and asked me to repeat a phrase on my own. She was amused that I was speaking German with a French accent. However, I soon lost my French accent and mastered the guttural German intonations, and got used to placing the verb at the end of the sentence. Yes, if nothing else, I proved to myself that I *did* have an affinity for foreign languages.

I was surprised when our teacher, Miss Comstock, told the class that she was a native of Germany. Like my mother, she spoke English with absolutely no trace of an accent. She described to the class her fond memories of growing up in Germany. She recalled how during a long train ride as a young girl she had climbed up into an overhead baggage rack to sleep, the fishnet rope structure of the rack being as comfortable as a hammock. Though born perhaps in the early 1940s, she never mentioned the war. She was disappointed when I told her at the end of the semester that I would not be continuing in my study of the German language. I would be moving on to graduate school at Temple University, where I would be majoring in psychology.

# DENMARK 1968

It was my father's first trip back to Denmark after his brief 1946 tour as an American soldier. Mother and I had taken a flight from Kennedy Airport two weeks earlier, and were at Copenhagen Airport to meet him. Before making his trip, Father had learned some useful Danish phrases. He had also memorized a few comical things to say in the event that the ice needed to be broken. "*Min hofteholder bedræber mig* (My girdle is killing me)." Meeting Lars Buus again after more than thirty years had passed, he began with a respectful "*God dag.*" Morfar, upon hearing his son-in-law making a creditable attempt to speak Danish, put Bob to the ultimate test, asking him to repeat the tongue-twisting Danish phrase; "*jordbær grød med fløde* (strawberry preserves with cream)." But this would require some more practice on my father's part. Bob still wore the wristwatch his father-in-law had presented him with in 1946. The two men hit it off very well, almost as if the long hiatus in their acquaintanceship had never occurred.

Bob also hit it off well with brother-in-law Knud, with whom he had never had a face-to-face meeting. They had a lot to catch up on—twenty-two years, in fact. Bob told Knud about his work for Gibbs & Cox. Knud was fascinated how a plan drawn up on flat sheets of paper could be transformed into a complex three-dimensional ship. He told my father about his own work. He was employed by a small company in Silkeborg called Pasilak. They manufactured milking machines, pumps, and storage tanks for a variety of fluids, including milk, which were exported mostly to Germany and England. Knud's job was to translate the very technical advertising copy into German and English. While Mother stayed home with Mormor to catch up on family affairs, Knud took Father and me on a tour of his workplace. As it was a weekend, the factory was deserted, except perhaps for a guard or two. My father was concerned that Knud might get into trouble for entering the unoccupied factory (back in Gibbs & Cox, security was elaborate; you needed to show your photo ID to the guard to be permitted to enter the building). Using his key to open the door, Knud had no qualms about entering the empty factory. If challenged, he would simply explain who he was and what business he had here. He expected no challenges, and indeed there were none. He gave us a tour of the factory. There were huge storage tanks ready to be loaded onto trucks and delivered. There were tanks of varying sizes, and equipment whose use Father and I could only guess at. Knud was still pondering my father's explanation of how a series of blueprints could be transformed into a ship. He could understand how, in his own workplace, even the largest storage tank could be manufactured, but to construct something as complex as a ship was almost beyond his comprehension. Knud directed Father and me to his small, windowless office. It was equipped with little more than a typewriter, a pile of advertising copy, and a stack of reference books. My father described the drafting-room floor at Gibbs & Cox: a hundred or more workers hunched over drafting tables, all overlooked by their boss stationed in his glass-enclosed office, who would call any employee to task for failing to apply himself. Knud shook his head. Working conditions were very different at Pasilak. Here you worked at your own pace; there was no one looking over your shoulder.

After the tour, Knud suggested that we pay a visit to Silkeborg Castle. I had been to Silkeborg on several occasions with my mother, usually on shopping trips or to visit the Silkeborg Museum, but we had never seen or heard of a castle. It was certainly news to me, and not in any of the guidebooks I had perused in preparation for our trip. As Knud parked his red Volkswagen in a small parking lot surrounded by tall pine trees, there was still no sign of the castle. Was he playing a joke on us? As it turned out there once had been a castle here, somewhere back in the twelfth century, but there was almost nothing left of it now except for an unimpressive square of foundation stones that marked the spot where the castle had formerly stood. The "castle" was disappointingly small. A border of low-clipped privet hedges ran around the area, considerable taller that the foundation stones of the erstwhile castle that they enclosed. So what had happened to Silkeborg Castle? Had it been sacked by brigands like the monastery at Øm Kloster? Knud explained that the castle had simply been abandoned and fallen into disrepair. Over the years, people had carted away the tumbling stones of its walls to construct new buildings, like the Silkeborg Museun where the Tollundman was now housed. The large foundation stones were all that remained of Silkeborg castle. Still, I thought, it had been a very small castle, not much larger than a private home in the present century.

Mother accompanied us on what had become an almost obligatory pilgrimage to Himmelberget. Driving there by car shaved off the two-hour round-trip boat ride. Who could resist the view over the Silkeborg lake district or the heather-covered slopes of the Sky Mountain?

The next day, when Anna Lise and Verner drove down from Tranum, Father tried out one of his ice-breakers, *"Anna Lise, du er en pige; Verner, du er en dreng* (Anna Lisc, you are a girl; Verner, you are a boy)." It was not something I would have attempted, but my father was always the charmer. He knew exactly when such levity would succeed, and used it appropriately.

Having settled into the house at Resenbro, we began a tour about the countryside in a rental car, accompanied be Anna Lise and Verner in their camping wagon. Our car was an Opal, which Father soon discovered, had a faulty reverse gear. After stopping in a parking space during our trip to Himmelbjerget, with the reverse gear grinding in protest, the car had to be pushed out. So Father thereafter made sure that wherever we parked we would be able to pull straight out. Problem solved. While my parents and I stayed overnight in hotels along the way, Anna Lise and Verner and their young sons, Erik and Peter, drove about in their new camping wagon, pitching a tent at the end of each day in a succession of campgrounds. For them, it was a working vacation. They had recently purchased a sizable tract of land behind the Esso station in Tranum and were planning to open a camping place of their own early in the following year. It was to be called "Camping Skovly (roughly, Forest Camping)." The general store had already been completed. It would cater to the daily needs of the campers, offering, among other things, various daily necessities, food, and Tuborg beer. A small auditorium would show old movies projected upon a screen. The bathhouse was still a work in progress. Anna Lise and Verner took notes at each camping place they stopped at, listing the amenities they would need to provide for their guests, amusements to keep the children entertained, and also the deficiencies they would have to avoid if they wanted to make a success of this venture.

One day we drove south to the town of Kollund, on the Danish border with Germany. Danes often went to Germany to purchase liquor, which Danish taxes rendered very expensive. Before passing through the checkpoint, my parents and I decided to take a stroll along the border. There was a water-filled ditch separating the two countries. A three-foot-high granite marker rose on the German side of the ditch. I could make out some writing on the marker. What did it say? I took a big step over the narrow ditch, planting one foot on the German side of the border. Suddenly a commotion arose from a guardhouse about three hundred feet away. There was the sound of barking. Two German soldiers and a ferocious German shepherd tugging on its leash quickly emerged from the guardhouse.

"Come back! Come back!" my parents urged me.

I stepped back onto Danish soil and gave a friendly wave to the soldiers, who promptly halted their advance. Obviously, to apprehend me for my transgression, they would have had to cross over onto Danish soil, which they were not permitted to do. This little incident took place when the Germans were still concerned with defending their border. Not so today, when you can enter or leave any country in the European Union without ever having to show your passport. And people wonder why terrorist acts are being committed with such shocking frequency in the new Europe—committed by recent immigrants who should be grateful for having been granted sanctuary from the pest holes in which they had been born. After the Nazi occupation of World War II, the European Union, with its policy of open borders, was the most calamitous thing ever to happen to Europe. Winston Churchill would have been appalled by the creation of this monster.

Anyway, back to our vacation. Still In Kolland, Anna Lise and Verner, their sons, and my parents and I boarded a so-called "spirit boat." Bound for Flensborg, Germany such boats provided a singular service: supplying passengers with all the duty-free booze they could consume during the crossing. One did not need to show a passport to board the spirit boat. Such a requirement would have no doubt have drastically reduced the number of Danish citizens making the trip. This was no doubt the beginning of Europe's open-border policy. It was the thin edge of the wedge. Economic realities dictated that if governments restricted the free passage between countries, their economies would suffer. There were no age requirements on the spirit boat. Unaccustomed as I was to alcohol, I had two double rums during the passage (which, in retrospect, seemed to take much longer than should have been necessary for the half-mile crossing). We disembarked at the harbor in Flensborg, where Mother, who did not care for alcohol, took a picture of the rest of us, standing on the sidewalk beside a redbrick church. My father and I have silly grins on our faces. Verner is supporting himself with one hand on the wall of the church. Soon after the picture was taken, all of the adult males had to scramble off to find a public restroom where they could relieve themselves.

After crossing back to Denmark on the spirit boat, we next headed for the town of Sønderborg, not far from the German border. In 1864 the Prussian army invaded the southern Danish province of Slesvig. The outnumbered Danish army put up a fierce resistance at Dybbol Mølle, but their heroics were ultimately unsuccessful, and the province of Slesvig was incorporated into Prussia. After Germany's defeat in World War I, the northern part of Slesvig was returned to Denmark. (But the Germans, as my mother well knew, would be back.) The restored windmill in Dybol Mølle is now a symbol of Danish resistance. A picture taken by my father shows Mother, Anna Lise, and me standing beside a pair of enormous cannons (with wheels over six feet tall) that are aimed at the German border. A Danish flag mounted on a towering pole waves proudly over the site.

We headed north to Billund, which had been an obscure little town in central Jutland until the Lego Corporation chose to make an amusement park there, called Legoland. People flocked to see the miniature city constructed entirely of Lego bricks. There was a harbor, complete with ships whose hulls were made with an advanced version of the classic Lego bricks. A train ran on a track around the harbor. A helicopter was poised for takeoff. There were rows of red-and-white houses and a seven-foot tall church (imagine how many bricks it must have taken to complete this fantasy). The city of Legoland was populated by miniature Lego people.

This updated version was a far cry from the original box of Lego bricks my mother had purchased for me on the occasion of my eighth birthday. In those days all of the bricks were white, with a number of elongated red caps that were intended to be placed atop the bare walls. With today's bricks you no longer had to restrict your imagination to a simple walled construction (without even a roof in the early days). Now you could design a truck with wheels, a ship that would float, or a helicopter—the makings of which were available in the gift shop. Excited children scampered about the park, no doubt dreaming about the things they would be able to construct with their Lego bricks—only to be disappointed when they got home with their purchases and found that they would need a good many more bricks to complete their masterpieces.

Nearing the end of our trip, we flew from Tirstrup Airport in Aalborg back to Copenhagen, where we stayed at the Alexandra Hotel. With only two days remaining in our itinerary, we confined our sightseeing to places in and around Copenhagen. Morfar had suggested that we see the Frilands open air museum, which was not far from the Sorgenfri summer palace where King Christian X had been held under house arrest by the Germans. There were more than one hundred historic buildings at the museum. Some had been moved from their original sites, others were meticulous reconstructions. Reflecting Danish rural life from the 1600s to the early 1900s, they ranged from thatched-roof farm buildings and simple peasant cottages to stately manor houses and windmills. It would have taken us a week to see everything, but we did not have that much time left.

The following day we followed the same route Mother and I had taken in 1961. Leaving our hotel on Radhusepladsen, we strolled past Amalienborg Palace, admired nearby Marmor Kirken (the Marble Church), whose massive dome had been inspired by St. Peter's Basilica. We stopped by the Gefion Fountain and proceeded on to Langelenie, where, to Father's delight, we toured a French destroyer and had a ride on a hydrofoil. Continuing our walking tour, we visited the Round Tower, climbing its circular ramp to get a panoramic view over Copenhagen. Our next stop was the stock exchange, which was of particular interest to Mother and me. It had been built in 1624 by King Christian IV, known at the greatest builder among the Danish monarchs. He also built the Round Tower, Rosenborg Castle, restored Kronborg Castle after a terrible fire, and had much of Fredericksborg Castle (his birthplace) torn down so he could build an even grander palace. The old stock exchange was topped by a slender green spire corkscrewing skyward. Inside, we were surprised by a scene that one might have witnessed a hundred years ago. Two or three traders sat on tall wooden stools, only occasionally stretching out to post the latest stock quote in chalk on a large blackboard. There was only a handful of stocks listed then on the Danish Stock Exchange. It was a far cry from the hustle and bustle on the New York Stock Exchange. But remember, this was half a century ago; today thousands of Danish stocks are traded in a new stock exchange. On our way back to Hotel Alexandra we witnessed another anachronism: a wagon drawn by two horses was delivering cases of Carlsberg beer to a restaurant.

After returning to our hotel to freshen up, we visited Tivoli Gardens, watched a free performance at the pantomime theater, played the slot machines for a while, then had dinner in the Nimb Restaurant. Afterward, we watched a thousand lanterns go on. All lit up, the Chinese pagoda looked more magical than ever. But now as the fireworks display began, it was time to go. It would be Father's last trip to Denmark, although he planned on making another trip after he retired. But that was not to be.

# ON HER OWN

I did not accompany my mother on her 1969 visit to Denmark. It was my final semester at Rutgers, and the following spring I would be attending Temple University, where I would earn a master's degree in psychology. Mother did not do much sight-seeing on this trip, dividing her time between her parents' home in Resenbro and her sister's home in Tranum. She took only a couple of pictures: the by-now obligatory pilgrimage to Himmelbjerget, and a trek up to Udsigten. Her parents remained in good health. She reported in a postcard that Morfar had cut the hedges in front of the house with a pair of hand sheers, and had set out new strawberry plants. I also did not travel with my mother in the fall of 1971. Muff was very sick; she was throwing up and had to be carried outside to do her business. Someone had to stay home to take care of her. As she had started turning up her nose at her dog food, I sought to tempt her with something a bit tastier than her usual bland fare. I cooked a turkey roll for her, and made a meat loaf loaded with peas. (Muff would eagerly scarf up the occasional pea that someone had accidentally dropped on the floor from our own supper.) But her appetite for such novel treats would wane after a meal or two, and I would have to come up with something else to tempt her. Back from Denmark, Mother thanked me for keeping Muff alive until her return. Unfortunately, Muff was rapidly declining. Soon, she slept for most of the day and would no longer eat or drink. A week or so after Mother's return, we brought Muff to her veterinarian to have her put to sleep. I remained in the car, unable to bear witnessing Muff's final moments. In the back of my mind I clung to the vague hope that the vet would have some miracle injection that would restore her, if only for a few more days. The last glimpse I had of Muff was of her paws hanging limply in Mother's arms as she and Father headed into the clinic. No, there was no miracle cure.

# TIME TO LEAVE THE NEST

My hard-working father never questioned my decision to try and make a living playing the stock market. After college and graduate school, when it became time for me to make my way in the world, I remained at home. Father was impressed by my serious approach to investing. Mother had her doubts about my not going out and getting a job, but she would be guided by my father. He shrugged off her objections, pointing out that there would be plenty of time for me to get a proper job if my efforts in the stock market did not pan out. I would spend whole weekends poring over the financial pages in the *New York Times* (the *Herald tribune* having recently gone bankrupt), and *Barron's*. I read *Forbes* and *Fortune*. Every Friday night I listened to Louis Rukeyser's *Wall Street Week*, taking notes on the latest recommendations. Before buying a stock I would carefully plot its price movements on a sheet of graph paper. (This was before the internet.)

Once, during a round of golf, Father confessed to me that he had aspired in his younger years to be a cartoonist. He had a definite talent for drawing, as was evidenced by a series of free-hand drawings he had produced in his high-school science class depicting each of the ten major phyla of the animal kingdom. He had also turned out a few prospective cartoon panels. But cartooning was a difficult business to break into. It would have been an enormous risk to leave a successful engineering career, especially with a wife and child to support. But he always regretted that he had not found a way to undertake his alternative career, even if on the side. I think that is why he respected my decision to try my hand in the stock market, which would leave me with spare time to pursue a writing career.

# CAMPING SKOVLY

On our 1973 trip to Denmark, I had a lot of catching up to do. Knud and Elly had had a second daughter in 1971, named Anni. Anna Lise's boy, Peter, was having his confirmation—a far more elaborate affair than the corresponding rite of passage held back in the States. Mother and I attended the church ceremony and a sumptuous dinner held in a local inn that was attended by relatives we had not seen for some time. (We had missed Erik's confirmation the previous year.) Mormor had had a close call in 1972. Arriving for what she had thought would be a routine appointment with her new eye doctor, she was astonished when the doctor dispensed with the expected examination her eyes. Focusing his attention on the side of her face, he told her that she had a melanoma, which would have to be excised without delay. Mormor was non-plussed. Her regular doctor had told her that the black spot in front of her left ear was nothing to be concerned about. She had had it for many years. It was completely harmless. Best thing was to leave it alone. But her eye doctor, a much younger man with more up-to-date training, was insistent. He telephoned a specialist in Aarhus and set up an appointment for the following week. Mormor admitted to being annoyed by her eye doctor's actions, but she reluctantly agreed to make the trip to Aarhus. The melanoma as well as an associated lymph gland were removed. A biopsy confirmed that the "harmless" black spot was, indeed, cancerous. Had Mormor not gone through with her operation, the cancer would have quickly spread throughout her body, and we would not be sitting at the dining-room table, as we were in April 1973, having a lighthearted chat about Mormor's narrow escape from death. She turned her left cheek to Mother and me to display the site of her operation. Her skin was firm and unwrinkled; there was no sign of the surgery.

"*Du har haft an ansigt loftening* (You've had a facelift)," Mother said, as she compared the left and right sides of Mormor's face.

Anna Lise and Verner were busy running their recently opened camping place. They had a dog now, a large black English sheepdog named Muff, in honor of the original Muff, the airedale terrier once owned by Morfar and Mormor. With Anna Lise and Verner unable to take time off for leisurely rides through the countryside, Mother and I confined ourselves largely to walking tours through the woods of Tranum and our usual visit to Udsigten. We would not be visiting Møns Klint on this trip. But I did not have to venture very far from Camping Skovly to hunt for fossils. They had come to me. The rough roads in back of the camping place were paved with loose stones, and If you had an eye for it, the occasional fossilized sea urchin could be found among them. The stones had likely been dredged up in the bay at Aarhus, where Mother and I had been a couple of times. There, I had come across a similar fossil or two.

With Verner and his brother Carl running the Esso station and the repair shop, it was primarily Anna Lise who saw to the needs of the campers, selling most anything they might possibly need in the general store.

("What's better than a Tuborg?" a poster on the wall read. "Two Tuborgs.") Most of the campers were Danes, but a few hailed from Germany. I recall seeing a couple of German men who were of the right age to have served in World War II. Anna Lise, Mother, and I wondered if they had done their military service here in Tranum. Why would these Germans tourists bother to drive all the way to the north of Denmark when there were beautiful vacation spots much closer to their homes in Germany? (Anna Lise was not complaining, mind you. The Germans' business was much appreciated.) Just south of Munich are any number of idyllic lakes suitable for boating or swimming. There is Lake Constance on the border with Switzerland. If you fancied mountains, you could venture into Bavaria and enjoy skiing on the slopes of the Alps. All without leaving your homeland. So what did northern Jutland have to offer to these German tourists? Swimming and boating on the often rough North Sea is a chancy proposition. There are no mountains to speak of, and absolutely no skiing. There is only one explanation for the presence of German tourists in the far north of Jutland: they had been here before, and for them this was very likely a sentimental journey. Did their climb to the top of Udsigten (no doubt with less of a spring in their steps than they formerly had) carry them back to more youthful days? Did they have fond memories of gazing out across Jammer Bugt from a camouflaged bunker on the beach, waiting for the Allied landing that never came? Anna Lise spoke German and could have tactfully asked them if they had been in the war. My mother and I could also have asked, but none of us chose to bring the matter up—although we all suspected that they must, indeed, be veterans of that terrible war. Nor did the Germans volunteer any information, for the most part keeping to themselves and not mixing with the other campers.

Knud and I took frequent walks together. We would discuss anything and everything under the sun. I pointed out that the sandy soil in Denmark was very different from the heavy clay soil we had in Pennsylvania. Back home, potatoes and other crops were prone to rot if they were not planted high enough. Knud expressed surprise as we passed by a used motorcycle that was up for sale when I told him that back in the States a new motorcycle would cost far less than this used and dented one. The difference was due to the high Danish taxes. After one had sold something in Denmark, be it a motorcycle, a house, or a farm, the state would take the bulk of the profits. Addressing my astonishment at this state of affairs, Knud explained to me, "We get something for our money. Everyone will be taken care of in their final years." Okay, I responded, but I'd rather have the responsibility of taking care of myself than relying on some anonymous government bureaucrat to look after me. During one of our walks Knud asked me what this Watergate thing was all about.

"It's a hotel in Washington, D.C.," I began. But to explain Nixon's crime to someone who had seen only the occasional newspaper headline and had not been subjected to a year-long press campaign to create a scandal was no mean task. Try as I might to make things clear, Knud simply couldn't follow the facts of the case. And as for myself, attempting to recall the specifics of Nixon's predicament from across the Atlantic Ocean, I felt as if I was peering through the wrong end of a telescope.

# FROM RUGBRØD TO RUBARBERGRØD

I can still picture Mormor standing over the kitchen counter and slicing *rugbrød* for our lunch. The sour rye bread was brown and came in a dense, firm loaf that had to be cut into individual slices. To do this, Mormor would place the loaf into something that resembled a hand-operated Guillotine. With the bread securely held in the v-shaped wooden rack, Mormor would push down the sharp blade of the cutter and slice off an eighth-inch thick slice of bread. When she had accumulated a sufficient number of slices, she would set a plateful down on the dining-room table. Each of us would then butter a slice of bread and apply a thick layer of liver paste. We had a varied selection of toppings to choose from: pickled herring, leftover slices of *frikedeller*, strawberry preserves that Mormor had canned the previous year, baby shrimp on a bed of lettuce, a round or two of Bologna, sliced boiled potatoes from Morfar's garden. We would eat our *smorrebrød* with a knife and fork. The men usually washed down their meal with a bottle of Tuborg; the women would have coffee. No one ever left the table hungry.

In the middle of the afternoon we would have a snack consisting of a slice of white French bread, thickly buttered and slathered with honey. This treat we would eat, not with a knife and fork, but by carefully holding the crust of the bread between our fingers.

Needless to say, I invariably put on a couple of pounds on each of our visits to Denmark.

Back in the States, Mother and I continued the tradition of open-faced sandwiches for our lunch. Rubschlager Danish-style pumpernickel bread proved to be almost as good as the *rugbrød* we had enjoyed in Denmark. Unfortunately, none of the several American brands of liver paste came anywhere close to measuring up to Danish *leverpostej*. American and Danish liver paste are both made with pork liver, but there the similarity ends. In a book on Scandinavian cooking that Mother bought many years ago, there is a recipe for Danish liver paste. Among the ingredients not included in the American version are 2 tablespoons of butter, 2 tablespoons of flour, 1 cup of heavy cream, 3 flat anchovy fillets, and 2 eggs. Some American brands add bacon to the mix, but they list some additional ingredients not found in the Danish recipe: sodium phosphates, sodium ascorbate, sodium nitrate, potassium lactate, and sodium diacetate. American Braunschweiger liverwurst is manufactured for a long shelf life, hence it is loaded with preservatives that are absent in Danish liverwurst, which is intended to be consumed within a week or two, not to sit on a grocery shelf for a month or more. We bought our *leverpostej* in a grocery store in Silkeborg, called Føtex. It was baked daily on the premises and would still be warm when we picked it up.

Incidentally, in Danish grocery stores, the cashier does not stand all day long as in America, but is seated on a high stool behind the counter. The customers are expected to bring their own bags (usually made of string) and bag their own groceries. If you forget to bring your bags, you're out of luck. You just have to pile your stuff into the shopping cart. But I never saw anyone forgetting to bring enough bags.

Nearing the end of our 1973 trip, Mother bought on a whim a loaf of fresh-baked *leverpostej* in Føtex. We brought it home with us, and managed to make it last for two or three weeks.

My mother's Scandinavian cooking book also included a recipe for *rubarbergrød*. She had circled the heading in ink, obviously intending to reproduce the dessert we had enjoyed in Denmark. Inspired by Morfar's rhubarb patch, from which Mormor would make *rubarbergrød*, I planted a small patch of rhubarbs in our garden back home. For the next couple of years we had rhubarb jam. However, the rhubarbs, which need to be planted deep in a heavily composted and well-fertilized soil did not thrive in our clay soil as they had in the sandy soil in Morfar's garden. Our little patch soon petered out, and we resorted to buying strawberry rhubarb pie in the grocery store. It was much less work.

Fortunately for me, Carlsberg and Tuborg beer were featured in most American liquor stores (Mother had no taste for beer and would make a face when offered a sip). Sold for export, the brews were identical to the Danish version. I have always bought Danish beer (or in a pinch, Heineken). Back in the mid-sixties, the Danish government had the good sense to resist American-sponsored attempts to foist fluoridated water on the rest of the world. Danish drinking water is by law unfluoridated (as is the drinking water of Holland). So if you're drinking American beer, and can't be certain of the source of the water it contains, you may well be subjecting yourself to a slow poison that will eventually erode your teeth (the exact opposite of its supposed benefit) and cause numerous other physical and mental symptoms. So much for the United States Public Health Service.

# A BLANK SPOT IN THE RECORD

Over the years, Mother kept a meticulous list of every trip she made to Denmark. She made a total of twenty-four trips—eleven with me, the remainder by herself. But as I went over her list to get the chronology of this memoir correct, there was one entry that had me puzzled: June 2 - June 29, 1975. I have absolutely no recollection of this visit. Mother's entry indicated that she made the trip alone. I looked through her photo album. There was not a single picture taken in Denmark in 1975. I went through our collection of thirty-five millimeter slides on the off-chance that I had neglected to convert any images from that year into glossy photos. No luck there. Was it possible that Mother had made a mistake? Had she confused 1975 with some other trip? I got out one of her old passports. It contained two visa stamps for that year: Indrejst 2 Juni, 1975, Rigspolitiet Kastrup, Danmark; Admitted U.S. Immigration New York, N.Y. June 29, 1975. You can't get a more official confirmation than that. I do not know what I was doing at the time that would have prevented me from accompanying my mother. There was no immediate health crisis in the family. Mother had saved all of all of Mormor's aerogrammes, writing the date on the cover of each one and noting briefly any salient developments. Mormor wrote in her letter of April 7 that her annual checkup (for her melanoma) had gone well. Morfar was looking forward to his upcoming seventy-ninth birthday. He tired quickly, but was otherwise in good health. Mormor wrote that they were all looking forward to Inge's visit, though there was some question as to whether or not Anna Lise and Verner, busy as they were with the reopening of the camping place for its spring season, would be able to pick her up after her connecting flight to Tirstrup Airport in Aalborg. Verner and his brother, Carl, partners in the venture, had acquired some additional land so they could expand the camping place. They had ambitious plans. Mother's trip came a month after her father's birthday, so that was not the reason for her visit. Perhaps Mother sensed that this might be the last time she would see both of her parents in good health. All the more reason for her to take plenty of pictures.

The only explanation I can come up with is that Mother forgot to bring the camera along with her, although it would have been uncharacteristic of her to have forgotten to pack something as important as a camera. Mother was always more organized than I was. When we were going shopping, I would often have to rush back up to my room to retrieve something I had left behind—my wallet, the car keys, some spare change. As far as I can recall, Mother never once had to go back upstairs to pick up a forgotten item. Unlike me in more recent years, she always had her shopping list with her; she never had to return home to discover that she had neglected to pick up an item or two on the list. Over the years, I would sometimes forget that my estimated taxes were due. Mother, sitting down to complete her own taxes, would have to remind me. So how could she have forgotten to bring her camera along with her? The alternate explanation is far more implausible: that she had her camera with her but for some reason chose not to take a single picture. Could the camera, a Kodak Retina IIIC with a fold-up flash attachment, not have been working? I doubt it. There are a couple of pictures in the album taken later that year on a trip to Cape May, and there are pictures taken the following year at Gettysburg. There was nothing wrong with the camera.

So why didn't you take any pictures, Mom?

# OFF THE BEATEN PATH

In 1977 Mother and I made another trip together to Denmark. A few things had altered since our previous visit. Both Mormor and Morfar had visibly aged—Morfar all the more so. He had very likely suffered a couple of minor strokes over the years. He had high blood pressure and hardening of the arteries. Moving slowly and stiffly now on his daily strolls, he seemed preoccupied with knocking the heads off of dandelions with the tip of his cane, even when he found them growing along the side of the road. He tired quickly and often had trouble remembering things. Mormor, however, remained in good spirits. She bustled about the house doing her chores, continued to tend the garden, and had no difficulty hanging up a load of wash on the clothesline. She amazed Morfar by knowing the name of every newscaster on TV. I soon learned that I had been dethroned as the tallest member of the family. Poul, Knud's son, had sprouted up like a weed in the five years since I had last seen him, and was now about six-feet-four-inches tall. Anna Lise and Verner had never been busier at Camping Skovly, but the daily grind was beginning to take its toll on them. One of Anna Lise's knees was giving her some trouble. And Verner found it increasingly taxing to deal with both the Esso station and the camping place. Perhaps it was time to consider selling Camping Skovly. It was a difficult decision to make when things were going so well. They had received an offer from a developer who wanted to build a housing development on the property. But what would Anna Lise and Verner do in their retirement years? They were both still relatively young. They were not yet ready to sell out. To give up a thriving business was a hard decision to make.

One day Anna Lise was driving Mother and me up to Tranum. We had packed some sandwiches to eat on the way. Around the halfway mark we parked at a rest stop. We had not been there for very long when a balding, middle-aged man came over to our picnic table.

"*Inge Buss!*" he called out, obviously recognizing my mother, despite the passage of time, by her red hair. "*Og Anna Lise!*," he said, now recognizing my aunt.

"*Jeg er Olaf,*" he said in response to the blank stares he received.

Now they remembered. Olaf had been a frequent visitor as a child to Klostergaarden. It had been what? Fifty years ago? They reminisced for a while about the good old days. Were Inge's and Anna Lise's father and mother still living? Olaf could recall the names of perhaps a dozen horses that Lars Buus had kept in his stables. He proceeded to rattle their names off as if he had been there only yesterday.

After Olaf took his leave, Anna Lise and my mother began to chuckle. Anna Lise turned to me to explain. "*Vi plejede at kalde ham Snot-Olaf, fordi hans næse var altid dryppende* (We used to call him Snot-Olaf, because his nose was always running)."

Mother confessed to me that she could not recall the name of a single one of the horses, despite having ridden them on numerous occasions.

We had arrived in Denmark in time for me to enter the annual forty-five-kilometer march (about twenty-eight miles) in Silkeborg, sponsored by the Silkeborg Judo Club. My uncle, Knud, had participated in numerous marches all over Denmark. These marches had their origin in the 1940s, when Danes marched through the streets of Copenhagen in open defiance of Nazi orders that no more than five people at a time could assemble in a group. Knud kept a corkboard on his bedroom wall, decorated with all the medals he had earned on his various marches. Would I be able to earn a medal? Not as fit as I would have liked to have been, I began training during our stay in Tranum, running up and down the steep slope of Udsigten, and jogging in the sandy beach along Jammer Bugt, where the long-abandoned German pillboxes continued their silent vigil for an Allied landing that was never to come. After a week I thought that I was ready for the challenge. Yes, I was ready. Or so I thought.

We started our march on a chill morning from the courtyard of Vestre Elementary School in Silkeborg. But setting off with brisk steps into the nearby woods quickly warmed us up. I had a plastic bag filled with a camera and some provisions for the journey—a rookie mistake. Experienced marathoners brought with them not an ounce of excess baggage. A young woman, bare legs pumping, jogged past us. (I think I was holding my uncle back.) We quickened our pace. I began transferring my increasingly heavy bag from one hand to the other. As we approached the lower slope of Himmelbjerget, not quite halfway through the march, Knud flipped a couple of medals out of his shirt pocked and let them dangle on his chest. "*Nu er det tid til at prale lidt,*" he said. ("Now it's time to boast a little.") On the top of the hill, which had never before seemed such an arduous climb to me, we paused to catch our breath. The most satisfying drink I ever had in my life came from a water fountain on the summit of Himmelbjerget. I had never been so thirsty. After splashing water all over myself, I was ready to continue on. Fortunately, the hike back to Silkeborg was mostly downhill. We had to put the brakes on to keep from tumbling headlong down the sandy slope of Himmelbjerget. Along the way we teamed up with a veteran marathoner. His name was Martin. In his early seventies, he was lean and fit. Like Knud, he had participated in numerous marathon marches. He expressed his surprise that I was able to tackle a forty-five kilometer-long march without prior training. We stopped at a refreshment stand and asked for three Tuborgs, which we consumed as we sat on a nearby picnic bench. While not quite as satisfying as the fountain water that had quenched my thirst on the top of Himmelbjerget, it was a close second. I snapped a picture of Knud and Martin sipping their beer at the picnic bench.

Back at Vestre School in Silkeborg, we presented our punched cards from the completed route to a judge, each checkpoint at which we had stopped bearing a neat round hole. Receiving our medals was something of an anticlimax, but a nice memento, something you would be proud to display on a corkboard.

My legs were unbelievably stiff the following day; I could barely lift my feet, which slapped noisily upon the floor when I attempted to walk. But I had earned my medal. Knud shook his head upon seeing my shuffling, old man's gait. "*Har du virkelig ødlelagt sig selv?* (Have you really ruined yourself)?" he asked as we prepared to drive over for a visit to an art museum in Silkeborg. Trained and fit after many marathon marches, Knud was experiencing none of the muscular aches and pains that I was. I shrugged off my temporary disability and told Knud that I would be fully recovered in time for next week's marathon march in Tranum—it was a mere forty kilometers. "*Jeg kan nemt klare det* (I can easily do it)," I said to my uncle.

When the Tranemarch came around on the following weekend, I continued to experience some minor stiffness in my legs, but I felt that I was now an experienced marathoner, and assured Mother that if my legs gave me any trouble, I would simply slow down and not be concerned with setting any speed record. This morning I was not burdened with our heavy Retina camera as I had been on the Judo March. But had I really learned my lesson? A picture taken by my mother at the start of the march shows me clutching a bulging plastic bag. I was about to set forth on a forty-kilometer trek. What on earth was I thinking of? Had I not learned my lesson? There were rest stations along the way where I could obtain something to eat or drink—no need to bring along provisions. Upon reflection, however, I recalled that a heavy rain was forecast for later in the day, seriously dampening the spirits of the participants on the longer marches. All that I had packed in the bag was a light-weight plastic raincoat. No problem there.

I had attempted to persuade my mother to accompany me on the Tranemarch—not the long march, but the shortest of the three marches, amounting to a mere fifteen kilometers. It was not to be. Although on our 1973 trip to Denmark, Mother and I, after taking the bus and spending the morning strolling about in Silkeborg, had walked all the way from town back to Resenbro—a distance of over five kilometers, and probably quite a bit more when you include the distance we had covered in Silkeborg. But I could not persuade her that she could easily walk the fifteen-kilometer route in the Tranemarch. She had done more than a third of that without any difficulty. And she had easily scaled the slopes of Himmelbjerget and Udsigten. Here in Tranum the terrain would be level. Furthermore, Anna Lise and a friend of hers were going on the fifteen-kilometer walk. Piece of cake. But Mother was adamant; she was not going. And that was that. I knew from long experience that once Mother had had made up her mind on something, no amount of persuasion or cajoling could get her to alter her decision. Come to think of it, my cousins, Erik and Peter, though we had enjoyed several long excursions through the woods of Tranum, evidenced no interest in accompanying me on the march. Were they aware of something that I wasn't? Was Erik's smile simply an expression of his good wishes? Or was he anticipating that this march would prove to be more than I had bargained for? Early on Saturday morning, Mother saw Anna Lise and me off on our journey. For the first few kilometers, my aunt and I walked together, then the trail markers pointed in different direction: this way for the fifteen-kilometer route, that way for the forty-kilometer route. (You could have done this, Mother: by now you would have been already halfway through with your walk.) Anna Lise and I went our separate ways.

There were wooden route markers to show the way, and the usual checkpoints at which you had to have your card punched. Just short of the halfway point, and before the checkpoint, a car pulled up near the trail and a man emerged with his card in hand to join the other marchers.

"*Han snyder sig kun sig selv* (He's only cheating himself)," said the man next to me. And when you think of it, what possible satisfaction could someone get from obtaining a medal for an achievement that he had obtained only through a base deception? Sure, he could boast to his friends that he had been on one of the long marathon marches, but would not his medal be a permanent reminder of his ultimate inability to toe the mark?

Early that afternoon, as predicted, a steady rain began. I had figured that I could complete the better part of the march under sunny skies. That proved to be a slight miscalculation. But this was all for the best, I thought. Now Mormor, back in Resenbro, wouldn't have to drag the hose around to water the garden.

I found myself all alone on one of the back roads of Tranum, most of the other marchers apparently having heeded the weather forecast and chosen one of the shorter routes. But I pressed on, donning my plastic raincoat as the downpour worsened and slogging along a now rain-slicked dirt road. I could have stopped in at one of the relief stations and asked for a ride home, but I did not. I was determined to tough it out. I would not be called a quitter. I took a spill on one of the slippery roads. It felt as if someone had kicked me in the in the back of my right knee. No big deal, I thought. I was able to hobble on, if at a slower pace than before. And although not setting any speed records, I completed the course in the middle of the afternoon (the local newspaper had heralded the arrival of of an American entrant in the yearly march, so I was in effect under a microscope), and I felt that I had logged in a respectable time, especially for a neophyte in a driving rain.

The next morning I awoke upon an inflatable air mattress on Anna Lise's and Verner's dining-room floor. It was sheer agony to stand. Try as I might, I could not straighten my injured right leg, and for the remainder of our trip I had to hobble around using one of Morfar's canes. "*Nu komme den hurtig løber*," Morfar joked as I limped into the living room. ("Here comes the fast runner.")

Mother commiserated with me for my injury, without stating the obvious: "I told you so." She was always more sensible than I was, but never once, in spite of all my many mistakes, did she ever rub it in.

A week later we flew back to Copenhagen, where we stayed overnight with my mother's aunt, Anna, (Ella Buus' sister) before heading back to the States. Nearly six months would pass before I would be able walk again without a limp. I remember walking the entire length of the boardwalk in Cape May that fall to strengthen my leg. At the time I thought that I had taken my last marathon march.

Before we left Resenbro that year, Morfar presented me with a brass horseshoe. When we got back to the States, I chose to hang it up over my bedroom door the easy way, with a single nail so that the arms pointed down. Looking up at my handiwork, Mother told me that I should have hung it the opposite way, using two nails, so that my luck would not run out. I wonder if it's too late now to turn the horseshoe around. But, hey, what else can go wrong?

# STROKE

For a number of years Morfar had followed a daily routine that included taking a walk into the nearby town of Resenbro. Steadying himself with his cane as he smoked a cheroot, he would likely have lingered at the end of his driveway to cast a glance across the Gudenaa at hr. Rasmussen's farm, then he would stroll past the little woods at the end of his property, past the local train station, past the nursing home known as Rødegaard. Sometimes he would stop in the grocery store and pick up a box of cigars or some razor blades. On this particular April morning, the dandelions would have been in full bloom. Morfar, as was his wont, very likely lopped off a few of the yellow flowers with the tip of his cane, pausing to take a puff on his cheroot before continuing on. But today he never made it all the way into town. He made it only as far as Rødegaard. A passing motorist spotted him lying on the sidewalk. The driver stopped and rushed into Rødegaard to call for an ambulance.

Put under intensive care In the hospital in Silkeborg, Morfar was diagnosed as having suffered a massive cerebral hemorrhage. His prognosis was extremely guarded. After awakening from his coma, he was unable to speak and had to be spoon-fed. It was uncertain how long he might survive.

Mother flew to Denmark to be at her father's bedside. In the month that she remained, there was no change in his condition. She thought from the fleeting smile on his face when she came into his hospital room that he recognized her. But she could not be certain. He would often give the same smile to his nurses. Mother and Mormor took turns spoon-feeding him. Seeing that there was nothing more that she could do, Mother returned home.

In August, two months after Mother left, Morfar was discharged from the hospital to Rødegaard, the very nursing home that he had passed every day on his morning constitutional. He remained unable to speak. But gradually he improved enough to be able to slowly feed himself with a spoon.

# CONDITION HOPELESS

The year after Morfar suffered his stroke, Mother and I made another trip to Denmark. There would be little time for sightseeing on this visit. Understandably, the house at 25 Resenbro had been neglected for the past couple of years. Needed repairs had been put off. In the bathroom, a trickle of water ran continuously onto the toilet from the overhead cistern. The backyard was overgrown with weeds. The once orderly hedges had grown straggly. I immediately saw that my task was to put things right. Upon our arrival, Mormor had handed me a couple hundred kroner to spend on whatever I chose. The next day Mother and I took the bus into Silkeborg. We located a hardware store, where I bought a light-weight push mower that Mormor would be able to use in place of the old one that weighed a ton and would be a challenge for Hercules to push through tall grass. I also bought a small scythe that I would be able to use instead of the unwieldy implement that Morfar had formerly used to clear the meadow on the lower slope of the property. Mormor was delighted with her new lawnmower. Now she would be able to mow the lawn herself, and would not have to wait until Knud found the time to do the job. I fixed the leaking cistern above the toilet. I puttied several long-neglected windows and painted the peeling trim around the front and back doors. I trimmed the hedges and dispatched the backyard weeds, discovering a bit too late that it was not a good idea to pull up stinging nettles with your bare hands.

"Why didn't you wear gloves?" Mother asked me when I came into the house with my fingers numb and swollen. I didn't have a good answer. I suppose it was a macho thing. No matter the pain, a knight of the Round Table ought to be "unwinceable."

Handily swinging the new light-weight scythe, I cut down the waist-high grass on the lower meadow. As I toiled away, taking one long stroke after another, Lancelot's refrain from *Camelot* came to my mind. I could hear Robert Goulet singing: "*C'est moi, c'est moi* the angels have chose to fight their battles below..."

Well, at least it helped keep me going. Perhaps more appropriate to the situation was Richard Burton's soliloquy as King Arthur at the end of the musical: "Each evening, from December to December, before you drift asleep upon your cot, think back on all the tales that you remember—from Camelot. And ask each person if he remembers the story, and tell it strong and clear if he does not, that once there was a fleeting wisp of glory called Camelot..."

A story of the profoundest loss. How do you move on after the once joyful kingdom has fallen into disarray? How do you escape when you're blue? Maybe by working yourself into a kind of trance. I would toil away after breakfast to put things right at 25 Resenbro, working steadily until my mother called me in for lunch. There were still a few small potatoes to be had from the garden. The last strawberries that Morfar had planted continued to bear fruit. But the asparagus had finally petered out. A slender stalk or two—small pickings.

After our lunch, Mormor would take a nap. I would resume whatever work I had left unfinished that morning. But by two o'clock I would have to hurry inside and get cleaned up. It was time. Mormor was ready to leave and would not wait for a straggler. On a couple of occasions, I had to run to catch up. Every day, Mormor, my mother and I would walk to Rødegaard. Morfar's condition remained unchanged. Usually, he would be lying in his bed, but sometimes we would find him in the downstairs common room, sitting in his wheelchair. The nurses would bring the residents into the common room to engage in whatever activities they were capable of. Most of them just sat there nodding off in their wheelchairs, Morfar included. When asked by one of the nurses if she wanted to take her man out into the garden, Mormor declined. What was the point? Lars no longer recognized her; he could no longer appreciate the beauty of flowers or trees. They might as well bring him back to his room where he could have his afternoon snack.

One day I was left alone with Morfar in his room. My mother and Mormor had been called into the office to discuss some minor administrative matter. Suddenly, Morfar became agitated, turning his head and gazing left and right. I asked him what he wanted to do.

"*Jeg vil ud af sengen* (I want to get out of bed)," he whispered.

I did not tell Mormor when she and my mother came back to the room that I had heard Morfar speak. It greatly distressed my grandmother that for the past year and a half Lars had not uttered a single word to her. How would she take it if I told her that after having made perhaps ten visits to Morfar's bedside, I had heard him speak to me? My hope was that one of these days he would say something to Mormor, too. But he never did.

On one of our visits, I brought a deck of cards along to the nursing home. For many years Morfar had enjoyed playing solitaire as he smoked his daily cheroot. On my last couple of trips to Denmark we had played numerous games of rummy. As I recall, Morfar had won the majority of the hands. A smile would come over his face as he got the final card he needed, and with a chuckle he would spread his hand out on the table and announce, "Rummy!" Today in the nursing home, I hoped that seeing a familiar deck of cards would stir old memories. I shuffled the deck several times, doing some flashy manipulations, which in the past had never failed to get a look of admiration from Morfar, whose own fingers were too stiff to perform any card tricks. Today there was no reaction. I peeled several cards out of the deck and placed them in Morfar's hand. He knew enough to hold onto the cards, but he just lay there staring blankly at the objects he held in his hands with not a clue what to do with them.

Another day, after completing my morning chores, I was sitting by the living-room window in my grandparents' house when I saw one of the nurses from Rødegaard pushing Morfar in his wheelchair. He stared straight ahead the whole time, not giving the faintest sign of recognition as he passed by the house he had lived in for more that twenty years.

I did not summon Mormor, who was in the kitchen with my mother getting something ready for lunch. It would only have upset her to witness Lars' total lack of response to the sight of his own home. I know it upset me.

# YANKEE GO HOME

Our trip to Denmark in 1979 would be for me, once again, a working vacation. My repairs to the house at 25 Resenbro had held up, but the grounds had become as overgrown as they had been on our previous visit. The property was clearly too much for Mormor to take care of. And Knud, busy with his work at Pasilak, did not have the time to maintain the place and care for his own property. Furthermore, there was trouble on the home front. His older daughter, Rita, was going through a phase.

"*Far og Mor duer ikke mere* (Father and Mother are no use any more)," Knud said ruefully, describing Rita's recent estrangement from her parents. One day I went to my uncle's house. Rita, listening to some loud rock-and-roll music in her room did not even acknowledge my presence. I noticed that on the bulletin board over her desk she had scribbled the phrase, "Yankee, go home." We would not exchange a single word on this visit. I thought it strange how the Yanks who had sacrificed their lives to free Europe from the Nazis held such little esteem with the upcoming generation.

While I'm discussing Rita, I might as well include another vignette concerning her. My mother had loved her favorite doll when she was a child. On one of her return trips to Denmark, she took the doll from her mother, who had carefully preserved it for all these years, and gave it to Rita, perhaps six or seven years old at the time. Mother was saddened to learn a few years later that Rita had decapitated the once-cherished doll, which was subsequently discarded.

Knud's daughter, Anni, had a very different personality than her older sister. Anni had a well-developed sense of humor for a young child, and sometimes I found it hard to believe that she was only nine years old. On one of our walks we were engaging in some light-hearted banter when she turned to me and made a remark that could be interpreted in two different ways. In Danish, the word *skæg* means beard, but in a different context it can also mean funny. I had neglected to shave for two mornings in a row, so there was visible stubble on my face. Was Anni asking me if I had a beard, or was she saying that I was funny? She just laughed at my question. I never learned which meaning she had actually intended, but clearly she appreciated the play on words. Yes, she got the joke.

Anni had a playful nature. We were walking along the road one day when she stopped to pick a dandelion. She wrapped the stem around her fingers and fired the head off at me with a flick of her thumb. It took me a couple of attempts, but soon we were shooting at each other with dandelions.

It was time again for the yearly Judo March in Silkeborg. Knud invited me to go along with him and Anni. As he did not want to tax Anni by going on one of the longer marches, he had elected to participate in the shortest, fifteen-kilometer walk. I'll admit that I was relieved that I would not have to tackle another forty-five kilometer march without any training. I was relieved, too, that I would be leaving Denmark before Knud's next march, the two-day, ninety-kilometer Hervejsmarch, the oldest and most famous marathon march in Europe. Had I been around at the time, I'd have gone on the march. Come hell or high water, I'd have been up for it.

It was a fine June morning when Knud, Anni, and I set off from the Vestre Elementary School in Silkeborg. I hadn't even tried to persuade Mother to come along with us this time. Even though the short course was on mostly level ground and was so easy that her nine-year-old niece was going along I knew what my mother's reaction would be. Hiking through the woods was simply not her thing.

The walk took us about two and a quarter hours. Anni was pleased to earn her first medal. But this would be my last march.

Morfar died the following year. Mother went by herself to attend the funeral. Lars Buus' body was cremated. Unlike in days gone by, there was no headstone to mark his grave in the communal cemetery in Silkeborg. You could buy flowers in the nearby flower shop, but as there were no markers or individual plots, it did not matter where you left the bouquet. In the end, what difference did it make? When you're dead, you're dead.

# A CELEBRATION

The year 1981 marked Anna Lisa's and Verner's twenty-fifth wedding anniversary. Relatives that Mother and I had not seen in years made their way to Tranum from Copenhagen and Falster. The morning began with the simultaneous firing of two shotguns (loaded with blanks, I presume). A three-man brass band played an upbeat tune as the couple emerged from the back door of their house, greeted by the applause of their guests. We all filed inside and settled ourselves on the extra chairs borrowed the day before from a couple of the neighbors. Anna Lise and Verner opened their presents. I believe that Mother and I gave them a blanket, because there's a picture in one of our albums showing Anne Lise unwrapping a blanket—why else would I have taken the picture? We had a light breakfast of coffee and rolls, topped off with a glass or two of Jägermeister. After a leisurely stroll about the neighborhood (there would be no lengthy treks up to Udsigten this day) we returned to the house for lunch. We had coffee and French bread slathered with butter and honey, and finished off the Jägermeister. I noted that Knud, sitting beside me and puffing on a cigar, bore an uncanny resemblance to England's Prince Albert in his latter years. My cousin, Erik, thought that with my large, black-rimmed glasses, I looked like Woody Allen.

I was still experiencing a pleasant buzz as Mother and I took a stroll past a nearby farmer's pasture, where a big white horse stood with his head hanging over the fence. With no fear of animals (I had been bitten as a young child by a snake and a dog with no ill-effects), I extended my palm toward the horse's mouth. I was not quick enough to react as the horse clamped its teeth down upon my fingers and drew blood.

Mother was astonished by my rash action. "Why did you let him bite you?" she said.

I had no ready answer. "I thought he would just lick my hand. He must have thought I had brought something for him to eat." (Interestingly, there is a picture in my mother's photo album showing my young cousin Anni petting the same white horse.)

Obviously, Jägermeister and horses are a bad mix. Lesson learned. Mother saw to it that I thoroughly cleaned my wounded fingers.

That evening we had dinner at a local inn. I believe there were two courses, one of which was some kind of fish. Concerning dessert, I am more certain, for a photo shows a sixteen-inch-tall marzipan tower set in the middle of each table. A waitress kept our wine glasses filled. We sang a tune celebrating Anna Lise's and Verner's anniversary that a local musician had written for the occasion; the melody was based on the American song, *She'll be Coming Round the Mountain.*

I was feeling good after several drinks. I drained my glass in anticipation of the the waitress returning with a refill when Mother leaned over to me and told me not to have any more. At first I was puzzled, for I was not displaying any sign of intoxication, but then Mother explained to me in whispered tones that Elly, Knud's wife, who was sitting directly opposite us, had a drinking problem. Off on one of her binges, she would go to a bar and pick up a strange man. Mother suggested that I set an example by not having any more to drink. So I waived off the waitress who was just about to refill my glass.

"*Jeg tage min maal, og saa ikke mere* (I take my measure, and then no more)," I said, pointedly addressing my remark to Elly.

This was the first and only inkling I had that there might be trouble in paradise. Whenever Mother and I visited Knud and Elly, Elly was the perfect hostess, eager to please her guests and always serving a delicious meal. She impressed me as a sensible and conscientious person, working the night shift in a local hospital. Perhaps in giving me the heads-up, Mother was more concerned that *I* not make a fool of myself, considering my unfortunate experience with the horse earlier in the day. As things turned out, neither I nor Elly had another drop to drink.

Looking back on that evening, I suspect that by encouraging me to set an example for Elly, and not simply telling me not to have any more to drink, Mother was avoiding the appearance of being a nag or a wet blanket. I would have balked at any suggestion that I had had too much to drink, and would likely have told the waitress to go ahead and fill my glass. And here *I* was the one with a degree in psychology.

Anna Lise was pleased to report the following day that no one had gotten sick in spite of the freely flowing wine. The anniversary dinner had been a complete success.

There are certain events that remain permanently etched in your mind. You recall where you were when you heard the news, what you were doing: the Kennedy assassination, the explosion of the Challenger spacecraft, the destruction of the World Trade Center. I will never forget when I heard the news of the shooting of Pope John Paul II. My mother and I were sitting in the living room in Resenbro, perusing the *Midt Jyllands Avis*, with Morfar's empty leather chair between us. Mormor was out in the kitchen, listening to the radio as she began to get things ready for supper. I can still picture Mormor suddenly looking into the living room and saying "*Nogen har skudt Paven* (Someone shot the Pope)." Mother and I dropped our newspapers and went out into the kitchen to listen to the radio. The reports came in dribs and drabs. Riding in his Popemobile in St. Peter's Square, the Pope had been shot five times. Though gravely wounded, he was expected to survive. A Turk, a Muslim, had been arrested at the scene of the attempted assassination. Mormor asked how someone could have shot a good man like the Pope. Mother suggested that the man must have been insane. But none of us could have anticipated that the twisted mind that was behind this act was not a lone gunman acting on his own. It turned out to be not an isolated incident committed by a madman, but a harbinger of things to come.

Religion, Morfar used to say, had been the cause of more wars than anything else.

But there was still one final road trip to make. Starting out from Silkeborg, Verner and Anna Lise set off with Mormor, Mother, and me on an excursion that would take us to Copenhagen. We did no sightseeing on this trip, driving straight across the islands of Funen and Langeland, stopping only when we reached the island of Falster. In Nykøbing, we visited my mother's cousin, Ragnhild, who, having worked as a hairdresser, gave me a much-needed haircut. We took a brief walking tour of the town, my mother and Mormor enjoying revisiting some of their familiar haunts. Continuing northward by car, we would not stop off this time to see the chalk cliffs of Møns Klint, but pressed on to Zealand. We visited Mormor's brother Sven in Helsingør, then headed back to Copenhagen to stay with Mormor's sister Anna Mørk, who lived near Kastrup Airport. Anna had grown frail since the last time we saw her. She now walked with the aid of a sturdy arm cane. She remained in good spirits, but recounted to us how, a few months previously, she had passed out on the kitchen floor. When she awoke and realized that she was still alive, she got up and put into the oven the tray of *boller* (biscuits) that she had been working on before she fainted.

No trip to Copenhagen could be considered to be complete without a visit to Tivoli. Mormor had not been there since she had liven in Paarup, on the island of Falster. Mormor particularly enjoyed her stroll through the flower gardens, which were in full bloom toward the end of May. With our appetites whetted after our morning walk, we stopped by a pushcart and bought three pølser (hot dogs). Settling ourselves at a nearby picnic table, we sank our teeth into our sausages, a longer, skinnier, and spicier version than their American counterpart.

That afternoon we returned to Anna's row house. She had baked some biscuits while we were out, and they were still warm. Her biscuits were just as good as Mormor's, which was no surprise as both sisters had learned their baking skills from their mother.

We spent the night in Anna's small flat. Mother and I made ourselves comfortable on couches in the living room, while Mormor and her sister slept in the bedroom. Mother and I could hear a murmur of voices from the next room as the sisters reminisced until perhaps one o'clock in the morning. It would be the last time that Ella and Anna would have a face-to-face talk. Anna passed away the year after our visit.

Things were winding down for Mormor. The house at 25 Resenbro was obviously too much for her to cope with. Furthermore, she was fearful of returning to an empty house at night, even when Knud brought her home. She would close all the blinds, and sometimes leave the lights off so no one would know that there was someone in the house. Her goal was now to sell the house and move into an apartment in Silkeborg, where she would be surrounded by other people. But it would be a wrenching move. All of her furniture and possessions accumulated over a lifetime would not fit into a small apartment. Much of it would have to be discarded or given away.

One day a neighbor dropped by to see how Mormor was doing. When Mormor introduced me to her, the neighbor glanced aside at me and asked Mormor if I spoke Danish.

"*Han taler bedre Dansk end du gøre* (He speaks better Danish than you do)," Mormor answered.

More than a little embarrassed, I laughed off this gross exaggeration, which greatly impressed Mormor's neighbor, as I could speak Danish with no appreciable American accent. She went on to ask me if I could not stay on in Denmark and help my grandmother with her house. (Mormor had told her how I had made necessary repairs and tamed the overgrown backyard.) I explained that I had to go back to Pennsylvania to take care of our own house. My parents would soon be going down to Houston, where my father had a new job, and it would be up to me to hold the fort until they returned. I did not realize it at the time, but this trip to Denmark would be the last time I would see Mormor. I was in a bind. I could have stayed on in Denmark for a few months, but I was needed back home. I had no choice.

Mother returned to Denmark that fall to help Mormor prepare for her move into an assisted-living facility in Silkeborg. The apartment she finally settled on was quite small, requiring her to part with more of her things than she had originally planned on. But she was content with the arrangement. Much of the furniture would go with the house. Sweetening the deal was the fact that the purchaser was a neighbor. His name, coincidentally, was Lars. Mormor and Morfar had known him since he was a boy and had watched him grow up into manhood. So there would still be a Lars living at 25 Resenbro.

# THE CAREGIVER

My father's uncle George was diagnosed with lung cancer in 1980. He had been a heavy smoker for most of his life, stopping only after a violent coughing episode. His doctor had suggested privately to us that George had had perhaps two months left to live, but well into the next year he remained surprisingly hale and hearty. His wife, Grace, and his brother-in-law, Walter, had died over the past two years—both, suddenly, of heart attacks. (The Peterson family was prone to sudden deaths from heart attacks.) Now George was awaiting his turn with the Grim Reaper. But his death would be a lingering one. Ever since his wife and brother-in-law had died, we had been driving George down to the Jersey Shore (usually to Evelyn's or Barr's) every Saturday for a fish dinner, and continued to do so. His favorite appetizer was clams on the half shell, which he would simply swallow, without chewing. (Ugh.) This would be followed by a main meal of crab legs, oysters, or fried lobster tails, accompanied by George's favorite drink, a black Russian. At home, he medicated himself with Southern Comfort, going through a bottle or two a week. By the summer of 1981, George's strength at last began to fail, and the Saturday dinners came to an end. He was admitted to the hospital for radiation treatment, which did nothing to reverse the course of the disease. He was bedridden after a brief stay in the hospital. My father and I brought him a commode, but it would fall to my mother to take care of him in his final weeks.

In those days, there was no home healthcare service. You either stayed in the hospital to die, or you went home to be cared for by a relative. My mother, having been trained as a nurse, served admirably in the role of caregiver. Within a matter of days, George had become too weak to get out of his bed to use the commode, so Mother had to change his adult diapers several times a day.

As Father was working in Gulf Oil's Chicago office at the time, I would drive into New Jersey a couple times a week to help out, staying with George while Mother did the shopping. The smell of a feces-filled adult diaper made me gag, but it did not seem to affect my mother. By now, George was sleeping most of the time, eating little except for an occasional spoonful of yogurt. The doctor prescribed Atavan for anxiety. After one or two tablets, George closed his eyes and died.

# MOVING ON

I need to go back in time for a while to tie up some loose ends. In 1971, as soon as I was finished with my studies at Temple University, Father could hardly wait to put our house on Winthrop Road up for sale. He had long aspired to live in the exclusive community of Chatham, so that is where we would now move. Though most of the houses in Chatham were out of our price range, we found a fifty-year-old, one-story house that had a large, unfinished attic—ideal for expansion. It was truly a rare find. In half a century none of the previous owners had thought to put down so much as a floorboard in the attic with its high, peaked ceiling. Someone had installed a powerful fan at the top of the stairs to vent hot air from downstairs into the attic, effectively blocking access, even for storage purposes. Unbelievable. We immediately pulled out the fan and arranged to have air conditioning installed. No problem with headroom in this attic. If you could only use your imagination, it was an impressive space. Father quickly saw the possibility of creating two large rooms, storage closets, and a full bathroom in the long-neglected attic. We had barely started in on the ambitious project, however, when Father left Gibbs & Cox and started working for Gulf Oil. Assigned the task of creating an innovative computer program to monitor the performance of the large fleet of Gulf Oil tankers, he would assemble reports from the various ships' captains regarding such factors as the speed of the vessels coming and going (fully laden and empty), the velocity of the winds working with or against them, their turnover time in port—all of these observations and many more were to be incorporated into the program. As part of his duties, Father was sent to the Oxnard Shipyard in Los Angeles, California. His task was to inspect the hulls of the tankers in the dry dock, to document with photographs how well the paint was holding up, whether or not the hulls were encrusted with speed-reducing barnacles. As insignificant as such factors might seem to the uninitiated, if not corrected, they could easily add millions of dollars to the yearly cost of operating a single tanker—by no means a trivial matter for a fleet comprised of several hundred tankers. Incidentally, during Father's stay at the Oxnard shipyard, Los Angeles was stricken by a magnitude-six earthquake. It came during the night. Father described hanging onto the bed in his hotel room for dear life, the chandelier swinging wildly over his head. The quake passed quickly, but there were aftershocks for the next few days, one of which Father felt deep in the hull of one of the tankers he was inspecting.

With my father away, inspecting Gulf tankers in dry docks along the West Coast, it fell upon me to complete the work in the attic, which took several months. Though I had not been an active participant in the construction of our house on Huyler Road, I had been a keen observer of my parents' efforts, and had learned many of the construction techniques that now served me well. (And of course, Mother, was always there to offer her suggestions when the task at hand eluded me.) After nailing down four-by-eight-foot sheets of plywood over the bare joists, I put up Sheetrock on the walls and ceilings, I tiled the bathroom floor and the shower stall,

I installed carpeting on the floors. The attic was largely finished when Father returned from his West Coast inspection tour.

Unfortunately, we did not have much time left to enjoy the improvements to our home. Mother's cousin, Olga, daughter of Lars Buus' brother, Alfred, stayed in the upstairs bedroom for several nights. She had come to visit her younger sister Inger who had emigrated to America to pursue a career in nursing, only to marry Ancho Gangwar, an émigré from India who was employed as a mining engineer. Olga had her doubts about this marriage. "*En Indianer*," she said incredulously. But the marriage worked out just fine, as had my mother's and father's marriage.

In 1973, a major reorganization at Gulf Oil made it necessary for my father to relocate to an office in Philadelphia. It was not the most opportune time to make a move, for housing prices were in somewhat of a slump. Nevertheless, with all the improvements we had put into the house, its sale turned a tidy profit. A new housing development had just been started on Tower Hill Road in Chalfont, Pennsylvania. It was within an easy commute by car to Father's new office in Balla Cynwyd. We selected a house, and that was that.

My father continued to refine his computer program, which had now expanded to include every ship in the Gulf Oil tanker fleet. At the same time, he was still making an occasional visit to the West Coast to conduct a ship inspection. In 1980 he flew to Palermo, Sicily, where he documented the buildup of those troublesome barnacles on the hulls of several ships, which significantly impacted the ships' speed. A special paint that would discourage the barnacles from attaching seemed an obvious remedy, but the paint was expensive, and repainting a tanker was not a simple matter. The entire hull would have to be stripped down to bare metal to avoid a buildup of paint, which would have increased the weight of the ship and reduced its speed. My father enjoyed his work. He enjoyed challenges. His computer program and his ship inspections were already saving Gulf Oil millions of dollars. As a result of his observations of the buildup of barnacles on tanker hulls, Gulf switched to the more-expensive brand of paint.

Our move to Chalfont was not to be our last. In 1981 my father was reassigned to Gulf's Houston office. He looked forward to his transfer, saying of Houston in a takeoff of Sinatra's *New York, New York*, "If you can't make it there, you won't make it anywhere." It was uncertain how long Father's job in Houston would last, so the best course of action was for me to hold into the house in Chalfont.

My parents drove down to Houston in a Buick Skylark, leaving me in charge of our house. I had the use of the Buick Regal, which gave me the better part of the deal. In hot and humid Houston, Mother spent most of her time indoors. Unable to find any crochet hooks in the stores (inexplicably, though the stores carried plenty of yarn, they did not carry the necessary implements to do anything with that yarn), Mother asked me to mail down her crochet hooks, which she used to make two large throws to pass the time. A bit too warm for the Houston climate, the throws turned out to be nice and cozy when laid over the back of a chair in Chalfont. Once, while Father was at work, Mother walked to a nearby grocery store, only to be alerted by a woman she met while selecting her purchases that she had passed through a high-crime area (right past Houston's Chinatown) to reach the store. Had she not heard? Only a week before, a woman had been assaulted in a nearby parking lot. This was not a good area in which to take a casual stroll. Everyone in Houston traveled by car—not just because of the heat but for reasons of safety.

I flew down to Houston to visit my parents for Christmas. We drove west on Route 10 during a morning of dense fog. You could barely make out the road signs. "Drive Friendly," was a frequent admonition. There were some unusual names along the way—Hollow Woman Road sticks out in my mind. We pulled into a rest stop for something to eat and wait for the fog to lift. As we waited for the waitress to bring us our orders, a man with a long white beard seated at a table across the aisle raised his right hand and pointed skyward. Mother comprehended his meaning from an expression that was popular in Texas at the time: "The way out is the way up."

The fog was rapidly lifting as we continued onward into San Antonio to see the battle-scared Alamo where Davy Crocket, Colonel Travis, Jim Bowie, and sixty others had sacrificed their lives in the battle for Texas' independence. We booked a room at the Menger Hotel. That evening Father and I visited the hotel bar. (Mother, never much of a drinker, stayed in our room watching TV and missed out on an interesting piece of history.) It turned out that the bar at which we were seated was where Teddy Roosevelt and his Rough Riders had hatched out their plans for an attack on Spanish-occupied Cuba. As we sipped our drinks, the bartender pointed out a deep gouge in the surface of the bar, made, he said, by one of the Rough Rider's knives. ("Remember the Maine," had been the troop-rallying buzzword after the U.S. Battleship Maine was sabotaged and sunk as it lay in its berth in Havana Harbor in 1901.)

Not far from the historic Menger Hotel was the River Walk, lined with numerous shops and restaurants, all of which were crowded with tourists. We stopped in a restaurant that specialized in pancakes—any kind of pancake that you could conceive, they had it. For dessert we had pancakes with an ice-cream filling. How they managed to keep the ice cream cold and the pancake warm is beyond me. One night we took a boat excursion down the length of the river. Lights had been placed all along the route on the edges of the sidewalks for the *Fiesta de las Luminarias*. The lights were nothing more than single candles set in sand-ballasted paper bags, but at night they lent a magical quality to the waterway. Out of curiosity, we mounted one of the few stairways that led from the touristy River Walk to the streets above. We quickly went back the way we had come. Paper trash littered the sidewalks. The buildings were dreary and run-down. Everyone was speaking Spanish. It was a different world from the River Walk a mere flight of steps down below.

On Christmas day, we visited the Houston Zoo. As one might expect, the zoo was not crowded on this, the holiest of Christian holidays. But it turned out to be a strange experience. My parents and I were the only "whites" enjoying the zoo. Most of the other visitors were Vietnamese, with perhaps a few Japanese scattered in. We did not hear a single word of English spoken. We might as well have been touring a zoo in some foreign country. Texas was truly a melting pot.

Out next trip was to the Johnson Space Center. A televised launch of a Saturn 4 rocket bound for the moon was an impressive sight, but to walk the length of a disassembled Saturn 4 with all of its various sections laid out end-to-end on the ground (as tall as the Statue of Liberty) boggled the mind. It took us nearly five minutes to pass from the huge booster to the small capsule mounted on the top of the massive rocket. (Admittedly, we walked slowly—this was not something you wanted to hurry through.) The display in the command center of a mockup of the lunar lander also gave us pause. Upon a closeup inspection, it was unbelievably tiny and flimsy looking, especially when you compared it with the earlier Apollo vessels with their thick, sturdy walls. The lunar lander looked like something a crackpot inventor had hammered together out of sheet metal in his garage. Mother could not comprehend how two astronauts could have survived in this tiny capsule on the airless moon, much less lift off and return to the relative safety of the command module.

A few days after Christmas, I flew back to Philadelphia. Mother remained in Houston until the following summer. One hot, steamy morning she went downstairs to get the morning paper from the vending machine. After depositing her quarter, she had to shake off the fire ants that were swarming all over the paper. Overnight, they had made a nest in the machine. Unsafe streets, heat and humidity, and now fire ants. That capped it. Mother returned to Chalfont in 1982. Father remained in Houston until the following year when his work there was completed. All throughout his stay in Houston he would play golf nearly every weekend, even on the hottest, stickiest day. After nearly freezing his butt off as he drove a tank across France in 1944, the hot, humid Houston summers did not faze him one bit.

# THE ROAD TRIP

By 1983 my father's work in Houston was completed. The computer program that he had designed to keep track of the Gulf Oil fleet was running smoothly. I flew down to Houston to help Father pack in preparation for his return to Pennsylvania. He sold the Buick Skylark and bought a large, white Dodge van, roomy enough to hold most of the furniture from the Houston apartment. Before leaving Houston, however, there was one additional site that Father wanted to see: San Jacinto, where Sam Houston had defeated Santa Anna in 1836, snatching Texas from Mexican rule. At 567 feet tall the little-known San Jacinto Monument is taller than the Washington Monument. But Father's interest in San Jacinto was more nautical than historical. Moored in the harbor at San Jacinto was the battleship Texas, which had seen action in both World War I and World War II. My father could not resist giving the ship an impromptu inspection, from the captain's wheelhouse (where he took hold of the wheel), the captain's cabin, and everything in between to the engine room. The next day we began packing. After loading the van from floor to ceiling with furniture (we had to leave behind two bedroom end tables), we set off on a thousand-mile road trip back to Pennsylvania. We took turns driving. For me, sitting high above the other cars and steering a heavily loaded van, it was a novel experience. But for Father, who had driven an M4 tank in the war, it was nothing out of the ordinary. I soon learned to speed up as we came to the base of a hill, lest the heavily laden van lose momentum before we reached the crest. The brakes had to be applied even before the traffic ahead began to slow down. We stopped at a succession of motels along the way home, parking the van as close as possible to our room so we could keep watch over it. Our first stop was in New Orleans, Louisiana. Walking downhill from our motel toward the Mississippi River, we quickly perceived that New Orleans was a disaster waiting to happen. The downtown business area resembled a shallow bowl. A fifteen-foot tall levee was all that separated the bottom of this shallow bowl from the mighty Mississippi. And to the north was Lake Ponchartrain, whose waters were also contained by by a questionable line of dikes. We learned later that New Orleans had pumps operating day and night to keep the seawater out. Not the best place to locate a city. (In fact, local indians who saw the original French settlers building houses in an area prone to periodic flooding laughed at their folly.) There were musicians on nearly every corner, often having to compete with a passing brass band, or the rumble of a streetcar. During the day, residential houses had an aura of domesticity, with hanging plants swaying gently in the breeze on wrought-iron balconies. Louvered wooden shutters covered the windows on the upper floors to let in the evening breeze, however, hinting a darker reality, the shutters on the lower floors had no louvers, presenting an impregnable façade. Horse-drawn carriages conveyed tourist around Jackson Square. We paused to listen to a black jazz musician playing a saxophone, dropping our spare change into the hat he had placed in the sidewalk. I imagine that he pulled in a fair amount of cash in the course of a day, considering the number of tourists passing by to listen to his music and snap his picture. (And his take, of course, was all tax-free.) In front of the nearby St. Louis Cathedral (somewhat incongruously) was a two-man Confederate submarine. It couldn't have been much more than fifteen-feet long, with a single torpedo tube mounted in the front. The men would have had to sit crouched over, as the compact cylinder was scarcely more than four feet high. It's doubtful that they survived their mission. We had our dinner, an authentic Southern dish of shrimp gumbo at the Two Sisters' Restaurant. I had my first piña colada. That night, with our shirts sticking to our backs from the hot, humid air, we strolled along honky-tonk Bourbon Street, lined with shops featuring tacky souvenirs and with music bursting out of a succession of bawdy clubs. Tourists, some of them looking slightly sloshed, milled about aimlessly—easy marks for pickpockets. Loud-voiced barkers sought to entice the passers-by to enter nightclubs featuring "Girls, girls, girls. No cover charge." The dives bore such suggestive names as "The Palace of Pleasure," "Topless and Bottomless," "Le Paree Orgy," and "The Absinthe House."

But we had to move on, traveling as we were in a van loaded from the floor to the roof with furniture, a tempting target for some opportunistic thief—providing that he could pull the tightly packed items out of the van. At each of our motel stops we would phone Mother and tell her where we were so she could follow our progress on a map. Our subsequent stops passed more quickly. I can recall nothing of Mississippi or Alabama, except when we stopped after sunset to stretch our legs on a hill just across Mobile bay and saw the lights of Mobile back in the distance. We stopped overnight at Pensacola, Florida and found time the following morning to stroll along the hot, white sandy beach on Santa Rosa Island to pick up a few sea shells. Along the way, a road sign identifying the Swanee River bore a couple of musical notes in honor of Stephen Forster's famous song. We stopped overnight at Jacksonville. The next day we made a quick stop at Fernandina Beach and continued on to spend the night in Savannah, Georgia, where on a walking tour we temporarily lost our way amid a succession of small, lookalike parks. A cemetery with trees festooned with Spanish moss had numerous graves all bearing the date 1853. The cause of death noted on many of the headstones was a terrible epidemic of yellow fever. A guide book told us that ten percent of the population had succumbed to the fever in that fateful year. New Orleans had suffered a similar attrition. (The indians had been right: this was a bad place to make a city. Build on high ground; avoid the swamps.) Father and I had originally planned to stop at Charlestown, take in Fort Sumter, and continue on up the coast. But the prospect of parking the van overnight at a succession of small motels seemed to be tempting fate. We both agreed that getting back to Pennsylvania in the shortest possible time overrode seeing the sights along the way. After leaving Savannah, we headed inland through South Carolina, cutting several days off our planned journey.

On our drive up from Houston we always paid attention to our surroundings, looking out for anyone who might be showing an interest in our packed van. One day in South Carolina we stopped at a convenience store to pick up a six-pack of beer, a can of Ravioli for supper, and some fixings for sandwiches. Next to us at the beer cooler were three or four young men, whooping and hollering and saying little that we could understand. We took them for Southern hillbillies. Their clothes were ragged: torn bluejeans, tattoos, and shirts with filthy stains. One of them had stuck an eagle's feather in his hatband. Had they taken note of our van? Were they looking us over to see if we would be easy marks on a lonely stretch of the road up ahead? We hurried out of the store with our purchases and started the van. Just as we were pulling out of the parking space the young men exited the store, each one carrying a six-pack. There was more whooping and hollering. They piled into a battered old car with a New Jersey license plate. So much for appearances.

Next stop, Richmond, Virginia. After consuming our sandwiches in the van, we took an hour-long walk around the Richmond State House, whose iconic, colonnaded facade, sitting on the top of a steep hill, has been featured in a couple of movies. In fact, on the day that we were there, a movie crew was onsite. But as the actors and crew were taking their lunch break, we did not get to see any of the filming. My father, with his usual enterprising spirit, no doubt acquired in his army days, suggested that we might follow the crew inside the State House building and pick up a couple of box lunches. But then, we had already had our sandwiches, so what would be the point?

Bypassing Washington, D.C., we headed straight for Pennsylvania, arriving home just after sunset. Neither of us had any regrets that we had not done more sightseeing along the way. It was a relief to finally park the van in our own garage and not have to worry about who might be watching our comings and goings.

# BULL MARKET

Neither I nor my mother had been trading stocks for a number of years, preferring to invest in the high-yielding CDs that were available during the seventies. (Imagine ten, even fourteen percent!) But by 1983 it became apparent that the stock market had finally bottomed and was now on its way back up. Bluechip stocks were offering dividends yielding as much as eight percent. So you could sit back, collect your dividend and wait for a capital appreciation in a year of perhaps ten or twenty percent. I opened an account at Merrill Lynch in Doylestown and began trading stocks again. It was like old times. Practically anything you bought went up. One financial commentator called this period in the eighties the Golden Age of stock market investing. By now, Mother had returned home from Houston. She was impressed by how well I was doing in the stock market, and opened her own account at Merrill Lynch. The chart of Xerox looked very promising. It was rising and falling in a predictable pattern, offering at least a twenty-percent return from the bottom to the top of its range—not to mention a seventy-five dollar quarterly dividend on your hundred shares. So in 1984 Mother and I both invested in shares of Xerox when the stock was near its low. The shares rose steadily, and we sold them for a hefty profit in 1985.

Having left Houston in 1983, Father was perhaps a little bit jealous at the trading partnership that Mother and I established. Previously, she had depended on him to pay for the cost of her trips to Denmark. But now, with the profits she had made in the stock market, she was independent, and would be able to afford to pay for subsequent trips out of her own pocket. Although it was Father who had introduced Mother and me to the New York Stock Exchange in the early sixties, he never trusted the stock market. He was not the gambler that I was. Mother was also a gambler; perhaps she was even a bigger risk-taker that I was. After all, she had decided at the age of twenty-four, after a week's acquaintance with an American GI, to pack her possessions into a wicker basket, say good-bye to her family and friends, and seek her fortune in America. That was a true gamble if ever there was one. I could have never have done such a thing. Stocks might have their ups and downs, but betting on people was another matter. As it turned out, Mother's gamble paid off, and so did her bet on Xerox. We were kindred spirits. We were a team. And I know it hurt my father that he was not cut out to be a member of this team.

Father had acquired a substantial number of shares in Gulf Oil over the years. But the stock price had languished due to a prolonged downturn in the oil industry. In 1984, with its shares undervalued, Gulf Oil was enmeshed in a hostile takeover offer. A bidding war developed between Mesa Petroleum (headed by Boone Pickens), and Standard Oil of California. Gulf's stock price ran up. My father became nervous about his shares. Fearing that the deal would fall through and the price would tumble back to its earlier depressed level, he decided to accept the first tender offer that came along. I advised him to hold on to his shares. But Father wanted out.

I could see from the concerned expression on his face that this was not a bet he wanted to let ride. Despite my proven track record in the stock market, Father rejected my advice. Nor did he follow my subsequent suggestion and sell just half of his shares. And Mother, though enjoying her profits in Xerox, chose not to back me up, leaving the decision entirely up to my father. Indeed, how would it have appeared if she had sided with me against her husband? Xerox was one thing, But Gulf Oil was personal. As things turned out, SOCAL's higher bid was successful, and Father, by selling out early, left over twenty dollars a share on the table. As the Kenny Rogers song says, "You've got to know when to hold 'em, know when to fold 'em."

It surprised me that my mother, who had grown up in a socialist country, enjoyed its benefits (until she left in 1946), and seen her parents receive "free" hospitalization and nursing home care, didn't put up much of an argument when I pointed out to her the superiority of capitalism. I can only attribute this to her independent spirit, which obviously must have rubbed off on me.

# DENMARK REDUX

I don't know if it was simply because she was needed back in Denmark, or because she could now afford to make as many trips home as she pleased without having to ask her husband for the price of a plane ticket. In any event, over the next six years, Mother made at least one trip every year to visit her mother. I would not accompany her on any of these trips, not because I didn't want to, but because now, with the house at 25 Resenbro having been sold, there was simply no longer a convenient place for two people to stay. Had Mormor continued to live in her old home, it might well have been a different story. After my parents' move up from Houston, I would have gladly spent a month or so every year doing whatever was necessary to maintain Mormor's house and property in Resenbro. Two people staying at a hotel for an entire month, however, would have been an extravagant expense—and to repeat this indulgence for six years in a row was out of the question. Mother made trips by herself to Denmark in 1981, 1983, 1984, and 1985. In 1986 she visited her mother in the hospital. Her first visit in 1987 was a bittersweet one. Experiencing increasing difficulty in getting around, Mormor had been transferred from her assisted-living facility in Silkeborg to Rødegaard in Resenbro, where Lars had spent his final years. In May, Mother sent a postcard describing a pleasant five days she and her mother had spent with Anna Lise in Løgstør. She wrote, however, that Mormor was glad when she returned to Rødegaard, where she could get around better and had nurses to assist her. In July, Mormor took a bad fall, resulting in a broken hip. Elly was taking her mother-in-law for a walk at the time and blamed herself for the fall. But Knud said after the incident that, given his mother's advanced osteoporosis, it was uncertain whether her hip had fractured before or after the fall. Mother returned to Denmark in the summer of 1987, visiting Mormor two weeks before she died of pneumonia.

"*Er jeg døde nu?* (Am I dead yet)?" Mormor asked, opening her eyes for the last time.

# THE GOLDEN YEARS

My father was restless after he retired from Gulf Oil in 1986. He continued to put a suit on every morning (though not a tie), and would pore through the want ads in the Sunday *New York Times*. Finally, through one of his contacts, he learned of a job opening. He made an appointment for an interview at the World Trade Center with one of his former bosses from Gibbs & Cox, who had started up a small design firm of his own. I accompanied him on his job interview. My father had undergone a recent operation to remove a cataract at Wills Eye Hospital in Philadelphia, and had a lens implant in his right eye. He was supposed to take eye drops every several hours. I had assumed that I would be administering the drops, but as we sat in the concourse of the World Trade Center to grab a bite to eat before Father's appointment, he tilted his head back and gave himself the drops.

The job was his. Unfortunately, the small firm that his former boss had started, competing as it was with much larger players in the shipbuilding industry, could not afford to pay a high salary. Getting home that day, Father made some calculations and concluded that it would not pay him to go back to work. His pensions from Gibbs & Cox and Gulf Oil, combined with his Social Security, paid slightly more his new job was offering. But if he went back to work, he would no longer be entitled to receive Social Security. Figure in the expense of a daily commute to New York City, and he would have ended up working for nothing, perhaps even losing money in the deal. He regretfully turned down the job offer.

At loose ends, my father looked for something to occupy his time. Playing golf at the Twin Woods Golf Course every day soon became a drag (at least for me). A ride in a hot-air balloon was a onetime adventure. Gambling junkets to Atlantic City lost their novelty once we had visited every one of the casinos. And you could go to Peddler's Village in nearby Lahaska only so many times before downing a yard of ale in the Cock 'n Bull Restaurant became old hat. Father, Mother, and I went to the Montgomery Mall, where artist Bill Alexander, who did a weekly series on public television, was giving a demonstration of his painting technique. The next day, borrowing Mother's paints and brushes, Father set up a canvas. But the flower he attempted to create did not look much like a flower, and threatened to spiral out of the canvas. So painting was out. Father began attending local craft exhibitions to see if there was some other hobby that he could take up. He became fascinated by an exhibition of carved decoy ducks. It proved to be the perfect hobby, for Father had always liked something he could do with his hands. So carving it was. He became quite proficient at his new hobby. Duck decoys were traditionally made from two hollowed-out sections of wood, so they would ride high in the water. A penny would be inserted inside the duck before the sections were glued together, thus proving that the decoy was, indeed, hollow. The completed decoy would then be painted in the colors of the particular duck that one was attempting to render as lifelike as possible. Working in the garage, Father made a mallard drake (the male of the species was always the more colorful), a buffleheaded drake, a blue-wing teal drake, and a wood-duck drake. Branching out, he also carved stylized bulls, realistic-looking birds (a bluebird, a wood thrush), and several turtles.

Often during our afternoon snack on a Saturday afternoon, Father and I would turn on the TV to watch Roy Underhill on *The Woodwright's Shop*. Roy's revelations about the hidden structure inside a piece of wood held a particular fascination for my father, who needed to know how the grain would respond to the action of a chisel when he was roughing out his ducks. We would then view an episode of *This Old House* as Mother began preparations for our supper.

Father's retirement clearly left him unsatisfied. He began to float the idea that perhaps a change of address would make a difference. Wasn't retirement the perfect opportunity to move on to greener pastures? We had been living on Tower Hill Road now for thirteen years, longer than we had lived anywhere else. A change of scenery would be good for us all.

# A HOUSE IS JUST A PLACE
# TO HANG YOUR HAT

So it was time for yet another move. My father always said that he had aspired to live in two special places. The upscale community of Chatham, which he had already checked off his bucket list, was one of them, the other was the Jersey Shore. We scouted out a new housing development in Howell, New Jersey, which was close to Spring Lake, where Father had enjoyed spending a summer vacation or two in his youth. After this peremptory search we put our house in Pennsylvania up for sale. Mother and I had suggested that before making such a drastic move, we should rent a bungalow, as Father's parents had done many years ago, or stay in a motel for a week to see how we liked the area. But Father had made up his mind.

"A house is just a place to hang your hat," he remarked after the sale had been consummated.

The house in Howell was but a twenty-minute drive to Spring Lake. Unfortunately, no homes had yet been built in this new development. We didn't know what we were getting into. Father was disappointed from the start. As houses went up on the fifty-foot-wide lots, the property looked far smaller than it had when the area was open space. People quickly had six-foot-tall fences erected to give them a modicum of privacy, as did we. Father noted the resemblance of the tiny, fenced-in lots to so many pig pens. He was not a happy camper. Built on a slab, the house lacked a basement, so there was no room to store things. We had had to leave some of our furniture behind in our old house on Tower Hill Road. Howell was turning out to be a big disappointment, and Spring Lake fell far short of Father's fond childhood memories. The traffic was another thing that we had not bargained for. It could easily take twenty minutes to drive from our house to the nearby grocery store, most of that time spent waiting in a long line of cars for the traffic light to change so we could cross the always-congested Route Six. Then there was the golf course. Quail Ridge Golf World was crowded, even if we arrived early in the morning when there was still dew on the grass. It was an eighteen-hole short course. There would often be a foursome coming up behind you, so you would either have to speed up your game or stand aside and let the faster golfers play through. And if you hit your ball into the rough you would just have to leave it there, unless you wanted to wade into the chest-high briars mercilessly attacking you with their sharp thorns. The last straw was when I discovered a deer tick crawling up my shoulder after we had spent the day playing eighteen holes of golf. Lime disease, spread by deer ticks was rampant in the area. We had been living in Howell for only two years when my father began itching to make another move.

In 1989 we decided to sell our house in Howell and moved back to Chalfont, Pennsylvania. The building lot we found in a development on Castlewood Drive was only a mile from our previous home on Tower Hill Road. Mother bore all these moves without a single word of complaint. I suspect that having made the initial move from her native Denmark, she clearly must have had a bit of the wanderlust in her blood, just like the man she married. For many years we had vacationed in Cape May, New Jersey, where we would usually take a room at the Stockholm Motel. Making our way home in 1989, we stopped off at Atlantic City. After feeding perhaps ten dollars in quarters into the slot machines, we took a stroll along the boardwalk. Suddenly, a voice called out to my father. It turned out to be a former colleague of his from Gibbs & Cox, accompanied by his wife. The woman smiled and gave a look of recognition when her husband introduced her to Bob Peterson.

"Oh," she said, "you're the one who moves around a lot."

Over the years, Mother kept a list of the various places where she had lived since she arrived in the States. It would have taken much detective work on my part for me to have compiled a similar list. So, thank you, Mother, as you always did, for keeping track of things.

Jersey City, N.J. --------------------------------- 1946
Huyler Rd., Branchburg, N.J. --------------------- 1955
Huyler Rd., N.J. ---------------------- sold 5/31 - 1965
Winthrop Rd., New Brunswick ------------ 1965 sold 1971
Center Ave., Chatham, N.J. --------------- 1971 sold 1973
Tower Hill Rd., Chalfont, PA ---------- 1973 sold 6-25-1986
Starlight Dr., Howell, N.J. ------------------ 1986 - 1989
Castlewood Dr., Chalfont, PA ------------------- 1989 -

Mother did not include the year (1981-1982) that she had spent in Houston on her list, most likely because it was not an "official" move, with me continuing to reside in our house on Tower Hill Road. Likewise, she omitted the six months that we lived in an apartment in Piscataway, New Jersey in 1965. Like the Houston apartment, it was evidently not a place that Mother considered "home." Nevertheless, both of these moves constituted significant upheavals in her life. But again, I never heard her complain about this series of disruptions. Getting each new house in order entailed months of work: first, put up curtains and blinds, order new appliances, paint the walls or put up wood paneling, wallpaper the bathrooms, decide where to hang our paintings and pictures, install carpets or hardwood floors, make multiple trips to the local nursery for landscaping plants. As Father was at work during the week, much of the decorating fell to Mother and me. But she did not mind, dutifully recording our places of residence on her list—including our move from Howell, where we had lived for barely two-and-a half years. (When we moved, I still had an unopened box of stuff stowed away in my closet that I had not found the time to sort through.)

Mother made another list, a much longer one, recording the dates of all her trips to Denmark. Over the years she made a total of twenty-three trips, on ten of which I accompanied her. Had my mother not made such a detailed list, I would have been hard-pressed to puzzle out the exact chronology. I would have had to resort to visas in mother's old passports to document when she made her trips. The dates of our moves from one house to another would have been even more difficult. I would have had to check the addresses on any old magazines that I had happened to save. So in a way Mother assisted me in writing this memoir. Looking at her two lists, the one pertaining to our moves in the U.S., the other pertaining to Mother's trips to Denmark, it is apparent to me that they are a record of two separate but parallel lives. Did Mother ever wonder about this curious dichotomy? If she did, I don't believe that we ever spoke of it. But as for myself, it was the oddest experience that when I was in Denmark, my life back in the States seemed no more substantial to me than a half-forgotten dream. And what of my parallel life in Denmark? Frequent letters from Mormor, Anna Lise, and Knud kept Mother and me appraised of developments across the Atlantic. I remember once holding one of Mormor's aerogrammes up to my nose in the vain hope of detecting a familiar scent from the house in Resenbro. So which one of the two worlds was the real one? I regret never having brought this perplexing subject up with my mother. Sometimes, when she was in a particularly good mood, she would sing some Danish tune that she remembered from her childhood. When we were in Denmark, the two of us spoke mostly in Danish, but when we came back to the States, we spoke only English, except to say "*God Nat*," and "*Sov godt*." ("Good night," and "Sleep well".)

# IN THE BLINK OF AN EYE

Father and I would make the drive from our little house in Howell, New Jersey a couple times a week to see how the work was progressing on our new home back in Chalfont. We watched the house go up, beginning with the laying out of the batter boards and the excavation of the foundation. Father took considerable satisfaction from the fact that we owned the biggest house on the biggest lot in the development. We would take pictures with an instant camera to show to Mother when we got back to Howell.

We moved into our new home on a cold winter's day in 1990. Father and I had loaded up the same van that we had driven up from Houston. Father drove the van while Mother and I followed in the car. The moving men brought the bulk of our furniture. Father spent the next several months making everything shipshape. He built temporary storage shelves in the garage, and makeshift storage cabinets in the basement—which he intended to replace with permanent structures as soon as he got the time. We had been living on Castlewood Drive for nearly three months now, and were more or less settled in. By now, everything had been unpacked. Most of our things were organized.

Did my father get any enjoyment from his retirement? It's difficult to say. His carvings served to fill his time. But although we never spoke of the matter, I suspect that it was quite a come-down from designing ships to designing duck decoys. Curiously, before he died, he was working on another duck decoy, whose roughed-out form was barely half the size of his previous creations. Did he have a premonition that he was running out of time and needed to scale back on his aspirations? Or was he simply intending to making a baby duck?

Father had ambitious plans for a finished basement: the ceiling and walls would of course be covered with Sheetrock; partitions would be put up to divide the space into two or three large rooms. There would be a basement bar (our third one). On a plot plan that he had drawn up of the property, Father indicated in the backyard where we would plant two willows for shade. He drew twin circles representing the spread of their branches when the trees had grown to full size. That evening, we picked up some Chinese food (egg rolls, wonton soup, fried rice) to celebrate our successful move. Father also said that this was an early celebration of his upcoming birthday in April. Was this some kind of premonition? For his actual birthday, on April 12, we were planning on going to the Cock 'n Bull Restaurant in Peddler's Village. After supper, as we stood in the dining room gazing out at the sunset, Father admitted that we would have been better off if we had stayed where we were on Tower Hill Road, sparing ourselves two unnecessary moves. He apologized to Inge and said that this was to be our last move; we would be staying here in Chalfont. Our wandering days were over.

The morning of March 28 was uneventful. Now that we were settled into our new home, Father was looking forward to going over to Twin Woods and playing eighteen holes of golf. We had driven past the course a week or two earlier, but were too busy to stop. (And I would later come to regret that I had not suggested that we throw our golf bags into the trunk and play a few rounds.) This morning, my father and mother were planning on going to Home Depot to pick up a few odds and ends; if time allowed, they would stop off on the way home to surprise our former next-door neighbors on nearby Tower Hill Road.

Wanting to get an early start, they made ready to leave around eight-thirty that morning. Sitting at my desk to take care of some paperwork, I saw them go downstairs. The house grew quiet. I assumed that they had left. Then I heard a rapid series of footfalls coming from the kitchen. I heard my mother call out in an uncharacteristically alarmed voice.

"Bob, are you in there?"

Silence.

Something was terribly wrong. I rushed downstairs into the hall. I could see my father's blue sweater pressed up against the bottom of the bathroom door. I tried to open the door, but I could not as my father lay stretched out on the floor, his back pressed firmly against the door, which opened into the bathroom.

"Dad, can you hear me?"

Again, there was no response. What to do? While Mother called 911, I ran out into the garage and found a screwdriver, which I used to pry the hinges off the bathroom door. Setting the door aside, I could see that Father was beyond help. His face was ashen; his lips were blue. I removed his glasses. A policeman came a few minutes later. The rescue squad arrived with a stretcher. The morning that had begun with such ordinary prospects was now hurtling to its inevitable conclusion. The rescue workers dragged my father out into the hall and placed him in a body bag. They lifted him up onto a stretcher and brought him out to the ambulance. And then he was gone. Mother would spend the next twenty-seven years without the love of her life.

I suppose it was a consolation the my father died before he and my mother had time to drive off in the car; a double tragedy had possibly been averted by mere minutes. With the house now empty and eerily silent, Mother and I both had to lie down. My mouth was dry. I remember a loud hum in my ears, reminiscent of an old TV set that was on its last legs. I did not know what to do, but Mother did. She dialed our former neighbors, Chick and Phyllis Chickirda, whom she and Father would have visited that very morning if events had not taken such a tragic turn. She told Phyllis that she and I had moved back to Chalfont.

Obviously sensing that things were not as they should be, Phyllis asked, "Where's Bob?"

I don't know how Mother kept her composure as she explained what had happened on this nightmarish morning. Phyllis was a big help. She suggested a funeral home and a lawyer, who happen to live just around the block.

In accordance with Father's wishes, we had him cremated. We saw him off wearing the blue sweater that Mother had knitted for him. We scattered some of his ashes off a dock into the waters of nearby Lake Galena. The rest of the ashes we buried in the backyard. I laid a length of driftwood that Father and I had picked up a year before at the Jersey Shore over his resting place. It made a good platform on which to place a pot of flowers, which I have done every year for the past twenty-eight years. Very likely a piece of ship's timber, the wood has not rotted or decayed in any way, despite being in contact with the ground. It looks no different today than it did on the day we hauled it off from the beach at Spring Lake, after sawing it into two manageable pieces. Perhaps, imprisoned in that block of driftwood is Father's idea for a carving or two that he would never get the chance to make.

# THE GUN

Soon after Father died, Mother revealed to me that he had told her that he had carried a gun in a side holster under his jacket during our tour of New Orleans. I had known nothing about this, but it would not have been out of character for my father, with his army training, to have been prepared for any eventuality, such as scaring off a thug one might encounter in the streets of crime-ridden New Orleans at night. As it turned out, we were quite safe in New Orleans and throughout the duration of our trip home. But did Father only pack a gun in the Crescent City, or did he have it with him during the rest of our journey. I wonder.

My mother did not like the idea of keeping a firearm in the house. I hid Father's gun and the bullets in separate places, but this simple stratagem failed to mollify Mother's concerns. I asked around and learned that it was permitted in Pennsylvania to keep an unregistered firearm in your home. But Mother remained uneasy about the gun; someone might break in and steal it, no matter how well I had hidden it. And if it was used in the commission of a crime, it might be traced back to us. I knew from long experience that it was useless to argue with my mother once she had made up her mind. So we took the gun to the local police station in Chalfont and turned it in. No questions asked.

# THE HUNDRED-DOLLAR BILL

From now on there would be no more long treks, just short trips to the grocery store, to nearby Lake Galena, or to a doctor's appointment. After Father's death, Mother worried about me. She was concerned how I was going to get by financially. On a visit to her safe-deposit box, she slipped a hundred-dollar bill into my birth certificate, just in case I should find myself short of ready cash some day in the future. Back home she suggested, quite sensibly, that I find some work for at least a couple of quarters so I would be able to put money into an IRA. I was, as a matter of fact, unemployed, and, indeed, had never held a job. I told Mother not to worry about me. Though she was no longer playing the stock market, I had continued to do so all through the eighties and now into the nineties. I showed her how well my investments were doing. During the nineties, I was netting an average of 40,000 dollars a year in the stock market. It would not have paid me to get a nine-to-five job and abandon my daily stock trades (which I now conducted online). True, I didn't have an IRA, a 401 K, social security, or Medicare. But neither was I shelling out any of my money to pay for any of these restrictive government programs that were designed to mollify "the little people." Without burdensome withholding taxes and other deductions to pay, I could plow all my money back into the stock market. I had a system. Online, I could download the moving averages of any number of stocks. I had discovered that when the ten-day moving average dropped below the thirty-day moving average, it was time to sell. Conversely, when the ten-day moving average rose above the thirty-day moving average, it was time to buy. At the end of the year I would take tax losses on my losing trades, thus offsetting my capital gains. In 1999 I had 240,000 dollars in capital gains, but paid a mere 45 dollars in federal income taxes. Despite my incongruous tax return for that year and others, I have never been audited. I had learned to play by the rules that the politicians had written for themselves and their millionaire investor friends. Mother never worried again about my financial well-being.

Unfortunately, the moving averages broke down in 2000. Quality technology stocks like Texas Instruments and Qualcomm were trading down as much as thirty per cent in less than a week, with no end in sight. Things would only get worse with the terrorist bombing of the World Trade Center on 9/11. Mother and I sat glued to the TV set watching the collapse of the Twin Towers. It seemed like the end of the world. But you could have predicted that something like this would happen after the previous bombing of the Twin Towers in 1996 and the attempted assassination of Pope John Paul II in 1981. The twisted ideology of Islam was on the rampage. Morfar had been right about religion. And once again, religion had reared its ugly head.

Alarmed by the broad sell-off in the stock market, Mother wondered if she should sell her Exxon shares and put the money into something safer. In a way, we were still trading partners, and she respected my advice. I told her to hold on to Exxon, even when left-wing politicians began attacking the oil companies for their role in causing "global warming." Any action taken against these oil companies would have plunged the American economy into a depression. The shrill campaign against "Big Oil" was doomed to fail. Global warming (later rebranded as "climate change") was a hoax. Mother followed my advice and did not sell her shares. And holding on to her Exxon stock was the best thing my mother could have done. After paying capital gains taxes, even on the stepped-up basis to which she was entitled, she would have been hard-pressed to get a decent return on what remained of her stake. The share price of Exxon eventually recovered. Mother was pleased to continue to receive her substantial quarterly dividends, which, I had explained to her, were subject to a lower tax rate as a qualified dividend (just follow the rules as set down by our duplicitous leaders, who make these rules to benefit themselves, and you won't go wrong).

# GROWING APART

Mother made another trip to Denmark by herself in 1991, the year after the love of her life died. She spent most of her time with her sister and brother-in-law. Having sold Camping Skovly and the Esso station, Anna Lise and Verner now lived in a roomy, two-story house with a sizable backyard. They had also purchased a summer house, about an hour's drove away in southern Jutland. Far from being a place where they could sit back and relax in their retirement years, however, they now had to spend much of their time maintaining the grounds. A video that Verner made shows that there was always work to be done, from trimming the extensive hedges, to digging up weeds. They would not keep the summer house for long, and they soon traded in their large house in Tranum for a much smaller one.

Mother and I made one last trip together in 1995. It was a taxing journey for my mother. You had to arrive at Kennedy Airport a full two hours ahead of your flight to go through all of the security checks. (And this was well before September 11.) Unlike in the old days when it was called Idlewild Airport and you would find yourself waiting all by yourself beside a couple of convenience machines, the place was crowded with hundreds of foreign tourists. You were lucky if you could find a place to sit while you waited for your flight to be called.

Anna Lise and Verner were now settled in their new home, which had everything on a single floor as opposed to the two-story dwelling my mother had visited four years earlier. The property was also smaller and more manageable. There was a shed and a couple of established plum trees in the backyard. Anna Lise and Verner had planted a small garden with peas and radishes. They were tending some new plantings in the front yard. Verner was not in the best of health. He had difficulty walking long distances, and often grew short of breath.

Mother and I made only short trips on this visit. There would be no more castle tours, no views over Copenhagen from the Round Tower, no more excursions to Møns Klint. Strolling along the beach at Tranum Strand, we took shelter from the blustery north wind on the leeward side of a thick-walled German bunker. Visiting Knud, still living in Resenbro, we made our usual pilgrimage to Himmelbjerget, arriving by car and walking only a short distance to the tower at the top of the hill. We would make, however, one final visit to Tivoli on our last full day in Copenhagen. While people came and went, Tivoli never changed. The flower gardens. Tivoli Lake. The dragon boats. The fountains. The pantomime theater. The concert hall. A new crop of children riding in miniature antique cars.

Good-bye.

My Danish cousins had moved on with their lives. Erik and Else now had two children. Erik's black hair was showing a few streaks of gray. He had inherited Morfar's sword from his days in the cavalry, and his leather armchair. Poul was married now and had two children. Rita was married and had a daughter. Knud's daughter, Anni, was now a young woman, taller than my mother. I barely recognized her. Her formerly straight hair was now curled and coiffured. She was working as a hairdresser. She had not gone on any marathon marches since the one we had taken in 1977. She did not remember how she had once fired dandelions at me. Separated by a thousand miles of ocean, I would not see Anni or any other of my cousins again, except for a visit by Erik's daughter Anne-Sofie and her best friend, who spent a few days with us in Chalfont in 2010. They were more interested in riding the duck boats in Philadelphia than they were in spending time with Mother and me.

So it goes. As with most émigrés who set off for a life in a foreign country, the bonds between my mother and her once-numerous relatives were steadily dissolving. Knud died of dementia in October 2010. Soon, the only connection with the homeland would be between my mother and her sister, Anna Lise. The occasional letter, a telephone conversation.

# HEALTH CONCERNS

On a visit to nearby Lake Galena, where we had scattered some of Father's ashes the previous year, Mother began to feel faint. Her heart was racing, pounding. Though it was not cold this morning, she was shivering, and her teeth were chattering. I had to help her back to the car. She wondered if she was having a heart attack. I drove her to her doctor. Doctor Lieberman assured her that she was not having a heart attack. Her symptoms were due to a low level of thyroxine—hypothyroidism. He prescribed a simple remedy, Synthroid, which she would be taking for the rest of her life.

Though she underwent a serious health-crisis or two, Mother enjoyed generally good health for the next twenty-five years. During a routine examination in 1993, Dr. Lieberman detected a microscopic amount of blood in my mother's urine. An X-ray showed conclusively that it was kidney cancer. The tumor, about two centimeters in diameter, was already beginning to deform the internal structure of the kidney. Referred to a specialist within a week, Mother had her left kidney removed. She was cured. Had her doctor not detected those few red-blood cells, the outcome might well have been different. Kidney cancer has a tendency to spread rapidly, and once it has spread, it cannot be cured with surgery or radiation.

The next crisis came on very suddenly. It was in 1995, about a month after our last trip to Denmark. Mother was reading the newspaper one morning when she realized that she could not make out the print with her right eye. She said that It was as if she was peering through a dark curtain. She was seeing zig-zag flashes of light. These flashes turned out to be a classic symptom of a detached retina. Her ophthalmologist referred her to specialist, who operated on her eye the next day. The operation was successful. Unfortunately, within a couple of days Mother was again seeing flashes of light in her eye. This turned out to be her retina tearing for a second time. A subsequent operation repaired the damage, but Mother was now legally blind in her right eye. She could just make out the large "E" on the eye chart. With poor vision in her one good eye, Mother's driving days were over. She would henceforth depend on me to take her where she wanted to go.

Once, on our way home from a morning visit to the Cherry Hill Shopping Mall in New Jersey, Mother had said to Father as he started up the car, "Home, James." The offhanded comment annoyed my father, who was sensitive about being retired, but some years later, as I drove Mother to and from her doctors' appointments and the grocery store, I did not mind playing the role of chauffeur. After all, she had chauffeured me to and from school for many years. Being a chauffeur for my mother was a job that I enjoyed. It required little effort. While Mother did her shopping, I would sit in the car and read a book. I got a lot of reading done. I would often bring a notebook along and get some writing done, too. Eventually, though, Mother began spending more and more time in the grocery store. I would check my watch. How could it take her over half an hour to pick up just a few items? Had she stopped to chat with someone or was she having trouble finding what she wanted? It became difficult for me to concentrate on what I was reading or writing; I felt compelled to glance every few minutes at the door of the grocery store to see if my mother was finally coming out. And so I began accompanying her into the store to speed up the process.

# THE CHRISTMAS-CARD LIST

Mother kept a typewritten list of all the people in Denmark that she exchanged Christmas cards with. The list covered both sides of two pages and spilled onto a third page. Originally, it had included over twenty names and addresses. Mother would write after each name the year in which she had last received a card. I noticed in the late seventies that she had crossed out several of the names. Some of the people had moved, and Mother had typed in their new addresses. Uncle Niels and his wife, Mette, had left Hessel and moved into a nursing home. So had Bedstefar's Johanne. But several of the people had died. Helge, who was my mother's age, died in 1976; his wife, Jenny, died in 1980. In the 1980s Mother was crossing off at least two or three names every year. Soon, the word *"døde"* appeared after more than half of the names on the list. Møster Anna *døde* 1982. Niels Buus *døde* 1987. Bedstefar's Johanne *døde* 1992 (after sending a last card the previous Christmas). In some cases Mother no longer recorded the date of death, simply indicating the passing with a red checkmark and the year in which she had last received a card. In 1997 there was a wave of cross-outs on Mother's list. She crossed out eight names and addresses. And Mother continued to cross off names on the list. She was buying fewer and fewer cards and international airmail stamps. The deaths continued to mount. Verner *døde* 1997. Knud *døde* 2010. By 2010 nearly two entire generations had been wiped out. Only my mother and her sister remained of what had once been a large family. The latest generation was smaller than the previous one as people were now having fewer children than was common in the past, and they had little interest in corresponding with a half-rememberer aunt who lived across the ocean. Indeed, the new generation was even remiss in keeping in touch with their own family in Denmark. During Anne-Sofie's visit to Chalfont in 2010, I asked her about one of my cousins, Claus, who was a year younger than I, and had made a trip to the U.S. back in 1979. Anne-Sofie shook her head. She had never even met him. Nor did she know Søren, Helge and Jenny's son, who with his wife, had visited us in the early seventies, when we were living in Chatham. It became obvious that our family back in Denmark was seriously fragmented. In some cases, Mother and I were the only remaining link between the different branches.

My mother had a second Christmas-card list of people she exchanged cards with in the States. It was shorter than her list of Danish correspondents. But like her other list, a majority of these names had also been crossed off by the time we reached the millennium. In most cases, Mother had simply recorded the last year in which she had received a Christmas card. (Perhaps the sender had simply grown tired of exchanging cards.) But she had also recorded a number of deaths, which she listed as "died" on the American list. Among the deceased were my cousins: Joseph, died February 1997; Peter, died September 1998. They were both more than ten years younger than I was. And so it goes. We never learned When Velma died. She had been suffering from dementia in her final years, and Joseph eventually had to lock her bedroom door to keep her from wandering off. After her husband's death, her brother-in-law took charge of her finances. He advised her to sell her Exxon shares and invest in something that yielded a higher return. A bad decision as it turned out.

I never really got around to discussing with my mother how she managed to cope with these steadily growing losses of her relatives and friends. Once, however, Mother asked me how I would get along after she was gone. I simply shrugged and said that I would not mind being alone. How wrong I was.

At this point in time, Mother was still able to leaf through the pictures in her albums and remember the lives of the people she had crossed off on her list. As long as she remembered them, it was as if they were not really gone. When we got her albums out of the drawer, Mother was able to recall the names of childhood friends she had not seen in over seventy years. (But unlike Snot-Olaf, she could not recall the names of her father's horses, even though she and Anna Lise had gone many times by horseback to cool off in the nearby bay.) She remembered growing up on Klostergaarden, trips by train to visit her grandmother at Risgaard. The pictures helped to bring all of these memories back.

By 2015, Mother was experiencing increasing difficulty attending to the daily influx of mail. Sitting at the kitchen table, she would use the bronze letter opener that had been presented to her when she left hr. Hansen's shop back in 1946 and open solicitations from multiple charitable organization. She would then put them on the dining-room table to be dealt with on some day in the future. But she never got back to them. It became my task to sort through these requests and select the few that were worthy of responding to. The solicitations continued to pile up. And then there were telephone requests for money. When Mother answered the phone, these shameless solicitors would cajole her into committing herself into making a contribution. They prey on elderly people, who can often ill-afford the twenty-five or fifty dollars demanded of them. But the solicitors rely for their commissions on the inability of people of advanced years being hesitant to simply say "no" and hang up the phone. I solved this problem by getting an answering machine (the so-called "do-not-call list" was a joke), and instructed my mother not to answer the phone. I then cleared the dining-room table of the accumulated solicitation letters and replaced them with Mother's photo albums. I left them open on the table, the pages turned to photos that recorded significant events in Mother's life: pictures from Klostergaarden, Risgaard, Paarup; pictures of my parents working on their dream house on Huyler Road.

Once, when we were looking through the photo albums, Mother noticed a picture from Huyler Road of Muff sitting on a nice 9' by 12' braided floor rug.

"Whatever happened to that rug?" she asked.

"We left it in the upstairs room on Tower Hill Road," I told her. "There was no room for it when we moved into the house in Howell." I chose not to remind her of the other once-cherished things that we had been forced to leave behind along the way: a kitchen table and four chairs, a folding bed, two armchairs, two or three couches, a couple of end-tables, a bookcase, and the two basement bars my father and I had constructed.

# EARLY SIGNS

Mother had always been very particular as to which drawers the pots and pans should go. Everything had its proper place, and she would chide me if I happened to put a pot in the wrong place, or even worse, in the wrong drawer. By 2014, though, she began to get the pots and pans mixed up unless I helped her. Increasingly, after we had dried things off, she would open the wrong drawer and attempt to put a pot in a space where it simply would not fit. When I opened the right drawer for her, she would nod and say, "I knew that." Which trays in which to put knives and forks was also becoming a problem for her, despite the fact that it was a simple matching task: like upon like. For many years we had used different towels for drying our hands and drying the dishes: the blue towel was for hands; the white towel was for dishes. Mother could no longer make the distinction. As far as she was concerned, a towel was a towel.

Mother was having increasing difficulty remembering what she was suppose to do in the morning when her alarm clock went off. She used to go through the ritual entirely on her own: at 6:00 A.M. she would get up and take her Synthroid (it had to be taken on an empty stomach), then she would go back to bed until 7:00, when it was time to come downstairs for breakfast. But now when I came into her room to see that she had taken her Synthroid, she would be completely in the dark as to what she was supposed to do. I began to write down instructions for her on a scrap of paper, which she would consult after her alarm went off. At first, we would leave the instructions on her dresser, propped up on a little ledge at the base of her mirror. But then the instructions began to disappear. I would find the scrap of paper in a drawer of my mother's dresser, or folded up in a pocket of her bathrobe. So I began making multiple copies of the routine that Mother was supposed to follow and left it up to her where she put them.

Mother's daily regimen of prescription medicine and non-prescription supplements became more and more problematic. In the past she would place her morning pills—Cozaar, Atenolol, Ecotrin—in a plastic cup next to her breakfast dish the night before. But now I had to take over the task. Mother would complain every morning at the number of pills she had to take, to which I had now added several supplements that were supposed to boost a flagging memory. But she was content when I showed her that I was taking the same supplements.

As it turned out, none of the pills I made her take seemed to be doing anything to stem the decline of her memory. Vitamin D, ubiquinol, resveratrol, tocotrienol, curcumin—not one of these promising remedies for the aging brain had as yet shown any appreciable effect. I bought some extra-strength Prevagen for her. The stuff was flying off the shelf in Rite Aid. Described as having been made from a protein derived from a jellyfish, it was supposed to reverse memory loss. Official-looking charts purported to show a steady improvement in brain function. Unfortunately, Prevagen is a cruel hoax. I soon remembered from one of my biology classes that proteins are broken down in the digestive track into simple amino acids. So you were not getting the advertised benefit of a jellyfish protein. This is why insulin must be injected into the bloodstream, and not administered by mouth. But there was no talk of injecting Prevagen. Why is the FDA silent on this matter? Follow the money.

Mother began to have trouble figuring out what day of the week it was. When she wanted to write out a check, she would often pick up a newspaper and look at the date, but this was of no help to her if the paper was a day or two old. I solved this problem, at least temporarily, by buying a large wall clock for her that gave not only the time but the date and day of the week as well. It wasn't long, however, before the task of filling out a check simply became too much for her. She would spend twenty minutes trying on different pairs of glasses so she could see better. Even with the stronger bulbs I had put in the light over the kitchen table, and with the Venetian blinds fully open, she would still complain that she did not have enough light. This was not entirely unexpected. In 1993 Mother had suffered a detached retina in her right eye, and the operation to repair it was far from successful. Her good eye was now beginning to develop a cataract. At first, I attributed Mother's increasing difficulty with her checkbook to her deteriorating eyesight. Okay. But was it really that simple? To spare Mother the distress of paying her bills, I began filling out all of her checks, leaving it up to her just to sign them. Curiously, her signature had changed. For most of her adult life she had written the letter "I" in the familiar American style. Now she said that she could no longer remember how to make such an "I" and reverted to writing the first letter of her name as she used to when she was a girl, the Danish style "I" looking more like a "Y".

Preparing dinner was becoming more and more of a chore for my mother. Increasingly, I would have to pitch in and take care of the main course, leaving her to simply cook the vegetables. It was not just that she lacked the stamina to stand over a hot stove and brown a panful of ground beef, or mix up the batter for the Sunday-night pancakes that we had enjoyed for many years. The process, the series of steps she needed to take to prepare a meal had become too difficult for her to follow. The problem was her memory. Now that I was preparing our meals, Mother would often ask me what we were having for supper.

"The same as last night," I would tell her.

"I can't remember what we had last night."

Although Mother no longer knew what day of the week it was and would quickly forget what she'd had for lunch or supper, she could still rattle off the phone number at Klostergaarden (Nykøbing Falster 9173), the farm that her father had owned in the twenties and thirties. In December 2014, Mother recalled a Christmas song from her youth. She remembered her family singing it as they circled about the tree on New Year's Eve and opened their gifts. She described how most of the farmhands came to the dining-room table to enjoy the dinner that her mother and the cooks had prepared. But some of the men, she recalled, had to stay in the barn to milk the cows. There was always work to be done on a farm.

# THE MEMORY TEST

In her appointment with Dr. Lieberman in April 2014, Mother said, as she usually did, that she had no complaints; she was feeling good. I brought up the matter of her short-term memory problem. Dr. Lieberman suggested that she might be treated with a drug. But he did not sound very hopeful. Unfortunately, any improvement would only be temporary, and there could be side-effects. So as Mother was currently in good spirits, we elected not to go the drug route. Her next appointment was in early December. Mother's condition was unchanged. Dr. Lieberman gave her a couple of memory tests. The first one she passed with flying colors. The doctor indicated three objects in the room—door, sink, computer—and asked my mother after a minute's conversation to recall the three objects. Mother unhesitating named all three. Next, Dr. Lieberman handed her a pen and a piece of paper and asked her draw the face of a clock and indicate that the time was a quarter to eleven. Mother drew a tiny circle, but the lack of space on her clock left her with not enough room to put in all of the numbers. The face of the clock wound up with only eight numbers; the time, however, a quarter to eleven, was not far off the mark. For the third memory test Dr. Lieberman gave my mother one minute to name as many different animals as she could. She struggled right from the start, slowly coming up with dog, cow, horse, Muff. Then she started repeating herself. This was very disappointing. The girl who had grown up on a farm could only name three of the animals that she had once been intimately familiar with.

The following spring, I replicated the clock test. I scribed a large circle on a full-sized sheet of paper and asked Mother to put in the hours. At first she balked at the task.

"Why don't *you* put in the hours?" she asked, obviously not comprehending the purpose of the task.

After I explained to her that this was the same test that Dr. Lieberman had asked her to do, she finally picked up a pen and began to place the numbers around the dial. Without any coaching from me, she worked in a logical fashion, beginning with 12 o'clock, then 3, then 6, then 9. She filled in the rest of the hours with reasonably good spacing between them, unlike her earlier performance in the doctor's office in which she had crowded the hours together and omitted four of them. I brought Mother's improved rendition of a clock to her next appointment with Dr. Lieberman. It seemed that if the parameters were set for her, and if she was presented with a familiar, structured environment, she could continue to function. The doctor again brought up the possibility of my mother taking a drug to help her memory, but mentioned again that the side-effects were not trivial. As Mother remained in good spirits and had no complaints, we decided that the harmless supplements I was giving to her would suffice for now.

# DOWNTON ABBEY

My mother had enjoyed watching the British TV series *Downton Abbey* from its inception. We had both grown teary-eyed over the death of Lady Sybil early in 2013. But by the fourth or fifth season, Mother often complained that she was having trouble understanding what the actors were saying. The thick accents spoken by some of the lower classes especially threw her. Putting on the subtitles was of no help, for then Mother would struggle with her poor eyesight to read the script, and be unable to follow the action on the screen. At the time I thought that the problem was due to her hearing, for now and then she would complain of wax in her ears, which would have to be flushed out with Debrox. Indeed, Dr. Leiberman had observed that she had narrow ear canals, which were prone to becoming obstructed with wax. So it was time again to get out the Debrox. Mother would lie on her side on the family-room couch and I would direct eight or nine drops into the blocked ear, telling her to lie still for ten minutes.

"My ear just popped," she would say after a successful treatment.

But even with her ear cleared of wax, Mother continued to have trouble hearing what people were saying on the TV (though she could understand me with no difficulty). So I bought her an amplifier, which enhanced human voices while simultaneously damping down the background noise. This seemed to work for her. But after watching an episode or two in 2015, the final season of *Downton Abbey*, Mother said that she had no idea who these people were or what they were doing. It was apparent that her problem was not simply due to her hearing or her failing eyesight.

Her brother Knud had died of dementia in 2010. But until then Mother and I would call him each year to wish him a happy birthday. Knud had once had a sharp and inquisitive mind. He enjoyed, as did my mother, perusing an almanac. But with each successive birthday, it became obvious that his memory was failing in a big way. It got to be that every conversation we had was essentially a repetition of the one we had had the previous year. Knud would ask where we lived in Pennsylvania. Was our house made of brick or wood? Was my mother's husband still living? Always the same questions. I no longer asked my uncle, as I had in years gone by, if he was still taking part in the marathon marches, for I knew he had given up that part of his life a long time ago. After Knud was no longer able to carry on a telephone conversation, we learned from Elly that he had fallen over his walker. He would sometimes confuse his wife's clothing with his own. A sad way to go.

Every day after lunch, Mother would stretch out on the couch in the family room and take a nap. Upon awakening, she would often be confused. She would be uncertain where she was.

"Are we in Denmark?"

When I told her that we were in Pennsylvania, she would ask, "Why did we move?"

Other questions followed. She would ask me if I had been born in Denmark. Where did I go to school? Once she asked me if we were related, but then quickly recognized me. Always the same questions.

But the hardest question for me to answer was when she asked, "When is Bob coming back?" I would gently tell her that he had died a long time ago. She would then ask about her mother and father, and I would have to tell her that they, too, were gone. I would have to go through this painful explanation on many different occasions. The similarity between Mother's symptoms and her brother's was beginning to alarm me. I dreaded the possibility that she was going down the same path.

At 3:00 we would settle down to watch a DVD and have our afternoon snack. By now it was becoming increasingly difficult for Mother to concentrate on the TV. She would gaze about the room, admiring the flowers I had brought in from the garden. She would look at the pillow she had made at the age of nine and point out the mistake she had made: a single row of stitches going the wrong way—which I always found difficult to locate, as this one wayward row in no way interfered with the precise floral design beneath it.

"We sure have a lot of Christmas plates," she would say, casting her gaze high up along the wall at the Bing & Grøndahl Christmas plates that her mother had sent us over the years. Shifting her gaze to the paintings on the wall, she would be unable to remember which ones she had painted and which ones I had painted.

One evening we were watching an episode of *The Amazing Race*, which was one of Mother's can't-miss shows. Before long, though, it became apparent that she wasn't paying attention to the various tasks that the contestants had to perform. When one of the teams boarded a helicopter and soared over the countryside, Mother turned to me and said, "I remember the first helicopter I saw. It flew past our school, and everyone ran to the window to see what it was." This would have been at her elementary school in the late twenties or early thirties. Mother's childhood memories remained intact. On another occasion, she recalled how they had to change trains to get to Risgaard, where her grandmother Severine lived and where her father had been born. While she might not be able to remember what she had seen on TV the night before, things that had happened eighty years ago were still clear in her mind.

*Survivor*, which Mother had looked forward to watching every season since its debut in 2000, no longer held her interest. She now found it impossible to keep track of the contestants, and shook her head when I pointed out to her this or that contestant had appeared as a villain or a hero in an earlier episode. She continued, however, to enjoy the game shows, *Jeopardy* and *Wheel of Fortune*. The predictable format and the bells and whistles held her attention. Increasingly, though, she would begin to doze off soon after the show had begun. In the past she had been able to supply a few of the answers, but now she sat in silence, often closing her eyes.

"I'm listening," she would say when I asked her if she was awake. "I just needed to rest my eyes."

To keep her awake, I began loudly calling out the answers on *Jeopardy*, whether I was certain of them or not.

"You know all the answers," Mother would say.

I could have been a contender, at least if my mother was the judge.

By the spring of 2015 even the simplest, everyday tasks were now beyond my mother. When it came to fixing lunch, she didn't know where to begin, and I would have to prepare her food. Formerly a finicky eater, with pronounced likes and dislikes, she no longer expressed any preference when I asked her what she wanted to eat. I would just have to judge by how much she left on her plate whether she had liked it or not.

"I'm losing my mind," she said. "I don't know what's happening to me. This isn't me."

Mother could no longer use the telephone to set up her doctors' appointments. Even though I set had down the particulars on a sheet of paper for her, she found it difficult to follow the menu (press 1 for an emergency, press 2 to renew a prescription, press 3 to set up an appointment). More often than not, as Mother became increasingly distressed by the confusing instructions, I would have to take the phone from her and finish setting up the appointment.

I shrugged off Mother's inability to make her own appointments. I did not much care for having to cope with a long menu myself, and would often have to listen to the instructions twice before I finally got them straight. So I began bringing Mother into her doctor's office, where we would ask the receptionist for an appointment. This was much more satisfactory for both of us than calling up on the phone. You left the office with an official appointment card in your hand. No chance of mishearing the date or time of the appointment. When we got home, my mother would line up her latest appointment card along with the others on the ledge at the bottom of her bedroom mirror. Another problem solved.

Mother took comfort in the hefty quarterly dividend she received from her Exxon shares. She wrote down the number of shares she owned on a scrap of paper so she would not have to keep asking me, though she would still inquire every few days what the current quotation was, then figure out how much her shares were worth using a calculator. Holding onto her Exxon shares had certainly paid off. Mother was pleased when I told her that between the two of us, we now had about 1.3 million dollars invested in the stock market. We were still, in a sense, investment partners, as we had been in the eighties when we both traded shares of Xerox.

For many years now, Mother had had no need to worry about me financially. But she was still concerned about my well-being. "It would be nice if you had a girl," she remarked one morning after breakfast as I settled her into her favorite chair in the family room, "but they're hard to find."

# NOT A BAD YEAR

My mother's memory decline appeared to have bottomed out by 2016. Were the supplements I was giving her finally beginning to kick in? She would look through the albums I had set out for her on the dining-room table. She continued to enjoy listening to music. Saturday evenings she would watch the *Lawrence Welk Show*. Sunday mornings she would listen to Sid Mark playing four hours of Frank Sinatra recordings. Though she had to ask me how to operate her stereo (which, frankly, with all of its black buttons arranged on a black console, confounded even me), she would enjoy listening to the records that she had brought home from Denmark. She appreciated the flowers I brought in every day fresh from the garden. She would take a newspaper or a magazine and sit on her chair on the porch I had constructed for her just off the kitchen. She would stroll out to the backyard shed that I had extensively rebuilt in 2014, adding a deck and a covered porch, under whose roof it was always six or seven degrees warmer than the ambient air, which made it cozy even on a cold day.

All throughout 2016, a single cane would suffice my mother on her perambulations around the backyard. Early in 2017, however, she began using two canes. She had formerly been able to go to the grocery store with the aid of a shopping cart. But now her back began to trouble her. For a while, a rollator provided a simple solution. She could wheel the vehicle around the store and then sit down on the seat if the pain in her back became too much for her. While she rested, I would scurry up and down the aisles to gather what we needed and place the items in a shopping bag. But my mother's back pain only grew worse. One day during a visit to Rite Aid to pick up a prescription, Mother could barely make it across the parking lot and had to sit down as soon as she got inside the store. "I wish I'd stayed at home," she said. This was close as she ever got to complaining. Thereafter, I would do all the shopping on my own. As Mother was now having difficulty walking even with the use of her rollator, I bought a folding wheelchair to bring her to her doctors' appointments. A specialist examined her and said that she had severe arthritis of the lower spine as well as mild arthritis in both hips. The prescription was Extra Strength Tylenol and a heating pad. Well, we had already been using those remedies. No injections. No cortisone. So much for modern medicine.

But Mother seemed content. When I asked her how she was doing, sitting there in her favorite chair with the heating pad on, she would invariably answer, "I'm doing good. I feel fine."

On her way upstairs each night, as she passed by the coffee table on top of which sat a pair of ducks that Bob had carved, she would pause to admire them and say, "Hello, ducks." Occasionally, if they happened not to be facing the right way, she would take a moment to reposition them. And then, continuing on, she would say, "Hello, ducks," to the pair atop the cabinet in the hallway.

I would generally lead the way up to her bedroom, taking two steps at the time.

"You're upstairs before I even get started," she would say to me from the bottom of the stairs.

I began leaving Mother at home when I did the shopping, hoping that her back would eventually get better so she could go out again with the aid of her rollator. But it was not to be. To keep her entertained when I was out, I would put the TV on for her. She enjoyed listening to the *Rachael Ray Show*. Cooking still interested her, even though she was no longer capable of doing any cooking.

On more than one occasion, Mother had told me how she had teased Anna Lise when they were children by making a marzipan bar last for several days, and then showing her sister, who had eaten hers all at once, how much she still had left. But such self-discipline was now beyond my mother. We had several bags of candy left over after Halloween in 2016. When I wasn't looking, Mother would open the closet where we kept the candy and take out a couple of pieces. She was still cagey enough not to leave any of the wrappers lying around where I might find them. It wasn't until I chanced to look in the closet and see that all of the bags were empty that I realized what she had been up to. I also discovered that one of the tins of Danish butter cookies that we were saving for Christmas was empty. When I confronted Mother, she claimed to have no recollection of having eaten the sweets. I hid the remaining tin of cookies on a high shelf. Mother was shocked when I got her onto the scale and told her that she weighed more than I did. One of her jackets could no longer be zippered up, and the pants I had bought her as a Christmas present (she used to take petite sizes) were obviously not going to fit her.

The worst part of my mother's weight gain was not that some of her clothes were now too small for her. She was becoming increasingly unsteady on her feet, and was falling a couple of times a week. Her falls resulted in no broken bones. Mother's knees would simply buckle and she would sink to the floor, landing on her bottom. Unfortunately, she was unable to get back up on her own after she had fallen. If she happened to go down while I was out, she would remain on the floor until I came home. I demonstrated to her how she could pull herself up onto a chair, then turn around and sit down. But this simple maneuver was quite beyond her. In the end I would have to hook my arms under her armpits and pick her up off the floor. She offered no help while I was lifting her to her feet. She was a dead weight in my arms—150 pounds of dead weight. We engaged in a series of exercises designed to strengthen her legs, but the knee bends she was capable of performing with the aid of her walker did not translate into an ability to stand up after a fall. Still, she was game to perform her fifteen to twenty minutes of daily exercises. The previous year, Dr. Lieberman had prescribed a physical therapist to help her overcome her shuffling gate, and I now incorporated many of these exercises into her routine.

# THE FINAL YEAR

Though she was now house-bound except for her doctors' appointments, Mother seemed to be holding her own through the first half of 2017. In March she called up her sister and wished her a happy birthday. She chatted with Anna Lise for a good forty minutes, laughing several times as they reminisced about the past. I overheard her ask if Verner, who had died ten years ago, was still living. After she hung up, Mother could not tell me what she and her sister had talked about. But she said that she would call her again in a couple of weeks. That summer, Mother's subscription to the AARP Bulletin came up for renewal. I persuaded her to renew for five years instead of just a single year in order to get the cheapest rate. I fully expected her to be around in five years. With the same rationale, I started ordering bulk supplies of Depends, and I soon had a supply of adult diapers that would last her for six months. But look at the money we were saving.

Meanwhile, Mother's memory problems continued to worsen. Early in June she could no longer find her way to the downstairs bathroom. She would open the closet door in the kitchen, then proceed to open the basement door. I would have to show her the correct door out in the hallway. Upstairs, it was a different story as the bathroom adjoined the bedroom. Unfortunately, it was not long before she could not even sense when she had to use the bathroom. I began asking her every hour or two if she had to go. More often than not she would say that she didn't have to go or that she had already gone. She would soil her pants while sitting in her chair and not be aware that anything was wrong. I would have to bring her into the bathroom and clean her up. Urinary and fecal incontinence soon became a daily problem. I would have to change her Depends three or four times in the course of the day, starting when she got up in the morning. She could no longer take a shower by herself, so I would have to turn the water on for her and put her into the tub, instructing her how to soap herself up. As the procedure was something of an ordeal for her, we eventually cut her showers down to one a week, unless she had made a mess in her pants, in which case she would have to be cleaned up in the shower.

Getting dressed was also becoming a serious hurdle for her. She found it increasingly difficult to distinguish between her pajamas and her day clothes. ("What's the difference?" she would ask.) Oftentimes I would go upstairs after finishing my breakfast to find that she had put her shirt on, but had left her pajama bottoms on, or else she had pulled her pants on over her pajamas, and we would have to go through the whole routine a second time. For many months now Mother had struggled when she had to bend over to put her socks and shoes on. So, pulling her chair up close, she would prop her feet up one by one on the wicker basket at the foot of her bed. Now and then, though, her morning stiffness made it nearly impossible for her to reach her feet, and I would have to buckle her shoes for her. More than once as I did this, Mother would tell me again the story of how, when she was preparing to leave Denmark, there were no suitcases available and she had to settle on this wicker basket to pack her things in. The basket served another function. With her shoes now securely fastened, Mother would grasp the handle on the side of the basket and pull herself up to a standing position. "What would I do without my basket?" she asked me one morning.

Mother's tendency to misplace her things was by now almost a daily occurrence. Concurrent with her inability to place knives and forks, pots and pans back where they belonged, she would lose her glasses, her ring, her wristwatch—which would invariably turn up in the wrong drawer, or squirreled away in a shirt or bathrobe pocket. One evening after supper, she could not find her lower denture. Trying to retrace her steps, I searched through the garbage pail under the kitchen sink. Nothing. I looked through the drawers. I checked the pocket of her apron. Where could she have put her teeth? I checked the cup in which she would put her dentures to soak every night before going to bed. Empty. I looked through the garbage pail in the bathroom. I plunged my hand into the toilet bowl and felt around. Nothing. It was a mystery. Had she flushed them down in the toilet? The thought crossed my mind that we would have to go to the dentist and get her fitted for another set of dentures. The following morning I continued the search, checking out possible hiding places that I had visited the day before. Again attempting to retrace Mother's steps, I looked in the family room at her leather chair with the heating pad draped over the back. I moved the heating pad aside and felt under the coverlet. There was her lower denture. At least now she would not have to gum her food. To prevent Mother from misplacing her watch and glasses when she retired for the night, I would tell her to place them in the bottom drawer of her night table, which was empty except for the watercolor she had done of Mickey Mouse and Minnie Mouse when she was nine years old. "The Mickey Mouse drawer," I called it to help jog her failing memory.

Mother's ninety-fourth birthday came in late July. She was proud of her red hair, pointing out to me that she still had only a single gray hair or two. Her face was unlined. She looked like a woman in her seventies. In the past Anna Lise used to call to wish her sister a happy birthday. With memory problems of her own, she had not called now for a year or two, leaving it to my mother to initiate the calls. Mother had rung once in June, but Anna Lise had not been home. I suggested that today, on her birthday, would be a good occasion to call, but as Mother did not seem particularly receptive to the idea, I did not press the issue. She would call her sister in her own good time, no doubt on a day when she felt more like talking. In any case, Mother enjoyed the Linzer torte I had baked for her birthday. Now that she had given up baking, I had become something of a baker in my own right, tackling a rather challenging raspberry-tart lattice pie that had originated in Austria. (I had researched German baking while working on a novel about Hitler's Germany.)

Unfortunately, Mother would never speak with her sister again. On September 11, she had seemed fine all day, eating her afternoon snack as we watched a DVD. But just before we were to begin our supper, she fell on her way into the kitchen. As she was unable to sit at the table, I decided to bring her upstairs to her bed. She fell going up the stairs and fell several additional times before I could make her comfortable. The following morning she was incoherent, so I called the rescue squad.

# A SIMPLE BLADDER INFECTION

In Doylestown Hospital, the nurses at first thought that my mother had suffered a stroke. A corner of her mouth was turned down, and her left arm was immobile. She would not respond to the nurses' questions, and would speak to me only in whispered Danish, so softly that I could scarcely understand what she was saying.

At last, lab tests were run and the proper diagnosis was made. My mother had a urinary tract infection. No big deal, I thought with relief. Mother had come down with a bladder infection six or seven years previously and had quickly overcome it. Now, for a ninety-four-old woman, she was still physically fit. Her only real problem was with her memory. Without exception, the books I had consulted concerning dementia or Alzheimer's presented a fairly positive spin on the outlook for a victim of this horrible brain disease—at least until the final stages. And my mother was nowhere near the final stages. She still knew who I was and recalled things from her past. But as it turned out, Mother's kidney cancer had been a walk in the park compared to what she would soon be facing. I had read up on urinary tract infections and how to deal with them. The books recommended flushing out your system with copious amounts of water and drinking cranberry juice, but they neglected to mention the fact that for an elderly woman suffering from dementia, fecal incontinence would inevitably result in a bladder infection, which, while little more than annoyance for a younger person, for someone of my mother's age and with her weakened immune system, would be a virtual death sentence. Mother was given antibiotics and hooked up to an IV pole with a saline drip. She quickly began to pick up, but remained very weak. As she was unable to get out of bed on her own, her doctors decided that she should be discharged to a local nursing home for rehabilitation. She remained at Pine Run for two weeks. When she first got there she had to be spoon fed. Wheeled into the activity room for a session with some of the other residents, she promptly threw up on the table. It was not an auspicious beginning, but little by little Mother began to improve. Within a few days she regained the ability to feed herself. I brought her boombox and some CDs into her room, a couple of framed photographs, and one of her photo albums. She was taken up the the fourth floor every morning for a physical therapy session. At Pine Run, the nurses used Attends instead of Depends. The Attends, opening on the side, could be more easily put on and taken off a bedridden patient, accomplished by the simple act of turning her from side to side—no need to stand up. Mother would flinch when any of her nurses felt her swollen ankles, and I would explain to them how her swollen ankles had forced her to give up a career in nursing when she was living in Denmark. As my mother was incapable of engaging in a detailed explanation, I showed the nurses a picture of the young GI she had met at a dance in Copenhagen after the war and accepted his proposal of marriage. They all remarked how handsome he was. Disregarding the nurses' instructions to call for assistance, I would help Mother out of her bed by myself when she needed to use the bathroom, for I knew that I would be on my own when she was discharged from the nursing home. On Mother's final day, her physical therapist took her out to the car in a wheelchair to practice transferring from the chair to the car seat. The transfer did not go especially well, even with two therapists assisting her. But I was confident that I would be able to manage when I got her home. And I did.

Upon My mother's release from Pine Run, the Renaissance home-health-care service that Dr. Lieberman had arranged kicked in. She now had a visiting nurse, a physical therapist, and an occupational therapist. An aid came in twice a week to give her a shower and wash her hair. The rest was up to me. As I had anticipated, Mother picked up quickly once she was back home in familiar surroundings. Her appetite improved and she got back into the routine of doing her daily exercises. In the beginning of October, I had a stair lift installed so Mother would no longer have to climb up and down the twelve steps that led to her upstairs bedroom. She was pleased with this development, smiling every time I put her on the chair. "This is new," she said more than once, even after she had been using the lift for a couple of weeks. She never quite mastered the simple hand controls that would have enabled her to use the lift on her own. Once, when I had gone out early to do the shopping and told her that she could remain in bed until I came home, she squeezed past the lift with her cane and walked down the stairs to sit on her favorite chair in the family room. Back home, I had mixed feelings about her exploit, but at the same time I was heartened by the fact that she could still negotiate the stairs on her own, something that she had not done without assistance in over two months.

The first order of business for the Renaissance aids was to go through the house with me and insure that conditions were appropriate for a person with my mother's disabilities. They were pleased to see that I had installed sturdy grab bars in the bathrooms and that I had placed similar grab bars next to any doorway where my mother had to take a step up or down. The aids were particularly impressed how I had cut down (and neatly patched) the side of Mother's bathtub so that she would have only a four-inch-high ledge to step over. Mother's strength increased steadily. Dylan, her physical therapist, was encouraged that she was able to walk longer distances on every one of his visits. Her performance on the get-up-and-go test had markedly improved—forty seconds to stand up, walk a measured distance and sit down again. Unfortunately, Mother's reprieve turned out not to be long-lasting. At six o'clock one morning in the middle of October, I found her extremely groggy when I attempted to wake her and give her her Synthroid. Instead of letting her sleep a while longer to see if she would pick up, I immediately called the rescue squad. Back in the hospital and diagnosed with another UTI, she began to recover faster than she had from her previous bout with e coli. Having her admitted at the first sign of trouble had made a considerable difference. Her mental state, however, lagged behind her physical recovery. On her first night at the hospital, she thought that she heard her brother, Knud, coming down the hallway. Once again, I had the sad task of telling her that her brother had been dead for seven years. A little later, during dinner, she asked me if Bob was waiting for us in the car. I shook my head and explained that, except for her sister, we were now alone in the world. Mother was released from Doylestown Hospital two days after she was admitted. I drove her home and she resumed her physical therapy sessions.

At first the distinction between a physical therapist and an occupational therapist eluded me. Though there was some overlap in the physical skills that both of them sought to enhance, the occupational therapist additionally focused on cognitive skills. Donna, her new occupational therapist, asked Mother to name the months of the year and the days of the week. How many colors could she name? Presented with pictures in a magazine, Mother could easily identify Donald Trump and Harry Truman. Eisenhower gave her a little trouble, but when told his first name she quickly came up with his last name. Looking around the house and seeing how my mother had enjoyed painting in years gone by, Donna tried to get her interested in a coloring book. I had had the same idea and bought Mother a coloring book and a set of colored pencils. As it turned out, Donna had no more success than I had in encouraging my mother to fill in the outlines of a flower. After a few strokes, she put away the colored pencil. But at least she had tried, and the activity had brought a smile to her face. Maybe on another day she would do some more coloring. Both Dylan and Donna observed that my mother was doing better than most patients her age. Physically, she was as fit as many patients in their seventies. Things seemed to be looking up.

Late in October Mother had another fall. This time, instead of landing harmlessly on her bottom, she fell headlong onto the carpet in the utility room, scraping the side of her face and dislocating the middle finger on her right hand. Despite her tumble, she remained in good spirits, simply switching over to using her left hand for the next couple of weeks as her injured finger healed in a cast that covered her entire hand. I purchased two motion detectors for her: one for her bed, the other for her favorite chair in the family room. Carrying the alarm on my belt, I would thus be alerted when my mother was on the move.

Toward the end of November, Mother had improved sufficiently to be discharged from the Renaissance home-health-care service. I breathed a sigh of relief as she signed her name with the outstretched index finger of her now fully functional right hand on the tablet proffered by her nurse, but for the next week or two the house seemed empty without all the health aids stopping in nearly every day.

We were on our own now, but Mother continued to do her twenty minutes of daily exercise with me. Her appetite was good. She remained in high spirits. The month of November passed without incident, although Mother regretted that she had not gotten me a present for my birthday. On December 11, I brought her to a routine appointment with her urologist. As usual, she told the doctor that she felt fine. I had to point out that she was continuing to be troubled by daily urinary and fecal incontinence. The doctor took a sample of her urine and said that the results would be available from the laboratory in about two days. I pushed Mother back out to the car in her wheelchair. As I opened the door for her and helped her into the front seat, she turned to me and asked, "Where's our little dog?"

I sensed at once that this was not a good sign. Although it is difficult with a person suffering from dementia to tell if any one particular comment is a departure from the "norm," this question of Mother's disturbed me. In the beginning of her hospital stay in September, she had been delirious, pointing to the ceiling and insisting that she could see a small dog. Why couldn't I see it? It's right up there. I had learned from experience that PH test strips and thermometer readings were less than reliable indicators for detecting the onset of a UTI. One needed to go by subtle changes in behavior: sluggishness or increased mental confusion. I hoped that my fears were unwarranted, and, indeed, Mother seemed all right throughout the evening. The following morning, however, she was confused and lethargic. I called 911.

It turned out to be a third bladder infection. The hospital routine was familiar by now: the IV pole, blood samples, antibiotics. It was only the doctors and nurses that were different. I arrived early each day at the hospital to help feed my mother, as she could not yet feed herself. She had no appetite, and to feed her a scrambled egg and some yogurt could take as long as two hours. Unlike on her last hospitalization, she was not ready to go home after two days. A week went by and she showed little improvement. She still had to be spoon-fed. She had been scheduled to be released on a Saturday, but her nurse said that she was not ready to go home. The nurse suggested that I call Pine Run and see if I could get her a room. This I did, but there was no one available on the weekend to handle an admittance. I would have to call back on Monday. I had barely gotten off the phone when Mother's hospital doctor asked me to accompany him out into the hall. I could not have been more stunned if he had punched me in the stomach.

"This isn't a matter of rehabilitation," he said, "It's a hospice situation." He gave her no more than a couple of months to live.

There were two options: place my mother in a hospice facility or bring her home to die with the help of home-hospice caregivers. I chose the latter.

# OUR LAST CHRISTMAS

On December 20 Mother came home in an ambulance. I ordered a hospital bed for her, which was not so much for my mother but to make things easier for me and her caregivers. A bed that could be raised and lowered and had an inflatable mattress made caring for a bedridden patient a less backbreaking task. I learned from Mother's visiting nurse how to roll her from side to side to change her soiled Attends, how to roll up a compromised bed pad so I could slip it out from under her. To keep her calm, I began giving her Atavan (the same medication that she had administered to uncle George thirty-six years ago as he lay dying from lung cancer). But even with the Atavan she would still become agitated when her nurse came in to tend to her, crying out when she was turned over, and flinching whenever her tender ankles were touched. Resorting to a stronger narcotic, I would use a syringe to give her by mouth a quarter milligram of morphine, timing the dosage to coincide with the arrival of her caregivers.

"I don't know what I'm doing anymore," Mother said as she settled into her newly installed hospital bed. She took only a few bites of the scrambled egg that I brought up for her breakfast. A sip of her cranberry juice. "I just want to pass," she said. "I feel all right, but I just want to pass."

At lunch she took only a single forkful of her leftover egg. She asked for some ice cream, so I brought up her favorite chocolate truffle ice cream. That afternoon I reheated her scrambled egg. She quickly finished it off as well as a half slice of banana, two cookies, and several potato chips. For supper she had a slice of the lasagna I had baked. Her appetite seemed to have returned. Was she on the mend?

I continued to entertain a vague hope that the doctor had been wrong in his negative assessment of my mother, and that she would again begin to regain her strength now that she was home. After her previous hospitalizations she had always picked up once she was back among familiar surroundings. One day she asked for her watch. That was a positive sign, wasn't it? Day by day, however, I could see that despite these brief periods of remission, she was slowly growing weaker. Her appetite began to wane again. It would take her an hour to eat half of a scrambled egg and half a banana. But at least she could still feed herself, even if I had to cut everything up for her. To keep her from dozing off, I would play Frank Sinatra CDs on her boombox. I put a DVD player on her food cart so she could watch episodes of the *Lawrence Welk Show* that I had recorded for her. On Christmas Eve Mother told me that during the morning she had been thinking back on when she was a little girl at Klostergaarden. She seemed content. That evening I had to unwrap her present for her. It was a knitted green sweater. I told her that it had come from Ireland. "From Ireland?" she said, smiling up at me. I draped the sweater over her shoulders. She would never get a chance to wear it. I raised up the head portion of of her hospital bed so she could sit up and have her turkey dinner. She was able to eat only one small slice of meat, spitting out the last mouthful. She could not finish her chocolate cake, and she spit out the piece of marzipan I offered her. She took only a single sip of Asti Spumanti and made a face. "It's too strong," she complained.

On Christmas morning she had more of an appetite. She finished all of her scrambled egg and half a banana. She had a Danish butter cookie for dessert. I took heart in these little flashes of improvement. By lunchtime, however, her appetite was gone. She kept spitting out her turkey sandwich, and could eat only a couple spoonfuls of yogurt. "I'm so tired of eating," she said. "I just feel so full."

"We're going to need a big moving van," she said after I took the uneaten portion of her lunch away.

"We're not moving," I told her.

"Good," she said.

In her confused state of mind, she had gotten the notion that we were planning a move back to New Jersey. Or, now that I think back on her remark, was it some other move that she was contemplating?

The next several days saw more of the same. Scrambled egg and half a banana for breakfast. No appetite for lunch or supper. I now had to spoon-feed her and encourage her to eat. On December 30 she saw a "cute little dog" up on the ceiling, and pointed to it just as she had done in the hospital several months before. For lunch she managed to finish half a cup of yogurt and two small slices of her favorite Havarti cheese. When I offered her some more yogurt, she said, "I couldn't eat any more. Thank you very much."

That would be the last complete sentence she spoke.

The following day she would not open her mouth. She pushed the straw away when I offered her a sip of cranberry juice. I continued to give her morphine several times a day, as she tended to become agitated when anyone tried to reposition her to prevent bedsores, or check to see if her Attends needed to be changed. In an effort to keep her hydrated, I gave her orange juice and cranberry juice using the same syringe that I used for her morphine. But she would accept only a syringe full or two before she stopped swallowing. Much of the liquid simply spilled out of the corner of her mouth and stained her shirt.

Mother clung to life for the next few days. She spent most of the time sleeping. The routine was now to try to get a few drops of orange juice or cranberry juice down her throat using the syringe, and administer a dose of morphine every few hours. As she was no longer eating or drinking any appreciable amount, I no longer had to worry about changing her Attends. She was no longer speaking, but would answer a whispered "yes" when I asked her a question.

About half-past four in the afternoon on January 5, I left Mother's bedside and went downstairs to get some more cranberry juice for her. When I returned, she was unresponsive. She had no pulse. Mother had drawn her last breath when I was not there to hold her hand; I had not been there to comfort her in her final moments. I called the emergency number the Doylestown hospice group had provided for me. Mother's nurse arrived with minutes and ascertained that she had, indeed, passed. She told me that it was not uncommon for a dying patient to choose to die when no one was around. A small comfort.

Two men from the Huff & Lakjer funeral home in nearby Lansdale arrived shortly after. I handed them a plastic bag containing Mother's clothes. They put her in a black body bag, zipped it up, and removed her from the house.

In accordance with her wishes, I had Mother's body cremated. Laid out in the funeral home, she wore the green Irish sweater I had given her for Christmas.

# AFTERMATH

A few weeks after Mother died, I noticed that several items were missing from the bookcase at the head of her bed. Most likely in early 2017, when she was still able to get around on her own, she had removed a number of books from the bookcase, perhaps in attempt to effect a less cluttered appearance. I found the missing books in the living-room bookcase, which left only two sets of books in the bedroom bookcase: the six volumes of John Galsworthy's *The Forsyte Chronicles*, which I had given to Mother as a Christmas present many years ago, and a six-volume collection of Danish short stories. There was also a Danish bible. But inexplicably missing was a small blank-and-white photo of Mormor that had been in Mother's bedroom bookcase for many years. Apparently it had been taken as an official ID photo, for Mormor, wearing a knitted hat and a fur collar, looked as if she had just dropped in on a cold winter's day to have her photograph taken. So where was the photo? I searched my mother's bedroom, went through every drawer, even looked in her sewing basket. Recalling how she had sometimes mislaid her watch and glasses, I opened her closet doors and went through the pockets of her shirts and bathrobes. Nothing. I continued my search downstairs. Perhaps Mother had brought the photo downstairs along with the books that she had removed from her bedroom bookcase. Early in 2017, she had rearranged the pictures in the living room and dining room, and had brought out a few additional photos from her photo albums, placing some of them in frames but most simply propped up against candlesticks, vases, or whatever was handy. But the small, framed picture of her mother was not among them. Whenever something turned up missing, my biggest fear was that Mother, in her confused state of mind, might have simply thrown it out. Indeed, apparently in an attempt to reduce clutter, she had thrown out my Lego bricks, which had been stored in a plastic bag on a closet shelf in her bedroom for as long as I could remember. Had her mother's photo gone out with the Lego bricks? It seemed so. Perhaps the photo, in which her mother looked so sad and wan, had upset her. Who knows what distorted thoughts go through the mind of a victim of dementia? Around the same time I discovered that Mother had secreted three tissues (one fresh, two used) between the pages of her November issue of the *Reader's Digest*, which she kept on a table next to her favorite chair in the family room.

Several months after my mother died, I happened to open the wicker basket at the foot of her bed, of which she had spoken of so many times throughout the years. I had never before looked through it. There on top, as I well knew, was the burlap Christmas blanket that Mother had embroidered in 1956. I laid the blanket aside. Underneath were clothes that my mother had obviously never worn, a couple of sweaters, blankets in their original wrappings, a brand-new bed sheet, a slightly used pair of her favorite slippers. (No sign though of my Legos.) But there, tucked away in the folds of a blue sweater, I discovered Mormor's missing picture. As I examined the picture, I found that the cardboard hinge that had supported it had given way and now flopped uselessly. Why hadn't Mother brought the picture to me and asked me to fix the broken support? It may well be a pointless question to ask of a person suffering from dementia. I repaired the support with a couple drops of glue and replaced the picture where it had formerly stood in Mother's bookcase.

So why had she hidden her mother's picture in her wicker basket? The basket was packed to the brim with things that she would have needed if she was planning on going on a trip. I suspect that from the day of her arrival in the United States, in the back of Mother's mind, was the thought that if she did not like her new life in America, she could always return to Denmark. The wicker basket had always been her link to her homeland. No need to pack, just grab the basket, hop on a ship or plane, and go home. So her basket, in effect, was permanently on standby. And now, facing the end of her life, Mother had been prepared to make one last journey with her precious wicker basket.

The basket still sits at the foot of her bed, waiting, waiting for what?

INGE'S OIL PAINTING OF HER GRANDFATHER'S FARM

Bedstefars hus
+ Stinkbergs på
Tingsted
I was born here

169

LARS + ELLA BUUS, INGE, KNUD + ANNA LISE 1925

FAMILIEN BUUS
KLOSTERGAARDEN 1928

170

INGE + ANNA LISE - MILKING TIME 1930

Klostergaarden. 1935.

↑
LARS BOOS

↑
INGE

INGE BUUS 1933    3 PHOTOS, 3 POSES, 3 KRONER

SEVERINE BUUS - RISGAARD 1937

INGE                                ANNA LISE

ANNA LISE, KNUD + INGE 1932

INGE BUUS 1937

ANNA LISE + ELLA BUUS
1941

OURUPGAARD 1943

AMTSSYGGEHUSET, GENTOFTE, KØBENHAVEN 1943

↑

INGE

BJØRNHOLM 1942

INGE + LARS BUUS
OURUPGAARD 1943

INGE BUUS 1945

CORPORAL BOB PETERSON 1943

BOB

FORGES LES EAUX, FRANCE DEC. 1944

SERGEANT BOB PETERSON FEB. 1945

Luxembourg
1945

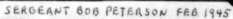

↑
BOB
FREDERICKSBORG CASTLE, COPENHAGEN NOV. 1945

176

M.S. GRIPSHOLM

INGE ON HER WAY TO AMERICA
M.S. GRIPSHOLM SEPT. 30, 1946

NIAGARA FALLS OCT. 1946

BOB & INGE - STATUE OF LIBERTY

FAR, MOR, GLENN + INGE 1948

GRIPSHOLM - KØBENHAVN 1948

2159 HUDSON BOULEVARD - CHRISTMAS EVE 1952

JULY 4, 1952 OUR BUILDING LOT
ON HUYLER ROAD

CLEARING THE LAND

THE 3 OF US WOULD SLEEP IN THIS SHED

HUYLER ROAD 1954

April 23 - 1954

1954

25 April 1954

1958

PAARUP 1955

↑ ↑ ↑
ANNA LISE LARS ELLA

MUFF GLENN ELLA

HUYLER ROAD

DEC 1960

JAN 1961

184

1968

IDLEWILD AIRPORT

1980

KENNEDY AIRPORT

1984

1962

EASTER 1962

INGE MADE THIS COAT - ALSO MUFF'S COAT

BADMINTON 1964

FINISHED BASEMENT 1965

HOUSE FOR SALE 1965

LARS, ELLA, INGE + KNUD   1968

188

25 RESENBRO 1968

1968

1968
FLENSBURG, GERMANY

1968

HIMMELBJERGET

1931
MORMOR, INGE, ANNI + GLENN

1968

1977

TRANUM - CAMPING SKOVLY GENERAL STORE

1973

TRANUM UDSIGTEN — ON THE WAY UP

UDSIGTEN — AT THE TOP

1977

LARS          INGE        VERNER        ELLA    ANNA LISE

25 RESENBRO

1979

1981

SILKEBORG

1979

VESTRE SKOLE, SILKEBORG-1979 JUDO MARCH
ANNI + KNUD

1981

TIVOLI, COPENHAGEN

1981

1981 CHRISTMAS IN HOUSTON, TEXAS

THE MENGER HOTEL - SAN ANTONIO

1983 TOWER HILL ROAD, CHALFONT, P.A.

1989 STARLIGHT ROAD, HOWELL, N.J.

1985 PEDDLERS VILLAGE

JAN 1986 STARLIGHT RD, HOWELL, N.J.

OCT. 24, 1989 CASTLEWOOD DRIVE, CHALFONT PA - LAST PHOTO OF BOB

1990 CASTLEWOOD DRIVE - THE PAINTING IS THE ONE THAT INGE BROUGHT
TO AMERICA IN HER WICKER BASKET IN 1946

MAKING PANCAKES

1995 LØGSTØR - ANNA LISE'S + VERNER'S NEW HOME

1995 TRANUM STRAND - A GERMAN BUNKER FROM THE 1940s

CHRISTMAS EVE 2012

CHRISTMAS EVE 2015

FEB. 18, 2015

FEB. 17, 2017

MAY 17, 2017

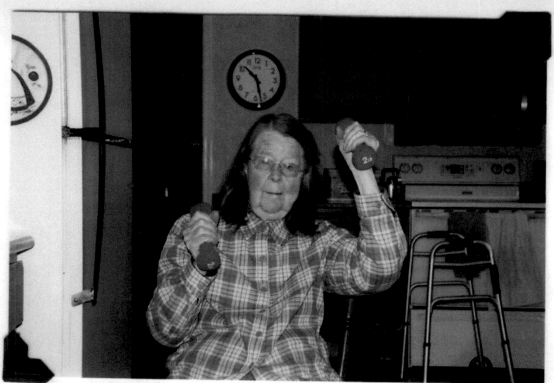

FEB. 16, 2017

INGE'S 94TH BIRTHDAY

NOV. 14, 2017

INGE'S WICKER BASKET ~ OVER THE BED: "SUNNY DAY IN COPENHAGEN"

Printed in the United States
By Bookmasters